THIS HOUSE OF SKY

Ivan Doig

THIS HOUSE OF SKY

Landscapes of a Western Mind

A HARVEST/HBJ BOOK

HARCOURT BRACE JOVANOVICH

NEW YORK AND LONDON

Printed in the United States of America

Library of Congress Cataloging in Publication Data

Doig, Ivan.
This house of sky.

(A Harvest/HBJ book)
1. Doig, Ivan. 2. Doig family. 3. Meagher Co., Mont.—Biography. I. Title.
[F737.M4D643 1980] 978.6'612'030924 [B] 79-18783
ISBN 0-15-689982-5

First Harvest/HBJ edition 1980
C D E F G H I J

To my wife, Carol.
Westward we go free.

THIS HOUSE OF SKY

TIME SINCE

Soon before daybreak on my sixth birthday, my mother's breathing wheezed more raggedly than ever, then quieted. And then stopped.

The remembering begins out of that new silence. Through the time since, I reach back along my father's tellings and around the urgings which would have me face about and forget, to feel into these oldest shadows for the first sudden edge of it all.

It starts, early in the mountain summer, far back among the high spilling slopes of the Bridger Range of southwestern Montana. The single sound is hidden water—the south fork of Sixteenmile Creek diving down its willow-masked gulch. The stream flees north through this secret and peopleless land until, under the fir-dark flanks of Hatfield Mountain, a bow of meadow makes the riffled water curl wide to the west. At this interruption, a low rumple of the mountain knolls itself up watchfully, and atop it, like a sentry box over the frontier between the sly creek and the prodding meadow, perches our single-room herding cabin.

4

Alone here on our abrupt tiny shelf, the three of us eased through May and the first twenty-six days of June secure as hawks with wind under our wings. Once a week, the camptender from the home ranch would come the dozen miles of trail to us. The blaze-faced sorrel he rode and the packhorse haltered behind would plod in from the shadows which pooled in our valley under the shouldering slopes, until at last the rider stepped off from his stirrups into the cabin clearing and unknotted from the packsaddle the provision boxes, dark-weathered in their coverings of rawhide, which carried our groceries and mail. My father, with his wise tucked grin, surely tossed a joke: *Hullo, Willie. Bring us that side of T-bones and a barrel of whiskey this time, did ye? I've told ye and told ye, our menu needs some fancying up* . . . As surely, my mother would have appeared from the cabin, her small smile bidding the caller to the tin mug of coffee in her hands. As surely again, I would have been at the provision boxes as my father began to unpack them, poking for the tight-rolled bundle of comic books which came for me with the mail.

Minutes later the camptender would be resaddled and riding from sight. For the next seven mornings again, until his hat and shoulders began to show over the trail crest another time, only the three of us nestled there in the clean blue weather of the soundless mountains.

Three of us, and the sheep scattered down meadow slopes like a slow, slow avalanche of fleeces. Before I was born, my mother and father had lived other herding summers, shadowing after the sheep through the long pure days until the lambs were fattened for shipping. *Ivan, you wouldn't believe the grouse that were on those slopes then. The summer we were married and went herding on Grass Mountain, all that country was just alive with grouse then. I'd shoot them five at a time, and your mother—your mother'd cook them at noon when the sheep had shaded up. We'd eat one apiece and seal the rest in quart jars and cool them in the spring water so we'd have them cold for supper. They were the best eatin' in this world. Lot of times we'd have them for breakfast too, before we moved camp. Y'see, on forest reserve you're supposed to move camp about every day. The first summer there on Grassy, we moved camp fifty-eight times in the first sixty days. We had a brand new box camera we were awful proud of, and we'd take a picture of our campsite every time. Your mother . . .*

The pair of words would break him then, and fool that I could be, I would look aside from his struggling face. In these afteryears, it is my turn for the struggle inside the eyes and along the drop of throat, for I have the album pages of those campsites along the ridgelines and the swale meadows of their first summer mountain.

Off the stiff black pages, two almost-strangers grin up into my eyes, like past neighbors seen again across too many years, and I wonder at all I know and do not know of this set of lives:

My father looks stronger than I ever knew him, and even more handsome, the straight broad lines of his face framed cleanly around the dimple-scar in the center of his chin. His stockman's hat has been crimped carefully, sits on his head at a perfect angle. His shoulders line out level and very wide for a man just five and a half feet tall, but this strength at the top of him trims away to a lower body slender as a boy's. I am reminded that he was so slim down the waist and hips that the seat of his pants forever bagged in, and the tongue of his belt had to flap far past the buckle, as if trying to circle him twice. Certain photos catch this father of mine as almost mischievous, cocking the dry half-grin which sneaks onto my own face as I look at him. In others there is a distance to him, a sense that except for accident he might be anywhere else in the world just now, and maybe a being entirely unlike the one I know here. In any pose, he looks at the camera squarely, himself a kind of lens aimed back at the moment.

To see him, the several hims encamped across the pages, is to begin listening for the burred voice, the retellings, the veers and jogs of his life:

Ivan, I think I'll take on those two bands of sheep for McGrath. He's a bearcat to work for, but the son-of-a-buck knows livestock and he knows how to turn money. . . .

That place was a haywire outfit from the start, or I'll put in with you. They had men on that place that by God you wouldn't send to fetch a bucket of water or they'd bring it back upside down. Cliff and I stood it for about a week, then we told the boss to write 'er out for us, we were heading for town. . . .

This doctor now, I don't know about him. If I was in as good a shape as he says I am, I wouldn't be sick atall. . . .

Again the sentences snap; I see the handsome steady mouth clamp itself, the chin-dot of scar come close beneath, small but deep like a tool mark nicked in when his strong head was carved. A single quick notch at the bottom of his face, as if it might be the first lightest scratch of calamity on him.

But my mother: my mother, here in some summer of early marriage, already seems frail, so slim—too light a being to last there so near the challenge of timberline. Again, because I know what was to come, I believe myself into the notion that I can read it all gathering on the album's somber paper. I print into my mind from her every pose how fine-boned she was, hardly more than tiny, with a roundish, slightly wondering face where most of my own is quickly read. I coax from the photos all detail which seems to tell the sickness eroding in her; the pinch across her slender shoulders, the eyes which are almost too calm and accepting.

But the one thing which would pulse her alive for me does not come. I do not know the sound of her voice, am never to know it. Instead she is wound in the other voices tracked through the years. Her teacher at the one-room schoolhouse in a sea of sage: *The first morning of school, here I saw this girl coming up on a black horse, just coming as fast as ever she could. And it was your mother, and she was rushing up to tell me there were mice in the well, and not to use that water.* The rancher's wife who had neighbored with her in some summer of haying: *I wouldn't see anyone for hours, and I would go across to your house and there your mother would be reading to you. She'd read by the hour, on a hot afternoon she'd keep you so cool and quiet just sitting there reading . . . She was so quiet, had such a soft fine voice.* The forest ranger who oversaw their range that early season on Grass Mountain: *She could do about anything a man could—ride, sling a pack, any of that. She even knew how to trap. We talked sometimes about runnin' a trapline, and I know she did in winters later on. But she had to be careful, y'know, anything she did, or she'd choke right down, short of breath.*

Yes. This album of summers again, as if I might finger through the emulsion patterns to the moments themselves. At the backs of my familiar photoed strangers, always a forest, and always sunlight spattering down through the pine boughs to their rough shirt fronts. The canvas slopes of their tent are triangled grayly at the back of the day camp. Two black herding dogs, ears up in dog surprise, study the lens. A pair of saddlehorses gawk in from the grassy fringes of camp as if afraid any attention might go by them. One creature in these early pictures does not fit, and this intrigues me—the pet which is being stroked in my mother's hands.

Those first seasons of following the sheep, my parents kept with them in their daily sift through the forest a cat, an independent gray-and-white tom they had named Pete Olson. Somehow, amid the horses and dogs and sheep, and the coyotes and bobcats which ranged close to camp, Pete Olson rationed out his nine lives in nightly prowls of the mountain. Then as camp was moved each morning, he would be cradled like a prince between somebody's lap and the saddle pommel as the horses shouldered through the timber. My parents were childless then, told by doctors that they might always be. If the prediction had held, if I had never been, would any but the astral glance of a cat ever have seen into those far summers of theirs? Would that time be different for not having met my eyes?

Yet the two are met, and in this season on the final mountain, the surprising drifter ducking through swags of pine branches on the back of a horse has become me. Later, my father would never tire of telling what a cantankerous source of pride I made in that riding family. *The only thing we could get you on was a sawbuck pack saddle. You know what they are, like a little sawhorse setting on top of the saddle rigging. Hard as a rasp to sit on, but you straddled in there like it was the only thing going. Ride sometimes half a day in it. You were a stubborn little dickens.* This, with the grin up at me as I loomed half a head over him. As I tried to find in myself that small flinty son from the past.

Wherever it may point, my own clearest moment of myself in that far summer has just the mood of sober cussedness he recalled. I had been given a bow and a few arrows, likely an early gift for my birthday. Time and again, my arrows whacked far from the paper target my father had tacked to the side of the cabin. I see myself pouting it out, kicking at the tan bunchgrass as I think, as the creek makes its shying mutter. Then I edge close to the cabin wall until the round sharp tip of the arrow hangs inches from the paper. I let go the bowstring, and the bullseye slashes open with a hard snapping sound.

That, with every instant of remembering clear as the noon air. Yet of my mother's death, whatever I try, just a single flicker, dim and hurtful, ever is called back: the asthma has claimed her, there are only two breathings in the cabin now, my father is touching me awake in lantern glow, his shadow hurled high up onto the wall, to say *she is dead, Ivan, your mother is dead,* sobbing as the words choke him.

The start of memory's gather: June 27, 1945. I have become six years old, my mother's life has drained out at 31 years. And in the first gray daylight, dully heading our horses around from that cabin of the past, my father and I rein away toward all that would come next.

Memory is a set of sagas we live by, much the way of the Norse wildmen in their bear shirts. That such rememberings take place in a single cave of brain rather than half a hundred minds warrened wildly into one another makes them sagas no less. By now, my days would seem blank, unlit, if these familiar surges could not come. A certain turn in my desk chair, and the leather cushion must creak the quick dry groan of a saddle under my legs—and my father's, and his father's. The taste in the air as rain comes over the city is forever a flavor back from a Montana community too tiny to be called a town. A man, the same alphabet of college degrees after his name as mine, trumps in a debating point during a party argument, and my grandmother's words mutter in me on cue that he grins like a jackass eating thistles.

Rote moments, these, mysteryless perhaps in themselves. It is where they lead, and with what fitful truth and deceit, that tantalizes. If, somewhere beneath the blood, the past must beat in me to make a rhythm of survival for itself—to go on as this half-life which echoes as a second pulse inside the ticking moments of my existence—if this is what must be, why is the pattern of remembered instants so uneven, so gapped and rutted and plunging and soaring? I can only believe it is because memory takes its pattern from the earliest moments in the mind, from childhood. And childhood is a most queer flame-lit and shadow-chilled time. Think once more how the world wavers and intones above us then. Parents behave down toward us as if they are tribal gods, as old and unarguable and almighty as thunder. Other figures loom in from next door and the schoolyard and a thousand lanes of encounter, count coup on us with whatever lessons of life they brandish, then ghost off. We peek into ourselves and find deviling there as well. Riddles are delight at its most tricksterish high chant: Thirty-two white horses on a red hill. Now they're tramping, now they're champing, now they're standing still. Where are they? *Bafflement to the other, triumph to you:* In your mouth! *And darker frolic: this first sudden set of years also is the one season of life, for most of us, when we can kill emotionlessly—or worse, simply from curiosity, to see how the tiny mice prodded from their field nest are different, dead, from the tiny mice, alive, of an instant ago. Cruelty comes new to us, and astonishing, yet we are at our cruelest to each other, mocking playmates home in sobs. Marauders, we are marauded, too. Darkness blankets down around a child as if the planet's caves have emptied all their shadows over him. Everything fights the child's ambitions—fences reach too high, streets stretch too wide, days too short and too long. Imagination is the single constant friend of the child, and even imagination does its share of betrayal, scowls itself in some stalled passage of time into scaredness and doubt.*

Just so does life blaze and haunt around us before we learn we are sober creatures of civilization. Just so, when childhood itself has passed into the distance behind me, does my remembering of the thirty-year story that begins with my mother's last breath go on the way it was recklessly shaped in me then.

VALLEY

The clockless mountain summers were over for my father. Forty-four years old, a ranch hand, now a widower, Charlie Doig had a son to raise by himself. He needed work which would last beyond a quick season. He had to fit us under a roof somewhere, choose a town where I could start to school, piece out in his own mind just how we were going to live from then on. It tells most about my father over the next years that I was the only one of those predicaments that ever seemed to grow easier for him.

Some homing notion said to bring us back to old ground; his mood, maybe, that we were lost enough without braving places he had never been. Beginning when his legs were long enough to straddle a horse's back, Dad had spent all but a few years of his life riding out after cattle and sheep across the gray sage distances of the Smith River Valley and the foothill country hunkered all around it. Any ranch in sight could start a story: *The winter of 'twenty-one, I helped that scissorbill feed his cattle. He worked a team of big roans on the hay sled. Oh, they were a pair of dandies . . . Diamond*

Tony was herding there on Grassy Mountain, and this one day he had a Wyoming scatter on the band, sheep from hell to breakfast . . . It was just up over the ridge, the two of us were ridin' fence. Pete started working over that mare with his quirt again. 'Damn ye anyway,' I says to old mister Pete. 'Beat up on a horse like that, would ye?' I cussed him up one side and down the other, don't think I didn't. . . . Into that remembered countryside, the two of us came now like skipping rocks shied across a familiar pond.

In the years beyond, when we would talk through that time and try to find ourselves there in the early lee of my mother's death, our tellings ended up athwart one another, like the stories of two survivors, each of whom had come out of blankness at a different moment and in a different corner of the scene. Such of each story, that is, as we allowed out of ourselves, for there too a difference sloped between us. It was my father's habit to say and resay a version as it had first taken shape in him. It became mine to mull and prod away at all versions. Yet between us, we could summon a kind of truth about that fierce season of bewilderment.

Angus wasn't done with his haying yet, you remember. After your mother's funeral, he asked me to come help out. Yes. The early weeks, the first act of rescue: Angus, my father's favorite brother, brought us to live with him and his family. We tucked ourselves into an upstairs room of the ranch house there. While Dad worked in the hayfield, I was left at the ranch buildings to play with my three cousins. This again was something new and unfair in my life. Before, the aloneness of the way we lived, out on a foothills ranch or in the Bridger peaks, had spread open my days for whatever I could think up. If I wanted to spend half the daylight hours face down over the creek trying to scoop my hand under tadpoles, I did it. If I wanted to play a pretend game of flipping rocks at a tree and making with my mouth the *kchew, kchew* sound of shooting, I did that. But now such lonesome pleasures were crowded away. Now, just as my mother had, my aloneness was dying, and that loss mourned hard in me, too.

Then, wouldn't ye know it, Clifford came up with the idea of us moving in there with him so you could start to school. More easily can I imagine my father's life without me in it than without Clifford. The two of them had been friends since before they could remember, left home together as youngsters to go off to a lumber town away out on the coast, cowboyed and drank and storied with one another, knew and liked each other in the automatic way that happens only a time or two during life. Clifford had come out of a homestead family as poor as the shale slopes crowding in on their shanty. He had never flinched from anything for very long ever since, and he did not flinch now to take in his saddlefriend and a bereft boy. *Well, hell, y'know, me an' Charlie was like brothers. Closer, maybe. I seen your dad was havin' a hard time gettin' over your mother's passin' away. I don't think he ever did get over it, in a way.* Clifford's ranch lay a few miles from the valley's town, White Sulphur Springs, where I now began school. Each morning came a too-quick trip to the schoolyard; a trudge from the pickup to the high brick box of a school; a trudge up the broad flight of stairs to the classroom where I would be cooped for the day with twenty small strangers, not one of whom had ever ridden a sawbuck packsaddle or shot an arrow in the Bridger Mountains. Those early weeks in the first grade, only two little blurts of excitement set off any interest within me. We went through a drill about how to line up and quick-march out of the old brick building if it caught fire, which gave me hope that maybe it would. And one morning when we were fanned around the teacher for reading, the blonde girl sitting next to me peed herself and set up a sobbing howl as the rest of us backed off from her puddle and watched to see how school handled something like this. The teacher's hankie ended the tears, and a janitor with a mop sopped up the other. I sat with my feet up on the chair rungs for the next few days of reading lessons.

Those first weeks of school, they were a kind of tough time for ye, weren't they? They were. Even before the alarming peeing, I was unimpressed with lessons, which seemed to be school's way of finicking around with things I could do quicker on my own. Already I could read whatever the surprised teacher could put in front of me, and add or subtract numbers as fast as she chalked them on the blackboard. How this had come to be, I had no idea; I only knew that I could not remember when I hadn't been able to read, and that the numbers sorted out their own sums before I had to give them any close attention. School struck me as a kind of job where you weren't allowed to do anything; I had free time in my head by the dayfull, and spent it all in being lonesome for ranch life and its grownups and its times of aloneness. To keep what I could of myself, I moped off on my own every recess and lunch hour, then sulked in some corner of the playfield after school until I could see Dad or Clifford driving up the street to fetch me.

I guess ye'd have to say that spell was none too easy for me, either. A tiny plopping sound of surprise, made by clucking his tongue against the roof of his mouth, might come from my father when he suddenly remembered something, or felt a quick regret of some sort. This time, the soft salute meant both those things. *Godamighty, Ivan, I did miss your mother.* That cannot begin to tell it. If it was Dad instead of Clifford who came to take me from the schoolyard, I stepped from the shadows of my mood into the blacker shadows of his. Years afterward and hundreds of miles from the valley, I was with him when he met a man in the street, backed away, and stared the stranger out of sight in wordless hatred. The man had worked at the ranch where my mother died, and a few days after her death told Dad bluffly: *Hell, Charlie, you got to forget her. That's the only way to get on with life. Don't let a thing like this count too much.* All that time and distance later, Dad still despised him for those clumsy words. Not until that moment did I entirely understand how severe a time it had been when he came for me after school in those earliest weeks after my mother's death and we would drive back to a borrowed room in a pitying friend's house.

Day by day as autumn tanned the valley around us, now with bright frost weather, now with rain carrying the first chill of winter, my father stayed in the dusk of his grief. That sandbagged mood, I understand now, can only have been a kind of battle fatigue—the senses blasted around in him by that morning of death and the thousands of inflicting minutes it was followed by. He might go through the motions of work, even talk a bit with Clifford, but at any time his eyes could brim and he would lapse off, wordless, despairing. I never knew either, when some sentence I would say, or some gesture I would make in the way my mother had, would send him mournful again.

Then coaxing began to finger through to us. My turnabout must have come first. The one classmate I knew at all was a black-haired, musing girl named Susan Buckingham; a few summers before, Dad had foremanned the haying crew at the valley ranch owned by her family, and Susan and I had become shy friends for the time, drawn together on the shaded afternoons when my mother would read aloud to us. Now in some one instant—amid the giggles from a game of tag, or the arc of a swing going so high it looked good and risky—Susan tugged me at last toward the center of the school playground and into more friendships. Also, several of my classmates carried their black tin lunchboxes to school as I did; we had to congregate to see which sandwiches or cookies could be swapped, and whether anybody had been lucky enough to get chocolate milk in his thermos instead of white. And when a too-early first snow came, draping across a few days of early autumn, all the rocks I had thrown at trees in the pretend games paid off: I could chunk a snowball hard enough to make even the sixth-grade boys flinch. Whoever chose up sides for the snow-fort game we played began to choose me first.

Suddenly the schoolyard no longer was a jail to me. And by luck, the teacher in that coop of a classroom was clever. She was a small, doll-like woman who, after she had done her first weeks of sorting, somehow could push twenty beginning minds at their separate speeds. For me, she began to get out extra books, put me to helping others with their alphabet and first words—anything to bring my eyes down into the pages, and all of it telling me that here, in as many words on paper as I could take in, stretched my new aloneness.

At the same time, Clifford was nudging Dad out of his sour haze. He heard of a small ranch for rent at the south end of the valley, and somehow drew Dad into promising he would look it over. The ranch never could amount to much—too little water, too many scabbed hillsides of glum rock—but it could carry several dozen head of cattle and maybe a few hundred sheep as well if a man knew what he was doing. And the true meld to be gained from the place, Clifford knew, was that the work demanding to be done there would elbow the grief out of Dad's days.

Somewhere in himself my father steadied enough to decide. *I didn't much want to do it, ye know. But Clifford got hold of me and took me down there to see the place and gave me a talkin' to, and I couldn't find enough reason against it.* He shook hands on the deal for the ranch. For the third time in a dozen weeks, the pair of us bounced across the Smith River Valley.

Little by little, and across more time than I want to count, I have come to see where our lives fit then into the valley. If Dad ever traced it at any length for himself, he never said so in more than one of his half-musings, half-jokes: *As the fellow says, a fool and his money are soon parted, but ye can't even get introduced around here.* Yet I believe he too came to know, and to the bone, exactly where it was we had stepped when we went from Clifford's sheltering. On the blustery near-winter day when we left the highway and drove onto the gray clay road of our new ranch, the pair of us began to live out the close of an unforgiving annal of settlement which had started itself some eighty years earlier.

It is not known just when in the 1860's the first white pioneers trickled into our area of south-central Montana, into what would come to be called the Smith River Valley. But if the earliest of them wagoned in on a day when the warm sage smell met the nose and the clear air lensed close the details of peaks two days' ride from there, what a glimpse into glory it must have seemed. Mountains stood up blue-and-white into the vigorous air. Closer slopes of timber offered the logs to hew homestead cabins from. Sage grouse nearly as large as hen turkeys whirred from their hiding places. And the expanse of it all: across a dozen miles and for almost forty along its bowed length, this home valley of the Smith River country lay open and still as a gray inland sea, held by buttes and long ridges at its northern and southern ends, and east and west by mountain ranges.

A new county had been declared here, bigger than some entire states in the East and vacant for the taking. More than vacant, evacuated: the Piegan Blackfeet tribes who had hunted across the land by then were pulling north, in a last ragged retreat to the long-grass prairies beyond the Missouri River. And promise of yet another sort: across on the opposite slopes of the Big Belt Mountains, placer camps around Helena were flushing gold out of every gravel gulch. With the Indians vanished and bonanza gold drawing in the town builders, how could this neighboring valley miss out on prosperity? No, unbridle imagination just for a moment, and it could not help but foretell all these seamless new miles into pasture and field, roads and a rail route, towns and homes.

Yet if they had had eyes for anything but the empty acres, those firstcomers might have picked clues that this was a somewhat peculiar run of country, and maybe treacherous. Hints begin along the eastern skyline. There the Castle Mountains poke great turrets of stone out of black-green forest. From below in the valley, the spires look as if they had been engineered prettily up from the forest floor whenever someone took the notion, an entire mountain range of castle-builders' whims—until the fancy stone thrusts wore too thin in the wind and began to chink away, fissure by slow fissure. Here, if the valleycomers could have gauged it in some speedup of time, stood a measure of how wind and storm liked to work on that country, gladly nubbing down boulder if it stood in the way.

While the Castle Mountains, seen so in the long light of time, make a goblin horizon for the sun to rise over, the range to the west, the Big Belts, can cast some unease of its own on the valley. The highest peak of the range—penned into grandness on maps as Mount Edith, but always simply Old Baldy to those of us who lived with mountain upon mountain—thrusts up a bare summit with a giant crater gouged in its side. Even in hottest summer, snow lies in the great pock of crater like a patch on a gape of wound. Always, then, there is this reminder that before the time of men, unthinkable forces broke apart the face of the biggest landform the eye can find from any inch of the valley.

Nature's crankiness to the Big Belts did not quit there. The next summit to the south, Grass Mountain, grows its trees and grass in a pattern tipped upside down from every other mountain in sight. Instead of rising leisurely out of bunchgrass slopes which give way to timber reaching down from the crest, Grassy is darkly cowled with timber at the bottom and opens into a wide generous pasture—a brow of prairie some few thousand feet higher than any prairie ought to be, all the length of its gentle summit.

Along the valley floor, omens still go on. The South Fork of the Smith River turns out to be little more than a creek named by an optimist. Or, rather, by some frontier diplomat, for as an early newspaperman explained in exactly the poetry the pawky little flow deserved, the naming took notice of a politician in the era of the Lewis and Clark expedition—*Secretary Smith of the Navy Department/The most progressive member of Jefferson's cabinet/ . . . thus a great statesman, the expedition giver/is honored for all time in the name of "Smith River."* The overnamed subject of all that merely worms its way across the valley, generally kinking up three times the distance for every mile it flows and delivering all along the way more willow thickets and mud-browed banks than actual water. On the other hand, the water that is missing from the official streambed may arrive in some surprise gush somewhere else. A hot mineral pool erupting at an unnotable point of the valley gave the name to the county seat which built up around the steaming boil, White Sulphur Springs.

But whatever the quirks to be discovered in a careful look around, the valley and its walls of high country did fit that one firm notion the settlers held: empty country to fill up. Nor, in justice, could the eye alone furnish all that was vital to know. Probably it could not even be seen, at first, in the tides of livestock which the settlers soon were sending in seasonal flow between the valley and those curious mountains. What it took was experience of the climate, to remind you that those grazing herds of cattle and bands of sheep were not simply on the move into the mountains or back to the valley lowland. They were traveling between high country and higher, and in that unsparing landscape, the weather is rapidly uglier and more dangerous the farther up you go.

The country's arithmetic tells it. The very floor of the Smith River Valley rests one full mile above sea level. Many of the homesteads were set into the foothills hundreds of feet above that. The cold, storm-making mountains climb thousands of feet more into the clouds bellying over the Continental Divide to the west. Whatever the prospects might seem in a dreamy look around, the settlers were trying a slab of lofty country which often would be too cold and dry for their crops, too open to a killing winter for their cattle and sheep.

It might take a bad winter or a late and rainless spring to bring out this fact, and the valley people did their best to live with calamity whenever it descended. But over time, the altitude and climate added up pitilessly, and even after a generation or so of trying the valley, a settling family might take account and find that the most plentiful things around them still were sagebrush and wind.

By the time I was a boy and Dad was trying in his own right to put together a life again, the doubt and defeat in the valley's history had tamped down into a single word. Anyone of Dad's generation always talked of a piece of land where some worn-out family eventually had lost to weather or market prices not as a farm or a ranch or even a homestead, but as a *place.* All those empty little clearings which ghosted that sage countryside—just the McLoughlin place there by that butte, the Vinton place over this ridge, the Kuhnes place, the Catlin place, the Winters place, the McReynolds place, all the tens of dozens of sites where families lit in the valley or its rimming foothills, couldn't hold on, and drifted off. All of them epitaphed with that barest of words, *place*.

One such place was where our own lives were compassed from. Southwest out of the valley into the most distant foothills of the Big Belts, both the sage and the wind begin to grow lustier. Far off there, beyond the landmark rise called Black Butte and past even the long green pasture hump of Grassy Mountain, a set of ruts can be found snaking away from the county road. The track, worn bald by iron wagonwheels and later by the hard tires of Model T's, scuffs along red shale bluffs and up sagebrush gulches and past trickling willow-choked creeks until at last it sidles across the bowed shoulder of a summit ridge. Off there in the abrupt openness, two miles and more to a broad pitch of sage-soft slope, my father was born and grew up.

This sudden remote bowl of pasture is called the Tierney Basin—or would be, if any human voice were there to say its name. Here, as far back into the tumbled beginnings of the Big Belts as their wagons could go, a double handful of Scots families homesteaded in the years just before this century. Two deep Caledonian notions seem to have pulled them so far into the hills: to raise sheep, and to graze them on mountain grass which cost nothing.

A moment, cup your hands together and look down into them, and there is a ready map of what these homesteading families had in mind. The contours and life lines in your palms make the small gulches and creeks angling into the center of the Basin. The main flow of water, Spring Creek, drops down to squirt out there where the bases of your palms meet, the pass called Spring Gulch. Toward these middle crinkles, the settlers clustered in for sites close to water and, they hoped, under the wind. The braid of lines, now, which runs square across between palms and wrists can be Sixteenmile Creek, the canyoned flow which gives the entire rumpled region its name—*the Sixteen country*. Thumbs and the upward curl of your fingers represent the mountains and steep ridges all around. Cock the right thumb a bit outward and it reigns as Wall Mountain does, prowing its rimrock out and over the hollowed land below. And on all that cupping rim of unclaimed high country, the Scots families surely instructed one another time and again, countless bands of sheep could find summer grass.

Exactly what had plucked up the Doig family line from a village outside Dundee in Scotland and carried it into these gray Montana foothills this way, there is no account of. Dad simply wrote it off to Scots mulishness: *Scotchmen and coyotes was the only ones that could live in the Basin, and pretty damn soon the coyotes starved out.* I have but the rough list of guesses from the long westering course of this country's frontier: poverty's push or the pull of wanderlust, some word of land and chance as heard from those who had gone earlier to America, or as read in the advertisements of booking agents. Perhaps some calamity inside the family itself, the loss of whatever thin livelihoods there had been in laboring on a laird's estate. Or it may truly have been an outcropping of the family vein of stubbornness. Some unordinary outlooks on life seemed to jaw out in my grandfather's generation, attitudes which might not have set well with a narrow village way of existence. Three Doig brothers and two sisters are known to have gone off from the Dundee area to risky futures, and at least two of them clearly went about life as if it was some private concoction they had just thought up.

The first remembered for doing entirely what she pleased was the sister Margaret, the one in the family who launched off from Scotland into the British Empire, alighting on some remote flood plain of India as a teacher or missionary, no one now is quite sure which. She is at the outermost edges of the family memory, a talisman of intrepidness glimpsed and gone in someone's reminiscences as remembered by someone yet again. The rememberers do tell that twice in her last years she came around the world alone to visit the relatives in Montana, a sudden spinsterly ghost from Victorian days in her long black dress and odd wooden sandals of India. She spent the rest of her life in India—died there, was buried there—and in her own way must have been entirely bemused with the existence she had worked out somewhere under the backdrop of the Himalayas.

The other original spirit was the eldest brother among those who packed up for Montana—David Lawson Doig, called D.L. The one clear fact about the route from Dundee is that a number of Scots came in succession, like a chain of people steadying one another across a rope bridge. Whoever arrived first—and no records name him—his letters talked the next one into coming to file on a homestead, and the one persuaded after that was D.L.'s own brother-in-law. Of course, D.L. stepped off next. By sometime in 1890, he had followed on with his wife and three children and set to work in Helena as a tailor until he could size up the Montana countryside.

He sized it up entirely backward to the way his heirs have wished ever since, passing over rich valleys to the west and south to adventure up into the remote Tierney Basin, where a homesteader who was giving up would sell him his claim. D.L. settled into his new site on Spring Creek, by long workdays and clever grazing made his small sheep ranch begin to prosper, and fathered hard until the family finally numbered nine children.

As promptly as he had enough offspring and income to keep the ranch going, D.L. devoted his own time to the hobby of raising brown leghorn chickens. He proved to be an entire genius at chicken growing. Before long, his bloodline of brown leghorns, with their sleek glosses of feather and comb, were as renowned as prize breeding stock. *He went to the big shows in California and all over the East,* a son tells it. *Beforehand he'd bring in his show cages into our front room and he'd have his chickens in there, and he'd prune 'em and pick at 'em with a pointer stick, make 'em stand certain ways and train their combs and everything like that, y'know. He had the best anywhere. When he was at the Coliseum Show in New York, the Russian government paid $1400 for three or four of those chickens. Something like that happened just a numerous lot of times. I didn't like no part of 'em—we all had to pitch in to take care of these blasted chickens—but he was one of the best hands in the world with his birds.* The trophies won at fairs and expositions covered most of one wall of the house, and D.L.'s wife sewed a quilt from the prize ribbons. Until the Depression and old age at last forced him out, D.L. could be found there in the Basin, a round deep-bearded muser fussing over his prize chickens, sending someone down to the railroad tracks in the Sixteen canyon to fetch the jug of whiskey consigned for him each week, and asking not one thing more of the universe.

D.L. was followed into his oddly chosen Montana foothills by two of his brothers. Another of the faintest of family stories has it that the brother named Jack came to D.L.'s ranch on a doomed chance that mountain air would help his health, and there patiently waited out the year or so it took him to die. His would have been the first Doig grave to be put down amid sagebrush instead of heather. The other brother, Peter Doig, somehow made his way from Scotland in the spring of 1893, just after his nineteenth birthday. He had been a tailor's helper, and in the new land at once began a life as far away from needle and thread as he could get. For the first few years, he did the jobs on sheep ranches that his son would do a generation later, and which I would do, a generation after that, as his son's son—working in the lambing sheds, herding, wrangling in the shearing pens.

There can't have been much money in the ranch jobs which drew my father's father in those first years. But what there would have been was all the chance in the world to learn about sheep—and sheep in their gray thousands were the wool-and-meat machines which had made fortunes for the lairds of the Scotland he arrived from. What was more, this high Montana grassland rimming the Big Belts had much of the look of the home country, and had drawn enough Scots onto ranches and homesteads that they counted up into something like a colony. The burr of their talk could be heard wherever the slow tides of sheep were flowing out onto the grass. Between the promise of those grazing herds and that talk comfortable to the ear, Peter Doig found it a place for staying.

Beyond the basics that he had relatives and countrymen in the new land and that he was medium height, slim, red-mustached, and had the purling lowlands way of speech, nothing can be found now of what young Peter Doig was like. Not a scrap of paper from his own hand, not a word from those who would have known him then, not one thing to show him head-on and looking out at the world. What he did for himself is likewise known only in scantest outline: he met and married D.L.'s sister-in-law, Annie Campbell, a young woman who had come from Perthshire by that chain of relatives and their relatives, and who now cooked for ranch crews. A year or so after the marriage, one son born, the young couple took up land a mile west of D.L.'s small ranch in the Tierney Basin.

Those homesteading Scots families of the Basin—Doigs, Christisons, Mitchells, a few who came later—could not know it at first, but they had taken up land where the long-standing habits and laws of settlement in America were not going to work. For one thing, this: the homestead staked out by Peter and Annie Doig lay amid the Big Belts at an elevation of 5700 feet. At first, the hill country did pay off with its summers of free pasture. In the bargain, however, came Januaries and Februaries—and too often Marches and Aprils—of hip-deep snowdrifts.

There was no help in law, of course, for the blizzards which bullied through the Tierney Basin. But little help derived, either, where law supposedly was shouldering its share of the load. Simply, it came down to this: homesteads of 160 acres, or even several times that size, made no sense in that vast and dry and belligerent landscape of the high-mountain west. As well try to grow an orchard in a window-box as to build a working ranch from such a patch. Quilt more land onto the first? Well and good—except that in an area of sharp natural boundaries, such as the Basin, a gain for one homestead could come only with someone else's loss. Simply go on summering the livestock in the shared open range of the mountains, as the Basin people did at first? Well and good again—except that with the stroke of a government pen which decreed the high summer pasture into a national forest, all that nearby free range ended. And promptly—*so fast it'd make your head swim*, my father would have said of such promptness—the allotments for forest grazing began to pass to the region's corporate ranches which already were big, and getting bigger.

Even if you somehow outlasted the weather, then, no foothills homestead you built for yourself could head off a future of national forest boundaries and powerful livestock companies. Like much else in the wresting of this continent, the homestead laws were working to a result, right enough, but not to the one professed for them. The homestead sites my father could point out to me by the dozen—place upon place, and our own family soil among them—in almost all cases turned out to be not the seed acres for yeoman farms amid the sage, nor the first pastures of tidy family ranches. Not that at all. They turned out to be landing sites, quarters to hold people until they were able to scramble away to somewhere else. Quarters, it could be said, that did for that region of rural America what the tenements of the immigrant ghettoes did for city America.

But that is my telling of it, across the gulf of a second generation after Peter and Annie Doig took up land in the Basin. They had other things in their heads than the years beyond tomorrow. The young wife from Perthshire could hear the howling of wolves and coyotes—and worse, the splitting cracks of thunder when lightning storms cut down on the Big Belts. To the end of her life, she claimed she never could forget those unruly sounds of the Basin, nor its isolation. The young husband was more the one for staying. Peter Doig built a house of pine logs from a nearby timbered slope and filed homestead papers for the 160-acre site—which ominously qualified best under a law for the taking up of "desert land." Over the next dozen years, the couple managed to double their owned acreage and to make a start in the sheep business, then used the profits to buy cattle, the easier livestock to pasture. As well, they added to the first son five more, until the names in the family began to resound like the roll call of a kilted regiment: *Edwin Charles,*

Varick John, Charles Campbell, James Stuart, Angus McKinnon, Claude Spencer.

Then, on a September day in 1910, a little past noon, Peter Doig stepped outside the log house. He had been spending time on errands—to the county fair the day before, where he had won prizes for his chickens and dry-land potatoes and treated himself to a fine rewardful drunk, this morning to his nearest neighbor's house on some small matter—and the ranch chores were piling up. He strode down the path to the garden to begin digging the rest of the prize potato crop. Going through the gate, he clutched at his heart, fell sideways, and died. He was four months short of his thirty-seventh birthday.

A few mornings later, a lumber wagon with a casket roped in place jolted out of the Tierney Basin and set off on the day-long trip to the cemetery at White Sulphur Springs. Behind the rough hearse coiled a dusty column of riders on horseback and families in spring wagons, neighbors and kin. They buried Peter Doig, tailor's helper in Scotland and homesteader in Montana, and rode their long ride home into the hills.

Charles Campbell Doig was nine when his father died, made old enough in that instant to help his mother and his brothers carry the body in from the dark garden dirt. It must have been the first time he touched against death. And touched ahead, too, somewhere in his scaredness, to the life he was going to have from then on in that lamed family, on that flinty Basin homestead.

That is as much as can be eked out—landscape, settlers' patterns on it, the family fate within the pattern—about the past my father came out of. I read into it all I can, plot out likelihoods and chase after blood hunches. But still the story draws itself away from the dry twinings of map work and bloodlines, and into the boundaries of my father's own body and brain. Where his outline touched the air, my knowing must truly begin.

He was, as I have said, not more than five and a half feet tall, and he had the small man's jut of jaw toward heaven about that. *I never saw anybody so big I couldn't take him on in a fight, anyway.* That would have been said from his declaring stance, standing flat-backed as if a strut had been stopped in midstride. Then the grin would have worked at the handsome straight mouth and the wryness come: *He might of cleaned my clock when I took him on, too, but that didn't matter. Oh, as the fellow says, I'm awfully little but I'm awfully tough.*

As the fellow says. That signal began seven of every ten of his jokes, the Dutch fellow or the Chinese fellow or the Irish fellow intoning one jape or another—and inevitably performed in Dad's dialect tries, all hopelessly but happily lost in his own heathery burr. My father had a humor unusual in a tense man, a casual gift of storying which paid no attention to the nerves twanging away in him. This may account for the way people sometimes have talked to me of him as if Charlie Doig were two separate men. *I remember Charlie could spiel with the best of us knotheads,* one will say, *had a story ready whenever he remembered to look up from his work.* And another, *He knew sheep ranchin', that feller did, but you know he could kind of get excited workin' cattle, he was too nervous to be the best cowman.* He divides like that in my own memory as well. Here, the natural pace of story which would have me listening without daring a blink. There, his marks of worry or tension, the tongue-click against the roof of his mouth or the spaced rhythm which began to parcel his words: *Damn-it-to-hell-anyway. . . .*

Too, I somehow see my father in different sizes at once—the box-jawed man so far above me as a boy, the banty of a fellow beside me when I had grown. But at whatever version, a remarkable economy of line about him. As if making it up to him for the shortness and a weight of only about 135 pounds, Dad's body went wide and square at the shoulders and then angled neatly down, like a thin but efficient wedge. His arms were ropy with muscle, yet not large; it was a mystery where the full strength of him came from, for he was as strong as men half again his size in lifting hay bales or woolsacks or wrestling calves down for the branding iron.

The quick parts of his brain, and they were several, mostly had to do with such ranchcraft. This came both from that Basin upbringing and from having flung himself out of it. *He was just pretty catty about anything to do with a ranch. And I knew Charlie when he wasn't much more than dry behind the ears, out and ridin' for these stock spreads. . . .*

So to me now, looking at my father's early life is something like the first glimpse ever into a stone-rippled reflection in a pond, and wondering how it can be that the likeness there repeats some of what I know is me, growing up at his side thirty years later, along with so much more that is only waver and blur and startlement, and so can only belong to some other being entirely. Crowding all his home hours in that log cabin beneath the Big Belts, five brothers, and a sister, Anna, born after Peter Doig's death; the one of me, alone and treasuring it that way. His eight years of school which, shying from those Basin winters, began with spring thaw and then hurried hit-and-miss through summer; all my summers until well into adulthood ending in earliest September quick as the bell at the end of a recess, school of one kind or another creeping on then through three entire seasons of the year. Some schoolmates of his came from families drawn back so far into the hills and their own peculiarities of living that the children were more like the coyotes which watchfully loped the ridgelines than like the other Basin youngsters. One family's boys, he remembered, started school so skittish that when someone met them on an open stretch of road where they couldn't dart into the brush, they flopped flat with their lunchboxes propped in front of their heads to hide behind. *Thought we couldn't see 'em behind those damned little lunchboxes, can ye feature that?* I barely could; my classmates always were town children, wearing town shoes and with a combed, town way of behaving.

Dad on horseback every chance he had, on his way to being one of the envied riders in a countryside of riders; me reading every moment I could, tipping any open page up into my eyes and imagination. He grew up with a temper fused as short as he was, but also with some estimates of himself considerably more generous than that; maybe because I held in all my temper and dreams, I filled out like a bucket-fed calf, bigger and solider and more red-haired every time anyone glanced in my direction.

Another wonderment at once follows this one, like a stone hurled harder into the pond. On his way to growing out of boyhood, my father came very near to dying. Then time and again after that, it would happen that he would draw alongside death, breathe the taste of doom, then be let live.

I have had to think much about how death has touched early into my family. It touched earliest of all toward my father. Why, if what is so far from having answer is even askable—why was his life so closely stalked this way? And how was it that he lasted as he did? The costs that this father of mine paid in all the surviving he had to do, I know enough about. But about why life had to dangle him such terms, not nearly enough.

That first slash at him, in 1918, came when the planet was dealing plentifully in killing. World War One had gutted open entire nations, the influenza epidemic now was ripping at family after family. Dad barely missed the war; he was seventeen and a half years old at armistice time. But only days later, he was closer to death than if he had been in the frontmost trenches.

The last year or so of the combat, Dad had been hired by Basin neighbors whose son had been plucked away by the draft board. That job, on a tatter of a ranch near the canyon where the railroad snaked through the Sixteen country, was a youngster's worst dream. All day, for one square meal—*oh, and they'd give me an apple to eat at bedtime, the honyockers*—and a few dollars a week which he had to pass along to his mother, Dad did a man's share of ranch work; on top of that, mornings and evenings he slogged through the chores of chicken-feeding and hog-slopping and kindling-splitting which a country child grows up hating.

It got worse. The soldier son was put on a ship to France, and now every day Dad was sent off on the mile and a half trudge down the railroad track to the Sixteen post office, to fetch a newspaper so the fretful parents could read through the list of battle casualties. *I tell ye now, it didn't take me long to be wishin' that the son-of-a-buck would be on that list, so I wouldn't have to fetch that damn newspaper.*

It was like my father to call down exasperation of that sort on somebody else, then undergo worse himself. The soldier son survived. But in mid-November of 1918, Dad set out on a day of deer hunting with a cousin, one of D.L.'s strapping sons, and the pair of them came down first with pneumonia, and then influenza. For days they lay delirious in the log ranch houses their fathers had built a mile apart. On the first night of December, the cousin died, and Dad's fever broke.

Those two had started out even when they put their first footprints in the snow on that hunting trip. Why death for one, and not the other? No answer comes, except that even starts don't seem to count for much. If that was what saved Charlie Doig then, he was going to need several such bylaws of fate before he was done.

That first siege on his health behind him, Dad went back to the hired work which each of the young Doig brothers started at just as soon as he was big enough. For years, their wages had had to be the prop under the family homestead, which at last was almost pulling itself up into a semblance of a ranch. By the autumn of 1919, all their cowboying and sheepherding and scrimping together had added up: *We'd got our debts paid off, and built up quite a little bunch of cattle. Sold 90 head that fall, put the money in the bank, laid in a winter's supply of groceries, bought a tremendous amount of oat straw a guy had there—it was just like hay, ye know. So we started in that winter with 190 head of cattle, and about 40 head of dandy horses. And also my mother just had inherited five thousand dollars from a relative that died in Scotland.* Luck, it seemed, could hardly wait to follow on luck. Then, weeks ahead of the calendar, winter set in.

It became the winter which the Basin people afterward would measure all other winters against. The dark timbered mountains around them went white as icebergs. The tops of sagebrush vanished under drifts. And up around the bodies of bawling livestock, the wind twirled a deadlier and deadlier web of snow. Day upon day, hay sleds slogged out all across the Basin to the cattle and horses as mittened men and boys fought this starvation weather with pitchforks.

By late January, the weather was gaining every day. The Basin's haystacks were nearly gone, and the ranch families shipped in trainloads of slough grass which had been mowed from frozen marshes in Minnesota. Fifty dollars a ton. Fifty-five. Then sixty. *We never heard of prices that high.* And there was no choice in the world but to pay them. *Godamighty, it was awful stuff, though. You had to chop the bales to pieces with axes.* Sometimes out of a bale would tumble an entire muskrat house of sticks and mud. *And cat-tails and brush and Christ knows what all.* Down to this brittle ration, the Basin country began to feel winter fastening into the very pit of its stomach. *I helped load what was left of a neighbor's sheep into boxcars there at Sixteen. Those sheep were so hungry they were eatin' the wool off each other.* And even the desperation hay began to run out. *If we could of got another ten ton, we could of saved a lot of cattle. But-we-could-not-get-it.* Cows struggled to stay alive now by eating willows thick as a man's thumb. And still the animals died a little every day, until the carcasses began to make dark humps on the white desert of snow.

It was early June of 1920 before spring greened out from under the snowdrifts in the Basin. *We had about 60 head of cattle left, and about half a dozen horses, and not a dime.*

The losses killed whatever hopes had been that the Basin ranch would be able to bankroll Dad and the other brothers in ranching starts of their own. Like seeds flying on the Basin's chilly wind, they began to drift out one after another now.

Dad did not neglect to savor his earliest drifting. An autumn came when he and his younger brother Angus went off to the Chicago stockyards with a cousin's boxcars of cattle. *For every carload of stock, see, you were entitled to your fare both ways. We were a pair of punk kids, out for a big time. So we took off to see Chicago.* On the cattle train with them was a valley rancher who celebrated such trips by spending his cattle profits and then papering the city with overdrawn checks. *Oh, he'd go back there and have a high old time.* He took the young cowboys in tow, and the three of them sashayed through Chicago. One morning after several days of cloudtop living, they were sprawled in barber chairs for the daily shave which would start them on a new round of carousing. The policeman on the beat—*a helluva big old harness bull*—paused outside the window at the sight of three pairs of cowboy boots poking from under the barber cloths. He sauntered in, lifted the hot towel off the rancher's face, and said: *Hello, White Sulphur Springs. When you get that shave, I want you.* Their financier on his way to the precinct station, the Doig brothers caught the next train back to Montana.

And some other autumn—it seemed to be his migration time—Dad and his friend Clifford Shearer talked each other into heading west for the Coast. What they were going to do out there, they had no idea whatsoever, but probably it would be more promising than the spot they were standing on at the moment.

Clifford and Dad made, as a valley man has said it to me, *a pair of a kind.* They both were under medium height, wiry, trim, Clifford with his own good looks more sharply cut than Dad's square steady lines. Both were what the valley called *well thought of.* The night before they left, the Basin people threw a farewell dance at the Sixteen schoolhouse. *Women were bawling and carrying on, you'd thought the world was coming to an end.*

Out in the unknown as job seekers, Dad and Clifford fizzed with more imagination than their first employment allowed for. They stopped in Washington's Yakima Valley long enough to try the apple harvest. The idea, they were told the first morning, was to pluck each piece of fruit with care—*now, you young fellers, give it this little twist so the stem don't come off, see?*—so it would go into the box unblemished for the market. But quality was not what they were being paid for; quantity was. Their orchard career hardly had got underway before they were caught efficiently shaking apples down into their boxes by the whole battered treeload, and were sent down the road. *We had five dollars apiece to show for it, anyway.* They headed west some more through the state of Washington. The Pacific Ocean stopped them at Aberdeen, where they hired on as pilers in a lumber yard.

Charlie and I didn't know what a stick of lumber was, hardly—this from Clifford, with his drawling chuckle—*we thought everything was made out of logs, y'know. But they asked us if we knew anything about lumber, and we said 'Well, sure.'* When the first rain of the Aberdeen winter whipped in, the pair of them slopped through their shift wondering to one another how soon the yard boss would take pity, as any rancher back home would decently have done, and send them in out of the downpour. By the end of that wettest day of their lives, they still were in the rain but had stopped wondering.

Well, hell, we needed the job, y'know. It was November and the streets was lined with men, and we was a long ways from home. So I said to Charlie, by gollies, I'm goin' uptown and see if they won't trust a feller for some rain clothes. Clifford slogged off and talked a dry-goods merchant out of two sets of raingear on credit. But a drier skin didn't ease Dad's mind entirely. *He got homesick, y'know. You never saw a guy got so homesick as Charlie.* Dad toughed it out in Aberdeen for some months, told Clifford he couldn't stand it and headed back to Montana. *That Aberdeen winter was the longest one in my life, and godamighty, the rain.*

When he came home shaking off the Pacific Coast damp, Dad was less interested in the world beyond the valley. He did some more cowboying, and some more time on sheep ranches; three seasons, he sheared sheep with a crew which featured a handsome giant shearer named Matt Van Patten.

The best looking guy I think I ever remember seeing. A sheep shearing sonofagun, too; he could really knock the wool off of 'em, went over 200 ewes on his tally every day. And a drinking sonofagun. Dad last saw him when the crew finished its final season and broke up. *Old Matt, he started hittin' the booze, he had a jug somewhere, along the middle of the afternoon. By suppertime he was so drunk he couldn't walk. The crew had a dead-ax wagon to haul its outfit in, and he was layin' in the bottom of that with his head hangin' out over the tailgate.*

When Clifford returned from the Coast, there was serious roistering to be caught up on with him, too. *I remember that me an' Charlie might get a little bit on the renegade side now and then, y'might say. This once, there was three of us—me an' Charlie and D.L.'s son Alec—caught the train from Sixteen up there to the dance at Ringling one night. We got our room from Mrs. Harder, the old German lady who run the Harder Hotel there. Then we went on down to the bootleg joint and bought a gallon of moonshine. So of course we got pretty well loaded off of it, and full of hell. Anyway, Mrs. Harder, she called up the sheriff's office and said for the sheriff to get down there: 'Dere's* sechs *boys from* Sechsteen, *and dey're wreckin' my hotel!' Well, hell, there was only three of us, but I guess she thought we was as bad as six.*

But the deep ingredient of my father's adventuring in those years of his early twenties was horses. It was a time when a man still did much of his day's work atop a saddle pony, and the liveliest of his recreation as well. And with every hour in the saddle, the odds built that there was hoofed catastrophe ahead. Built, as Dad's stories lessoned into me, until the most casual swing into the stirrups could almost cost your life: *I'll tell ye a time. I was breakin' this horse, and I'd rode the thing for a couple of weeks, got him pretty gentle—a big nice tall brown horse with a stripe in his face. I'd been huntin' elk up in the Castles, and I'd rode that horse all day long. Comin' home, I was just there in the Basin below the Christison place, and got off to open a gate. My rifle was on the saddle there, with the butt back toward the horse's hip, and it'd rubbed a sore there and I didn't notice the rubbin'. When I went to get back on, took hold of the saddle horn to pull myself up, ye know, the rifle scraped across that sore. Boy, he ducked out from under me and I went clear over him. I caught my opposite foot in the stirrup as I went over, and away he went, draggin' me. He just kicked the daylights out of me as we went. It was in a plowed field, and I managed to turn over and get my face like this—* cradling his arms in front of his face, to my rapt watching— *but he kept kickin' me in the back of the head here, until he had knots comin' on me big as your fist. And he broke my collarbone. Finally my boot came off, or he'd of dragged me around until he kicked my head off, I guess.*

The accident of flailing along the earth with a horse's rear hooves thunking your skull was one thing. Courting such breakage was another, and it was in my father not to miss that chance, either. Most summer Sundays, the best riders in the county would gather at a ranch and try to ride every bucking horse they had been able to round up out of the hills. It was the kind of hellbending contest young Charlie Doig was good at, and he passed up few opportunities to show it.

The hill broncs which would be hazed in somewhere for this weekend rodeoing—the Doig homestead had a big stout notched-pole corral which was just right—were not scruffy little mustangs. They were half again bigger and a lot less rideable than that: herds grown from ranch stock turned out to pasture, with all the heft of workhorses added to their new wildness. Eventually there came to be a couple of thousand such renegades roaming the grassed hills around the valley. Some would weigh more than three-quarters of a ton and measure almost as tall at the shoulder as the height of a big man. A rider would come away from a summer of those massive hill broncs with one experience or another shaken into his bones and brain, and Dad's turn came up when the last two horses were whooped into the Doig corral at dusk one of those Sunday afternoons.

Five or six of us were ridin', all had our girls there and were showin' off, ye know. Neither of the last horses looked worth the trouble of climbing on—a huge club-hoofed bay, and a homely low-slung black gelding. Someone yelled out, *That black one looks like a damned milk cow!* Dad called across the corral to the other rider, *Which one of those do you want, Frankie, the big one or that black thing?* The bay was saddled, and thudded around the corral harmlessly on its club hooves. Then the corral crew roped the black for Dad and began to discover that this one was several times more horse than it looked. *Oh, he was a bearcat, I'm here to tell you.*

The gelding was so feisty they had to flop him flat and hold him down to cinch the saddle on, the last resort for a saddling crew that took any pride in itself. Dad swung into the stirrups while the horse was uncoiling up out of the dirt. When the bronc had all four feet under him, he sunfished for the corral poles and went high into them as intentionally as if he were a suicide plunging off a cliff. Horse and rider crashed back off the timbers, then the bronc staggered away into another quick running start and slammed the fence again. And then again.

He like to have beat my brains out on that corral fence. Then, worse: *He threw me off over his head upside down and slammed me against that log fence again, and still he kept a-buckin'. I jumped up and got out of his way and tried to climb the fence.* Dad had made it onto the top of the fence when the battering caught up with his body. Blacking out, he pitched off the corral backwards, into the path of the gelding as it rampaged past. The horse ran over him full length, full speed. *One hoof hit me in the ribs here, and the other hit me in the side of the head here, and just shoved all the skin down off the side of my face in a bunch.* The gelding would have hollowed him out like a trough if the corral crew hadn't managed to snake Dad out under the fence before the horse could get himself turned. By then, someone already was sprinting for a car for the forty-five-mile ride to a doctor. *I was laid up six weeks that time, before I could even get on crutches.*

That was his third stalking by death; Dad himself had invited most of the risk that time, although in the homely black gelding it came by the sneakiest of means. But the next near-killing hit him as randomly as a lightning bolt exploding a snag. It began with the yip of coyote pups on a mountainside above the Basin. *I was workin' for Bert Plymale, and we lambed a bunch of sheep over there near the D.L. place.* Coyotes, sheep killers that they were, were hated as nothing else in that country, especially on the lean foothill ranches where any loss of livestock hurt like a wound. *They were eatin' the lambs just about as fast as we could turn 'em out. And we could hear these coyotes in a park up on the side of the mountain, yippin' up there early morning and evening. So I had a young kid workin' with me, and we decided we'd go up there and find that den.*

When they reined up in a clearing in the timber where the yips were coming from, Dad stepped off his horse and walked ahead a few steps to look for the den. *I was carryin' the pick and the kid was carryin' the shovel—in case we found the den, we could dig it out. I'd stepped off of this bay horse, dropped the lines and walked several feet in front of him, clear away from him. That sap of a kid, he dropped that shovel right at the horse's heels. And instead of kickin' at the shovel like a normal horse would, ye know, he jumped ahead and whirled and kicked me right in the middle of the back. Drove two ribs into my lungs.*

Dad hunched on the ground like a shot animal. *I couldn't get any breath atall when I'd try straighten up. When I was down on all fours, I could get enough breath to get by on. The kid, he was gonna leave me there and take off to find everybody in the country to come get me with a stretcher. I said no, by God, I was gonna get out of there somehow.* Spraddled on hands and knees in a red fog of pain, he gasped out to the youngster to lead his horse beneath a small cliff nearby. Dad crawled to the cliff, climbed off the ledge into the saddle. Then, crumpled like a dead man tied into the stirrups, he rode the endless mile and a half to the ranch. *That was one long ride, I'm-here-to-tell-you.*

Getting there only began a new spell of pain—the pounding car ride across rutted roads to town and the doctor. By then, Dad's breathing had gone so ragged and bloody that the doctor set off with him for the hospital in Bozeman. Two gasping hours more in a car. At last, by evening, he lay flat in a hospital bed. *But I always healed fast, anyway,* and a few weeks later, he climbed stiffly onto a horse again.

He wouldn't have thought, when he was being battered around from one near-death to the next, that he was heading all the while into the ranch job he would do for many of the rest of his years. But the valley, which could always be counted on to be fickle, now was going to let him find out in a hurry what he could do best. Sometime in 1925, when he was twenty-four years old, Dad said his goodbyes at the Basin homestead another time, saddled up, and rode to the far end of the Smith River Valley to ask for a job at the Dogie ranch.

More than any other ranch, the Dogie had been set up—which is to say, pieced together of bought-out homesteads and other small holdings—to use the valley's advantages and work around its drawbacks. Wild hay could be cut by the mile from its prime bottomland meadows; a crew of three dozen men would begin haying each mid-June and build the loaflike stacks by the hundreds. Cattle and sheep—like many Montana ranches of the time, the Dogie raised both—could be grazed over its tens of thousands of acres of bunchgrass slopes along and above the north fork of the Smith River, and sheltered from winter blizzards in the willow thickets cloaking the streambed. And the trump card of it all: hard years could be evened out with the wealth of the Seattle shipping family who owned the enterprise and ran it in a fond vague style.

The Dogie readily put Dad on its payroll, but that was the most that could be said for the job. He was made chore-boy, back again at the hated round of milking cows and feeding chickens and hogs and fetching stovewood for the cook. But he had come to the Dogie and was biding time there because the owners were signing into a partnership with a sheep rancher from near Sixteenmile Creek. The "Jasper" at the front of his name long since crimped down to "Jap" by someone's hurried tongue, Jap Stewart had arrived out of Missouri some twenty years before, leaving behind the sight in one eye due to a knife fight in a St. Joe saloon, but bringing just the kind of elbowing ambition to make a success in the wide-open benchlands he found a few miles east of the Basin. Drinker, scrapper, sharp dealer and all the rest, Jap also was a ranchman to the marrow, and he prospered in the Sixteen country as no one before or since. Now he was quilting onto the Dogie holdings his own five thousand head of sheep and the allotted pasture in the national forest for every last woolly one of them. He also moved in to kick loose anything that didn't work, such as most of the Dogie's crew.

Jap began by giving them a Missouri growling at—*most of you sonsabitches 've worked here so goddamn long all you know any more is how to hide out in the goddamn brush*—and ended up sacking every man on the ranch except Dad and a handful of others. While Jap's new men streamed in past the old crew on the road to town, Dad, at the age of 25, was made sheep boss, in charge of the Dogie's nine bands grazing across two wide ends of the county. *In another six months, I was foreman of the whole damn shebang.*

What one-eyed old Jap Stewart must have seen, watching Dad as he grew up in those ranch jobs which Annie Doig's sons were always pegging away at, was that he would know how to work men. Skill with horses and cattle and sheep were one thing; Dad had those talents, but so did every tenth or twentieth young drifter who came along. The rare thing in the valley was to be able to handle men. Ranch crews were a hard commodity, a gravel mix of drifters, drinkers, gripers, not a few mental cripples, and an occasional steady worker. No two crews were ever much alike, except in one thing: somebody was going to resent the work and any foreman who put him to it, and sooner or later trouble would be made. Anyone who had spent time on a ranch crew knew the stories—of a herder who sneaked the stovepipe off his own sheepwagon while camp was being moved so he would have something to be mad about and could quit, or of a tireless hay stacker who packed up and left on the first rainy day because he couldn't stand the hours of being idle. Darker stories, too, of a herding dog bashed to death with rocks in some silent coulee, a haystack ablaze in the night when there had been no lightning, a man battered in an alley after an argument with a broody crewman.

It would have been something to mutter about, then, for ranch hands who came onto the Dogie to find this kid foreman barely five and a half feet tall parceling out orders in a soft burred voice. Plainly Dad was too short and green to handle the crew of a 45,000-acre ranch. But there was the surprising square heft across his shoulders and down his arms—more than enough strength to be wicked in a fight, and, remember, *I never saw anybody so big I couldn't take him on.* But along with muscle and feistiness, Dad had a knack of handing tasks around in a crew reasonably, almost gently: *Monte, if you'd ride up to the school section and salt those cows there. Jeff, if you'd work over that fence along the creek. Tony, if you'd . . .* That soft *if* of his seemed to deal each man into the deciding, and it was a mark of Dad's crews that they generally went out of the bunkhouse to the school section and the creek fence and a dozen other jobs just as if the work had been their own idea all along. *Oh, he could handle us 'rangutangs, all right*—this from a Dogie man, a half century on—*no ructions on a crew of your daddy's.*

These years when my father began to ramrod crews were amid the era when the homesteaders' valley was dimming away, and the lustrous wealth of big new ranch owners had begun to show itself. President Woodrow Wilson's son-in-law toyed with a section of land on Battle Creek for a while. A family named Manger began to quilt together vast sprawls of valley grassland for its sheep. John Ringling of Wisconsin and New York and Florida put some of his circus fortune into buying 60,000 acres of range, erected a mammoth dairybarn near the White Sulphur Springs stockyards, and financed the twenty-mile rail-line which squibbed down the valley to connect with the main track of the Milwaukee and St. Paul railroad. *John's railroad may be only twenty miles long, but it's just as wide as any man's railroad,* the other Ringling brothers joshed, but John Ringling was serious as any squire about his sagebrush empire. He held to his investments in the valley for a quarter of a century, and the valley people talked casually about the Ringling family, as if they were neighbors who had happened to come into a bit more flash and fortune than anyone else.

But one name was beginning to be spoken most often in the valley: *Rankin.* It would be spoken in contempt nearly all of my father's remaining years there, and through my own boyhood and beyond. Wellington D. Rankin was a lawyer in Helena, a courtroom caricature with flowing silver hair and an Old Testament voice. And, be it said, a pirate's shrewdness. When the Depression began to catch up with John Ringling's indulgences, Rankin was there to buy the every acre—*the so-and-so got that Ringling land for a song, and did his own singing*—and then further ranch after ranch in the hills hemming the Big Belts, until a ducal new style had come into the valley.

Rankin poured in cattle by the thousands—his herd eventually was said to be ten thousand head—and then evidently skimped every expense he could think of. His cowboys were shabby stick figures on horseback. The perpetual rumor was that most of them were out on prison parole or other work release somehow arranged by Rankin; *old Rankin's jailbirds,* the valley people called them. More forlorn even than the cowboys were the Rankin cattle, skinny creatures with the huge Double O Bar brand across their ribs like craters where all the heft had seeped from them.

These wolfish cows roved everywhere: *That bastard of a Rankin always had more cattle than country. . . . I tell you, I'm afraid of 'em. A storm'll come and here Rankin's cows'll come up the road from Rock Creek, and they reach through your fences eatin' weeds and willows, and if they break in they can eat you out in one night.* Mile upon mile,

Rankin's land ran unfenced along the valley highway, and his herds grazed along the shoulders of the road and regular as the dark of the moon were smashed by cars cresting the route's inky little dips.

As the giant ranches took more and more of the country, then, men such as my father became more valuable as foremen—the top sergeants for the country's regimenting. A few of them held the same job for decades, the seasons of haying and lambing and calving as steady and ceaseless in their lives as the phases of the moon. Dad was of the ilk more contentious than that. The valley ranches often were miserably mismanaged—few owners having the deftness it takes to budget the grazing of thousands of animals across rough miles of sage country, in a chancy climate—and it was common for a feisty foreman to give his job one last thunder-blue cussing, quit, and move on somewhere else in the valley. Dad seared himself loose that way a number of times, even from the Dogie when the hand of ownership would get too clumsy there. His quittings, as he told and retold them, would take on all the shape and pace of a pageant. It would begin with the rancher swaggering into the bunkhouse after breakfast to have his say about the work to be done that day. Dad would listen, never giving a sign, until the rancher had finished. Then Dad would casually answer, No, someone else could line out the crew on those jobs, he was through.

Puzzled, the rancher would ask what he meant.

Dad would reply that he meant he was quitting, that's what.

Unbelieving, the rancher would begin to stammer: For bejesus' sake why, what was wrong?

This was Dad's cue to tell him with all barrels blazing—that he'd never worked on a haywire outfit with such broken-down equipment, or that he'd had enough of daylight-to-dark days with no Sundays off, or that he'd never been on a place before where he'd been given so damn few men to put up the hay.

The rancher next would plead: Hell, he didn't need to quit, they'd fix it up somehow.

This was the trumping time Dad had been waiting for: No, by God, he wouldn't work on any ranch run the way this one was, not for any amount of money. Write 'er out, whatever salary he had coming; he was going to town.

That the event did not always happen in just this fashion did not matter; it held that shape in Dad's mind, and left him free to revamp his routine of foremanning as promptly as he felt like it. Go to town he would, and in a day or so on to the next job as foreman—never for Rankin, *I'd rather scratch with the chickens than work for that bastard*—because the bedrock fact under young Charlie Doig's life was that he knew nearly all that was worth knowing about ranch work in the valley. It came of an irony: the one thing that hardscrabble Basin homestead had done for Dad and his brothers was to teach them how a ranch *ought* to operate. From having had to take that homestead apart and put it together time and again as they tried to make it go, the Doig youngsters could not help but learn more than they could forget. Out of that way of growing up and some unhaltered ability all his own, then, this young ranchman who would become my father had a feel for the valley's seasons and each of their tasks and the crews needed to achieve them, and it made him some reputation early.

My father, now, nearing thirty. Three or four times back from death's borderlines. Some time as foreman of the Dogie before pushing off for another of the valley's ranches, and others after that, whenever he was unfractured and in the saddle. Still putting a quick hand to the Basin homestead every so often with a couple of the other brothers, as if they couldn't stand to let the sage hills take back that grudging patch of ranch. If he was headed nowhere grand in history, at least he seemed not to mind the route. But now, as it had that way of doing, his life swerved hard. He met Berneta Ringer, my mother.

Some Saturday night in the spring of 1928, he danced with her in the community hall at the little town of Ringling, where John Ringling's branchline railroad wandered down the valley from White Sulphur Springs. Berneta was a slim high school girl, not much more than five feet tall, with a fragile porcelain look to her—pale skin set off by dark hair, a dainty way of arching her head forward a few inches as if listening to a whisper. She had a straight, careful smile, her lips just beginning to part with amusement. Her face was too round and the nose too broad to allow beauty, but a tidy prettiness was there. And she carried admiration from anyone who knew her situation: her family, which skimped along in a life hard and poor even for a country which had tumbleweeded so many families out of desperate foothills ranches, had come west from Wisconsin some years before, in the hope that the crisp Montana air would ease her asthma. That dainty thrust of her head came from breathing deep against the clutching in her lungs.

Probably Dad liked the grit Berneta showed against such odds. More than likely Berneta was flattered by the attentions of the clean-featured cowboy. Romance seems to have perked fast in both of them, and a few months later, the first full set of days they spent together brimmed with it.

It was the Fourth of July celebration in White Sulphur Springs, and they took the town. In my mother's photo album, that holiday's snapshots show up in a happy flurry; every scene has been braided to its moment by her looping writing. *Ready for the Big Day:* Dad and his brother Angus have doffed their black ten-gallon hats for the camera, grins in place under their slicked hair, and bandannas fluttering at their necks like flags of a new country. *The Wildest Bunch in W.S.S.*—seven of them from Ringling and the Basin are ganged along the side of a car, handrolled cigarettes angling out of the men's mouths, my mother and her cousin small prim fluffs in the dark cloudbank of cowboy hats. Angus, in showy riveted chaps, slips an arm around the cousin. Dad looks squarely as ever into the camera from where he has tucked down on the running board; the halter dangling over his crossed arms must mean he is about to bronc-ride. My mother stands as close beside him as she can, tiny and very girlish in a flapper's dress. She is a few months past her fifteenth birthday.

Then a pose which didn't need her words: the two Doig brothers in the rodeo corral, the pair of them straddled onto Angus's star-faced roping horse. Angus sits the saddle deep and solid, the loose ready loops of his lariat held by a pommel strap. Dad straddles snug behind him, and as they both turn toward my mother's camera, all the lines of their bodies repeat one another in such closeness—down the two of them, the same crimped curves of hat, nip of sleeve garter, sweep of chaps, pointed lines of boot. It is a picture which has caught, in this middle of a moment, how young they were, and how good at what they could do, and how ready they were to prove it.

All of this which paraded through those few quick days of celebration told my mother what she wanted to know about Charlie Doig. There is another photo taken soon afterward, in which my father grins cockily, hands palmed into hip pockets, dressy new chaps sweeping back from his legs as if he were flying. On this one is written: *My Cowboy.*

Yet marrying didn't develop. Berneta was too young, and her mother seems to have had doubts about cowboys. The courtship settled down to a slog. Dad would come horseback twenty miles along a rim of the valley and ease up to a ramshackle ranch house. Inside, with the three younger children looking on gap-mouthed, the mother telling him with cold eyes all the doubts there ever were about footloose cowpokes, and the talky father who could gabble by the hour, he did whatever wooing he could.

This slow courtship went on for six years. At last, just before my mother turned 21 years of age in 1934, they married.

From then, their story tells itself in a rush, just as Berneta Doig's life was hurrying to an end. Their first summers of marriage were the quiet, wandering ones they spent herding sheep in the mountains. Other seasons, Dad hired on and moved on as he had always done. Old age and the Depression were dislodging his mother from the Basin homestead she had come to so doubtfully forty years before. The next years brought Annie Doig's death, and the emptying of the Basin of its very last diehard settlers, the bowl of immigrants' dreams now become the fenced pastures of a cattle company. Brought, too, another of the close licks of death: Dad's brother Jim, his closest in age and as deft a stockman, was thrown from a saddlehorse and killed.

The sale of the Basin homestead for a few dollars an acre closed the circle back to the landlessness the Doigs started off with. By then, Dad had found his way around that lack of footing. Notching up from the jobs as foreman, in the late 1930's he began to run other men's ranches for them—all the responsibilities and decisions his, and the profits divided between him and the owner.

The South long and long has had its word for this system: *sharecropping*. Our West was edgier about that, and called it instead *working on shares*. But either way, the notion was that the landless man did the labor for the landed, and said his prayers that the weather or market prices wouldn't nullify his year's effort. For my father, going *on shares* was both an opportunity and an exasperation. He knew the work of raising livestock, and could do as much of it as any man in the valley. But even if he sweated forth stout shares of profit—and a number of times, he did—there was little bidding he could do for ranchland wanted by any of the valley's big ownerships. *And I decided I'd be damned if I'd scratch along on a dab of a place like we did back there in the Basin.*

By the time I was born in 1939, Dad had settled into managing, on shares, a cattle ranch owned by Jap Stewart's brother, beneath the east slope of Grass Mountain. The years there made steady money, but my mother's asthma was clenching worse and worse. The final winter of World War Two, the three of us went to Arizona to try the climate for her there. Dad started work in an aircraft factory, and almost before he was in the door was made a foreman. It may have been that my parents would have chosen Arizona for good, once the war was over and they could have had some time to talk themselves into a new direction of life. But they had arranged to run a thousand head of sheep on shares the next summer, and to give themselves one more season of the mountains. And so we came back to Montana and rode the high trail into the Bridger Range, one to her last hard breaths ever and the other two of us to the bruised time after her death.

This journey of life, then, my father had come by the autumn of 1945, when he and I began to blink awake to find ourselves with the stunted ranch he had managed to rent, and with my situation as the boy he now had to raise alone. It seems to me now that the ranch, even though it was our entire livelihood, counted little in this time. A few thousand acres hugging onto the Smith River just as it began kinking through sage foothills into the southern edge of the valley, the place had more to offer me than it did a man trying to coax a profit from it. Its shale gulches and slab-rocked slopes pulled me off into more pretend games alone than ever, more *kchews* of rock bullets flung zinging off boulders, more dream-times as I wandered and poked and hid among the stone silences. For Dad, the reaches of rock can only have been one more obstacle which cattle and sheep had to be grazed around, and my wandering games the unneeded reminder that he had a peculiar small person on his hands.

It may have been that he thought back to what his own boyhood had been like after his father died, how quickly he had grown up from the push of having to help the family struggle through. It may have been only habit, out of his years of drawing the fullest from those reluctant crews. Or maybe simple desperation. From whatever quarter it came, Dad took his decision about me. My boyhood would be the miniature of how he himself lived.

That policy of his corded us together at once, twined us in the hours of riding to look over the livestock, the mending of barbed-wire fences, all the prodding tasks of the ranch. But more than that. Dad's notion that I was fit for anything he himself might do carried me, in this time when I was a six-seven-eight-year-old, on a journey which stands in my memory as dappled and bold as the stories I heard of his own youth. For after our early months on the ranch, Dad had mended himself enough to enter the life of the valley again in full—and in the valley's terms, and his, this meant nights in White Sulphur Springs and its nine saloons.

Although he could tip down a glass of beer willingly enough, Dad was not what the valley called *a genuine drinking man.* With him, alcohol stood a distant second to the company he found along the barstools. The pattern is gone now, even from White Sulphur Springs, but in its time it was as ordered and enlivening as a regimental trooping of the colors. I come to it yet, even as Dad with me at his waist did, a night or two in mid-week and Saturday nights without miss, as a traveler into a street lit with festival.

The Stockman Bar started us for the night. Just walking through its door stepped you up onto a different deck of life. Earlier the lanky old building had been the town's movie house, and it stretched so far back from the sidewalk that its rear corners began to sidle up the hill behind the main street of town. The builder could have scooped out at the back so the floor would have come out level with the street at the front. Instead, he saved on shovels by carpentering from back to front much the way things were, and when the floorboards came out at the street about the height of a man's waist, a little ramp was angled up through them from the doorway.

It made a fine effect, the customers all at a purposeful tilt as they came climbing toward the long dark-brown span of bar. Then, sitting up on one of the Stockman's three-foot stools, you could glance out and down through the street window at passersby going along below your kneecaps. In early evening, it was a chance to look out at humanity as unseen as if you were hidden away on a shed roof, and Dad and I would settle in to watch the town's night begin to take shape.

The Stockman had other likable lines besides its lofty floor. From end to end, the wall behind the bar was almost all mirror and whiskey bottles, held in regiments by a great dark-wooded breakfront. Glass and liquor and liquor and glass reflected each other until my eyes couldn't take in the bounce of patterns. The label print and emblems would have added up to a book, and the ranks of bottles with their mirror images shouldering behind them seemed to crowd out toward us as we sat at the bar. But in gaps along the bottom shelf, saved for the clean glasses which rested mouth down on white towels, were propped the curiosities I would pick out to look at long and often—the tiny cellophane packs of white salted nuts or smoked meat strips. Every so often, someone might buy a packet and share it along the bar. Every time, the white nuts tasted as chalky as they looked, and the smoked meat let loose a seasoning which made us work each piece around in our mouths as if our tongues were gradually catching fire. These samples would disgust us all for a while, but before long I would forget just what the tastes had been, and start all over again the staring at the packets and the wondering what the snow-colored nuts or the blades of meat must be like.

Untasty as it was, the cellophane food offered the harmless choice I could focus on back of the bar. What I would look at with a peeper's stealth a hundred times an evening was the nakedness of the calendar lady.

You could depend on her year after year: some passing salesman from a brewery would provide the saloon with a long calendar to put up next to the cash register, and on the calendar just above the brewery's name would be a figure big as a sitting cat—the naked lady with breasts coming out like footballs. The style then was to photograph the kneeling calendar lady under a bluish-purple light. The play of this cold tint onto her breasts shaded the nipples down to dark pointed circles like the ends of ripe plums, and tended to make a brunette—as calendar ladies generally seemed to be, across the years—look as if she were only waiting for the shadows to deepen one notch more before lunging points-first right at you.

The single thing I knew about women was that I wasn't supposed to be seeing them in this condition. I felt I had to resort to great casual sweeps of looking: start my eyes at a high innocent corner of the whiskey shelves, work like an inventory-taker along the bottle labels until the neighborhood of the cash register, loiter around the cellophane snacks while trying to sense out of the corners of my eyes whether anyone was watching my peeping. Then straight and fast as I could, the peek right onto the glorious purplish-blue breasts. Hard-earned gazes, every one, but I was willing to work at it.

The Stockman had even another night-in, night-out attraction. Against the wall opposite the bar, a smeary rainbow of colors glowed out of the jukebox. Each shade slid in behind the fluted glass front as you watched, maybe a dim red followed by a tired green, a mild orange forever chased by a bruiselike purple, which was likely to remind a person of the calendar lady again.

This slow spin of colors seemed to be the chief job of the jukebox, because it rarely put out music. A song from it meant either there were strangers in the saloon, or one of Dad's friends had pressed a dime into my hand and steered me off to play a tune while he said something I shouldn't hear. Months on end somewhere in that span of time, I spent each bonus dime on *Good Night, Irene.* The record would slide out of hiding and flip into place, I would press my nose against the jukebox glass to see the needle jab down, and then I would feel the sound strum out: *Sometimes I live in the countreeee, sometimes I live in townnnn. . . .* A lot of times, men would turn sideways along the bar to listen as the sad chorus went on. *Sometimes I take a great notionnnn, to jump into the river and drownnnn . . .*

With its movie house length—long enough, in fact, to make the trip back to the toilet a hazard for a drinker too full of beer—the Stockman at dusk would be as open and uncrowded as a sleepy depot. And like a depot, it had someone veteran and capable in charge when the clientele did start showing up. Always, Pete McCabe would be waiting, watching. His soft gray shirt and the long oval of his face and bald brow seemed fixed behind the spigot handles which thumbed up at the center of the long bar. A dozen barrels of beer a week purled out of the spigots under his steady pull, and never a glass of it came along the bar without a good word from Pete McCabe.

There are listening bartenders, who are the storied ones, and there are talky bartenders, trying to jaw away the everlasting sameness of their hours. Pete was neither, and better—a bartender who knew how to visit with his customers.

When the two of us straddled onto stools across the slick bar wood from him, Pete would push a schooner of beer in front of Dad, listen close as a minister to whatever he had on his mind, and in turn begin quietly telling Dad who had come into town that day and what price they were getting for their lambs or wool or calves and how far along they were with the haying, and on into bigger currencies: *Hear they had a little flabble down the street last night. Couple of fellows squared off and pushed each other around a little. I just don't care too much for that fightin', Charlie. I don't let it get goin' in here, just have to slap 'em a little before they start in on it . . . Hear a lot about turnin' this into a big gamblin' state. I don't want to see that. It's just a sharpshooter's game, that gamblin'; you'll see the cross-roaders comin' in here like they were flies after a bunch of dead guts. . . . Government trapper was through, said they got an early snow down in that Sixteen country. About six inches of wet, heavy as bread dough. . . .*

Pete's rich ration of talk wasn't done for the business of it. In White Sulphur Springs there was steady thirsty commerce no matter how a bartender behaved. Pete simply had made it a hobby to size up people, and to work out a routine of friendship with those deserving. He had a tribute for the few best men he knew. Glancing off into the glass hodgepodge behind the bar, Pete would say slowly: *He's a nice fellow*. Slow nod, and slower again: *A real nice fellow.* When that was said, you knew the fellow must be a prince of the world. And plainly enough, Pete deemed this wry-smiling father at my side a real nice fellow.

Only now do I understand how starved my father was for that listening and gossip from Pete McCabe. Nowhere else, never in the silences of the life we led most of the time on the ranch, could he hear the valley news which touched our own situation, and in a tone of voice which counted him special. Nowhere else, either, did Dad's past as a ranchman glow alive as it did in the Stockman. Just then in its history, White Sulphur was seeing the last of a generation of aging sheepherders and cowboys and other ranch hands. Several of them, I remember, had nicknames of a style which would pass when they did: Diamond Tony, who had a baffling Middle European name and an odd, chomping accent to go with it; Mulligan John, called so for the meal which had become a habit with him in the aloneness of sheep camps; George Washington Hopkins, the little Missourian who insisted he was from Texas, and insisted too on being called simply Hoppy; a dressy little foreigner who had been dubbed Bowtie Frenchy; other immigrant herders who rated only Swede, Bohunk, Dutchy; towering Long John and silent Deaf John. Maybe half a hundred of these men, gray and gimpy and familyless, making their rounds downtown, coming out for a few hours to escape living with themselves. Any time after dusk, you began to find them in the saloons in pairs or threes, sitting hunched toward one another, nodding their heads wise as parsons as they reheard one another's stories, remembering them before they were spoken. *Just waitin' for the marble farm,* Pete McCabe said of them with sorrow, for he enjoyed the old gaffers and would set them up a free beer now and again, *you know they'd like to have one and don't have the money for it and I never lost anything doing it for 'em.* Dad had worked with most of these men, on the Dogie or elsewhere, and their company seemed to warm him from the cold agony he had been through.

Other valuable friends could be met in the Stockman. The two I remember above the rest were as alike and different as salt and sugar. Lloyd Robinson was the unsweetened one. Some time before, he had pulled out of his saloon partnership with Pete McCabe, but he still strolled in at least once a day like a landlord who couldn't get out of the habit of counting the lightbulbs. Lloyd was a nondrinker, or at least a seldom drinker. He came by the saloon just to give his tongue some exercise. His wolfish style of teasing kept me wary, but also taught me how to put in sharp licks of my own. Usually a mock uproar broke out between us. When Lloyd glared down the slope of his belly at me and rumbled that if he had been unlucky enough to have Scotch blood in him he'd have cut his throat to let it out, it was my cue to chirp back that he might as well get at it because a Missourian like him was nothing but a Scotchman with his brains kicked out anyhow. He would glower harder and I would try to squint back through giggles, until our truce came with Lloyd's grump that he might as well buy me a soda pop as argue with a redheaded Scotchman.

Nels Nelson had a spread of belly to challenge Lloyd's, but the disposition of a kitten. Nellie drove the grader, the huge bladed machine which scraped down the ruts or cleared the snow from the county's hundreds of miles of dirt roads. He handled machinery with the touch my father had for livestock, and it may have been this turn of skill they recognized in each other that made them friends.

This big open man Nellie had almost all that a small town could offer: a job he liked and did as if born to it, a pretty home of shellacked logs looking across the end of the valley to the Castle Mountains, a wife as handsome and spirited as the palomino horses which she pastured behind their house. He also had an almighty thirst.

It was said in admiration that Nellie was a happy drinker. Each fresh head on a glass of beer delighted him more, until it seemed the next spigot's worth would send him delirious. He would parrot dialects, spiel jokes, greet any newcomer as if the fellow were his long-lost twin, spread every generosity he could think of into the knot of friends around him—and of course was destroying himself. One particular episode of Nellie's that we all laughed about when it happened was actually the worst kind of omen. One midnight, he had wobbled home, lost his footing on the kitchen linoleum, and passed out where he crashed. As he went down, one forearm flopped into the slop bucket beside the sink. He came to in the daylight to find that forearm still dangling into the curdled gray swill of greasy dishwater, potato peelings, and table scraps. A man who could wake up to that in the morning and be back downtown the very evening again drinking—and worse, telling the story on himself—was a man doomed.

Side by side with a friend splintering apart this way, I suppose my father was in a mood to simply accept that life is fatal to us all, one way or another. If he ever tried to warn off Nellie from the fierce drinking, I never heard the words. The flow of booze into his best friend or the behavior of anybody else in the Stockman, Dad took without a blink of judgment. I cannot know whether he ever thought it out entirely, but I believe that in him was the notion that anyone who began his night along the bar with us must have been tussling life in his own right, just as we were. Pete McCabe's Stockman offered a few hours of neutral ground, and the wrong words, even wise ones, might snap that truce.

Three more saloons elbowed into each other on the same block with the Stockman. Next door stood the Melody Lane, with a neon cheeriness about it which probably was supposed to go with the name. Only about a third the size of the Stockman and with plump booths where couples might be sitting and cooing, the Melody Lane seemed always to be showing off its manners more than we liked. It was the kind of enterprise better suited to mixed drinks than beer, and Dad and I seldom invested much time there. But next on the block came a favorite of ours, the Maverick, hard drinking and rollicking. Under its low ceiling the air hazed into a murky blue, probably as much from accumulating cusswords as cigarette smoke. Opening the door from the street was like finding yourself in a sudden roaring fog. But if you had lungs and ears for it, the Maverick was the inevitable place to find one old friend or another bellied up sometime during the night, and it made a good sociable stop for Dad after the warmup beer at the Stockman.

For a time, the Maverick even offered gambling. Other saloons might slyly slip in a poker table or two, but the Maverick set up an entire side room. If you could wedge your way in, your money might change hands several different ways. In my memory is all of one evening spent perched on a corner of the roulette table, boosted kindly by someone who noticed me teetering on tiptoe as I tried to see across to the white marble whirling around the wheel. Roulette impressed me. I liked the practiced flip of the wheel man's thumb as he sent the marble whirring around its rim of circle, the hypnotic slow fan of the wheel moving the opposite direction, the surprise drop and glassy clatter as the marble fell onto the wheel and skittered for a slot. I probably liked to watch the stacks of silver dollars being pushed bravely onto the hunch numbers, too. It was noticeable even to me that roulette players suffered out loud, and hard, while the poker players farther back in the side room spoke only to raise, call, and ask whether everybody had put in their ante.

You can see that the Maverick could take up all of a person's night, if you would let it. But there were six more saloons in town, and Dad liked to keep on the move. Across a rutted alley from the Maverick stood a big square-fronted saloon which had earned a hard name even in this damnless town—the Grand Central. Generally, only spreeing sheepherders and the most derelict of drunks drank at the Grand Central, and you could catch a case of brooding glumness just by being around them. The upstairs floors served as the town's flophouse. *It's a stiffs' outfit,* Pete McCabe said down his nose. The bleary way of life there was beyond the understanding of anybody who hadn't sprawled into it, and the ragtag men of the Grand Central were known to the rest of us only by the stories which reeked out of the place like the stink of vomited wine. It was told, and thoroughly believed, that one time the undertaker had been called about a body lying head down across the stairs leading up to the flop rooms. He was baffled to find the corpse wedged hard in the stairwell, stiff as a side of frozen meat and apparently dead for at least the past twenty-four hours. He was exactly right. Thinking the sprawled victim was only drunk and sleeping it off upside down, the other inhabitants had been lurching carefully across him on the stairs for the past day and night.

Even without tales of this sort, the Grand Central made me uneasy. Almost anything else we might meet up with while I was downtown at Dad's elbow had its excitement for me. But not the hopeless sag of those sour-smelling men. We deigned into the Grand Central only when Dad had to find someone to herd sheep or do the lowest ranch chores for a few days, and that was often enough for me.

The saloons went quicker after the Grand Central, as if we were hurrying on from its sights and smells. The place on the next block, the Mint, was the first new saloon in town in years and stood out like a salesman in a white suit. It took up half of a long stucco building, side by side with the dry goods store under a single square front as if they were the facing pages of an argument in an open book. The Mint was inky inside—which must have been thought to be modern—with the light for the entire saloon washing pale and thin from a few tubes of fluorescence behind the bar. The owner was a three-chinned man in a white shirt, which always looked milky-bluish as he bulled around carrying glasses in the squinty light. This was the one saloon in town besides the uppity Melody Lane where drinkers used the booths almost as much as the bar stools. Some Saturday nights the Mint would have two or three people plinking music at the back of the room, and couples would crowd into the booths to sit with their sides snuggled into one another from knee to shoulder.

The Mint made a start toward the politer behavior across on the south side of Main Street, which counted only four saloons to the north side's five. Politest of any in town was the saloon tucked away at the rear of the big brick hotel. Always near-empty, it seemed to have given up to the pack of busy competition down the street and simply forgotten to tell the bartender to stay home. Dad and I dropped in only when he wanted to telephone long distance to a livestock buyer in Bozeman or Great Falls. The hotel lobby had the only phone booth in town, and it did a business steadier than the house saloon ever seemed to have done.

A block or so from there stood a mix of saloon and short-order cafe, as if the owner was absentminded about just what the enterprise was supposed to be. The town long since had supposed that the size of his stomach meant he really preferred the cafe side, and so had nicknamed him Ham and Eggs. Ham and Eggs' shacky little building stood almost squarely across from the Grand Central, and seemed to have caught a pall from over there. Night in, night out, there never would be anyone on the bar side of this place except Ham and Eggs himself and a few blank-eyed old sheepherders as unmoving as doorstops, and the short-order side made your stomach somersault just to glance in through the fly-specked window at it. Dad and I generally steered clear, as did anybody who had standards about saloons.

Close by, but a mile further up in likeableness, stood the Pioneer. Oldfangled but not coming-apart-at-the-heels like the Grand Central, earnest enough but not as hard drinking as the Maverick, the Pioneer felt and looked most like a cowtown saloon. Its enormous dark-wood bar and breakfront had been carved and sheened like the woodwork for a cathedral, and at the back, poker tables caught the eye like pretty wheels of green velvet. A small, sad-faced bartender stood on duty at the row of beer taps. *Hullo, Charlie; hullo, Red,* he would murmur as we stepped in, silently pull a glass of beer for Dad, and say no more until a quiet *Take it easy, Charlie; take it easy, Red,* as we went out the door.

Perhaps because of the stony bartender who had nothing else in the world on his mind except what somebody happened to recite into it, the Pioneer served as the town's hiring saloon. Ranch hands looking for a job would leave word with the bartender. Knowing this, ranchers would stride in to ask about a haying hand or somebody who knew how to irrigate. The ranch hand might have his bedroll right there along the back saloon wall, and minutes later be in the rancher's pickup on his way to the new job.

The Pioneer did its businesslike chore for the valley, and the last saloon of all, the Rainbow, did a darker one. The Rainbow gathered in the hardest drinkers of the valley and let them encourage one another.

The middling-sized saloon seemed innocent enough at first glimpse. Next door was one of the town's two cafes, also named the Rainbow, and in back, a large hall where dances were held every month or so. A sizeable portion of the county's social life took place inside the two Rainbows and the hall behind them. But soon enough, you noticed that the drinkers who came to the Rainbow night after night did not take their beer slowly and with plenty of talk, as most of the Stockman's regulars did. The Rainbow crowd—several of the town's professional men, some big ranchers, some of the showy younger cowboys—tossed down whiskey shots and quickly bought one another a next round.

The Rainbow was the one place of this night route which made me uneasy for Dad. Whenever I got sleepy in one of the other saloons, I would go out to our pickup, clutch the gearshift up away from the edge of the seat, and curl myself down, the steering wheel over me like a hollowed moon, beneath Dad's winter mackinaw. If even that didn't keep me warm or something woke me, I would blink myself up again and hunt down Dad to start asking when we were going home. Most times his answer was, *We'll go in just a minute, son* and three or four of these automatic replies later, we would be on the road. But the rule didn't seem to hold at the Rainbow. Whatever he told me there about how soon we would be leaving, the drink buying would go on, and time stretched longer and longer into the night.

Yet not even the Rainbow became the peril to us that it could have. Dad never enlisted as one of its night-after-night drinkers; he must have seen the risk clear. Every fourth or fifth trip to town, he might end up there and we would be in for a later stay, but otherwise the routine which carried us through the other saloons and their attractions was enough for him.

For me, this span of episode at my father's side carried rewards such as few other times of my life. I cannot put a calendar on this time—more than a year, less than two—but during it, I learned an emotion for the ranchmen of the valley which has lasted far beyond their, and my, leaving of it. Judging it now, I believe what I felt most was gratitude—an awareness that I was being counted special by being allowed into this blazing grownup world, with its diamonds of mirror and incense of talk. I knew, without knowing how I knew, that there was much to live up to in this.

Past those first hard-edged months after my mother's death, then, and on into my father's wise instinct of treating me as though I already was grown and raised, my sixth-seventh-eighth years of boyhood became lit with the lives we found in the Stockman and the Maverick and the others. The widower and his son had begun to steady. But one more time, something turned my father's life, our life. A woman stepped inside the outline where my mother had been.

Winter, long white winter. Then a pale quick sprig of spring. Then unsteady too-hot-too-damp-too-dry summer. Next an overnight autumn, and suddenly the breadth of winter once more.

This skewed rhythm of year that the mountain weather sent down on the valley, I can call to mind as if watching coastal waves comb in before me this minute. And recall, too—such is the eddying but detailed power of memory—precisely the crinkled dance of air as July's sun snaked moisture up from green windrows of hay. And the dour slapping push of a gray afternoon's wind, which I dread to this day. And the scenes out of the indelible ninth winter of my life, with its shadowless smothering snow across all the hills of the Sixteen country. And: our own storm-within-the-walls, the family struggle which broke over us again and again. I can feel its touch even amid that vastest winter, as my father is beginning to harness the workhorses for our journey to town. In the half-dark of the sunless forenoon, the horses' heads loom great and patient above me as I hold down on their halters. Dad works the stiff web of leather across each span of back, fastens the procession of buckles and snaps, murmurs his horse palaver: Here now, Luck, stand steady . . . Move a step over, Bess, can't ye? . . . *He backs the pair of horses to the sled bob, hands me the reins to tug steady as he does the quick hitching.* Done. Tell her we're ready to go. *Then, his too-deliberate tone, like a man paying out rope:* If-she-hasn't-changed-her-mind-in-the-last-five-minutes. *I hurry through the snow to the ranch house, past the gullies where whips of wind have cut into the deepest drifts, beneath the porch roof daggered with icicles, open the door and say in, as if reciting:* Dad says we're ready when you are.

FLIP

Let me call her Ruth here.

She came to the ranch on one of the first pale chilly days of an autumn, hired to cook for us for a few months, and stayed on in our lives for almost three years. Her time with us is a strange season all mist and dusk and half-seen silhouettes, half-heard cries. There is nothing else like it in the sortings of my memory. Nor is there anything now to be learned about why it happened to be her who became my father's second wife and my second mother, for no trace of Ruth—reminiscence, written line, photograph, keepsake—has survived. It is as if my father tried to scour every sign of her from our lives.

But not even scouring can get at the deepest crevices of memory, and in them I glimpse Ruth again. I see best the eyes, large and softly brown with what seemed to be some hurt beginning to happen behind them—the deep trapped look of a doe the instant before she breaks for cover. The face was too oval, plain as a small white platter, but those madonna eyes graced it. Dark-haired—I think brunette.

Slim but full breasted. And taller than my mother had been, nearly as tall as Dad. A voice with the grit of experience in it, and a knowing laugh twice as old as herself.

Not quite entirely pretty then, this taut, guarded Ruth, but close enough to earn second looks. And the mystery in her could not be missed, the feeling that being around her somehow was like watching the roulette wheel in the Maverick make its slow, fanlike ambush on chance.

Even how Ruth came to be there, straight in our path after Dad turned our lives toward the valley, seems to have no logic to it. Never before or since did I see anyone quite like her on a ranch. Ranch cooks generally were stout spinsters or leathery widows, worn dour and curt by a life which gave them only the chore of putting meals on the table for a dozen hungry men three times a day. So alike were cooks usually that the hired men seldom bothered to learn their names, simply called each one *Missus.*

But Ruth didn't fit Missus, she was Ruth to everybody. Those eyes were the kind which caught your glance on the streets of Great Falls or Helena, where young women went to escape to a store job and the start toward marriage and a life they hoped would be bigger than the hometown had offered—city eyes, restless eyes. Yet here Ruth was in the valley, passing the syrup pitcher along the cookhouse table, and for all anyone could tell, she seemed ready to stay until she came upon whatever she was looking for.

Her first reach had been badly out of aim—a marriage, quickly broken, to a young soldier. *He was home on a furlough one time,* a voice from his family tells it, *and met her and married her in such short time; really they weren't even acquainted.* Dad must have known about that jagged, too-quick marriage; the valley kept no such secrets. But living womanless had left us wide open for Ruth. To me, an eight-year-old, she was someone who might provide some mothering again. Not *much* mothering, because she kept a tight, careful mood, like a cat ghosting through new tall grass. But the purr of a clever voice, fresh cookies and fruit added to my lunchbox, even a rare open grin from her when I found an excuse to loiter in the kitchen—all were pettings I hadn't had. And for Dad, Ruth must have come as a sudden chance to block the past, a woman to put between him and the death on the summer mountain.

It happened faster than any of us could follow. This man who had spent six careful years courting my mother now abruptly married his young ranch cook.

Ruth, Dad. They were a pairing only the loins could have tugged together, and as with many decisions taken between the thighs, all too soon there were bitterest afterthoughts.

I remember that the drumfire of regret and retaliation began to echo between them before we moved from the ranch in early 1948, only months after the wedding. The ranch itself had plenty of ways to nick away at everyone's nerves. Any sprinkle of rain or snow puttied its mile of road into a slick gumbo, the pickup wallowing and whipping as Dad cussed his way back and forth. Yet the place also was too dry for good hay or grain, and too scabbed with rock up on the slopes where the cattle and sheep had to graze. Dad had begun to call it *this-goddamn-rockpile,* the surest sign that he was talking himself into dropping the lease. For her part, Ruth likely was ready to leave after the first night of howling coyotes, or of a cougar edging out of the Castles to scream down a gulch. Working as a cook on the big ranches out in the open expanse of the valley was one thing, but slogging away here under the tumbled foothills was entirely another. Ruth's mouth could fire words those soft eyes seemed to know nothing about, and the ranch primed her often. I can hear her across the years:

Charlie, I don't have to stay here, I didn't marry this hellforsaken ranch . . . I got other places I can go, don't you doubt it. . . . Lots of places, Charlie.

And Dad, the jut notching out his jaw as it always did when he came ready for argument: *Damn it, woman, d'ye think we can walk away from a herd of cattle and a band of sheep? We got to stay until we get the livestock disposed of. You knew what you were getting into . . .* And always at the last, as he would hurl from the house out to another of the ranch's endless chores: *Will-ye-forget-it? Just-forget-it?*

But nothing was forgotten, by either of them. Instead, they stored matters up against one another. *The time that you . . . I told you then . . .* There came to be a full litany of combat, and either one would refer as far back as could be remembered.

If they had fought steadily the marriage might have snapped apart before long and neither would have been severely hurt. But they bickered in quick seasons. Weeks, maybe a month, might pass in calm. Saturday nights, we went to dances in the little town of Ringling. Dad and Ruth whirled there by the hour. Often my Uncle Angus called the square dances, and I would watch Dad in a circle of flying dancers while a burring voice so close to his cried: *Swing your opposite across the hall, now swing your corners, now your partners, and promenade all!* Sometime after midnight, I would stretch on a bench along the dancehall wall with a coat over me and go to sleep. I would wake up leaning against Ruth's shoulder as the pickup growled down the low hill to the ranch buildings. The murmurs I heard then between Dad and Ruth would go on for a day or two. But eventually, a blast of argument, then no talking, sulking. Sometimes Ruth would leave for a day or two. Sometimes Dad *told* her to leave, and she wouldn't. At last, one or the other would make a truce—never by apology, just some softened oblique sentence which meant that the argument could be dropped now. Until Ruth felt restless again; until Dad's unease twisted in him once more.

I watched this slow bleed of a marriage, not yet old enough to be afraid of exactly what might happen but with the feeling creeping in me that the arguments in our house meant more than I could see. Joking with me as she sometimes did, Ruth would grin and her face come down close to mine: *If your hair gets any redder, you're gonna set the town on fire, you know that?* Dad talked in his usual soft burr when I rode in the pickup with him: *Son, let's go fix that fence where Rankin's cows got in. There's not enough grass on this place for our own without that honyocker's cows in here, too. Hold on, I'm gonna give her snoose to get up this sidehill . . .* But when they were together, I so often heard a hard edge in what they said to each other, a careful evenness as they talked over plans to leave the ranch as soon they could.

For what was happening, I can grasp now, was the misjudgment greater by far than their decision to be married: their mutual refusal to call it off. Each had a fear blockading that logical retreat. Dad would not admit his mistake because he wanted not to look a fool to the valley. On that he was entirely wrong; the only mystification anyone seemed to have was why he kept on with a hopeless mismatch. *I couldn't see that, going on with that marriage, with that little child you in the midst of it,* a woman of the valley once cried to me. *Ruth thought everything should come in a cloud for her. But she had hate in her, she was full of hatefulness . . . What was Charlie thinking of to let that go on?* For her part, Ruth would not face up to another split, would not let another broken marriage point to her as an impossible wife. Since neither could see how to call a halt to the mismarriage, it somehow was going to have to halt itself. But before it did, the pair of them would make two mighty exertions to stay together.

Perhaps because this arrival of Ruth in our lives is a riffle of time which everyone around me later tried to put from mind, memory hovers stubbornly here. Memory, or the curious nature, perhaps, that keeps asking exactly what the commotion was about. For on the edge of this fray between Dad and Ruth I begin to see myself, and here at the age of eight and nine and ten I was curiosity itself. If I inscribe myself freehand, as Dad did with the unfading stories he told me of his own young years, the words might be these: *I was a boy I would scarcely know on the street today. Chunky, red-haired, freckled—the plump face straight off a jar of strawberry jam. Always wearing a small cowboy hat, because I seared in the sun. Under that hat, and inside a name like no one else's. Ivan: EYE-vun, amid the Frankie-Ronny-Bobby-Jimmy-Larry-Howie trill of my schoolmates. Dad was amazed with himself when he at last discovered that he had spliced Russian onto the Scottish family name; he and my mother simply had known someone named Ivan and liked the sudden soft curl of the word—and besides wanted to show up Dad's least favorite brother, who had recently daubed 'Junior' onto a son.*

The name, together with the hair and freckles, gave me attention I wasn't always sure I wanted. At Dad's side in the saloons I sometimes met men who would look down at me and sing out: 'Now the heroes were plenty and well known to fame/Who fought in the ranks of the Czar/But the bravest of all was a man by the name/Of Ivan . . . Skavinsky . . . Skavar!' I consoled myself that it was better than being dubbed Red or Pinky, which I also heard sometimes in the saloons. And once in a great while, in his thoughtful mood as if remembering a matter far away, Dad would call me 'Skavinsky.' It made a special moment, and I prized it that way.

People who remember me at this age say I was something of a small sentinel: 'You always were such a little sobersides.' 'You was always so damned bashful it was hard to get a word out of you.' All right, but how jolly was I supposed to be, with a mother dead and the next one in a sniping match with my father? I believe that much of what was taken to be my soberness was simply a feeling of being on guard, of carefully watching life flame around me. Of trying not to be surprised at whatever else might happen.

I can tell you a time, as my father storied so many of his into me: Dad and Ruth and I are walking toward the movie house, on some night of truce in the family. We are at the end of the block from the building when I notice Kirkwood coming down the street. Kirkwood is a school classmate, but a forehead taller than I am, and with that head round as a cannonball and atop square shoulders you could lay bricks on. Kirkwood can never be counted on to behave the same from one minute to the next, and now he bears down on us, yelps 'Hullo, Ivy!' and takes a swipe at my hat.

The worst prospect I can think of is coming true: the great given rule of boyhood is not to make you look silly in front of your grownups, and Kirkwood is toe-dancing all over it. Now he has put on a hyena grin and falls in step with me. He glances toward Dad and Ruth, then skips at me and knocks the hat from my head.

'Kirkwood-I'll-murder-you!' I rasp as lethally as I can and clap the hat down over my ears. It sends his delirium up another notch, and he skips in for another whack at the hat. Dad and Ruth no longer can pretend not to notice and begin to glance back at the sniggering and muttering behind them.

Kirkwood giggles; this time when I hear him scuffling close, I swing around with my right arm stiff in what I now understand was a right jab. Kirkwood runs his round jaw into it and bounces flat onto the sidewalk. He wobbles up, looks at me dazedly, then trots off in a steady howl. I hustle toward the movie house where Dad and Ruth are waiting and watching. Both are grinning as if they have mouths full of marshmallows.

But I was less sure of my feelings. It was as if I had been through a dream that I knew was going to happen. Not in every detail—who could foresee even Kirkwood gone that batty?—but in its conclusion: that from the instant Kirkwood rambled into sight, he was aimed onto my fist. It somehow seemed to me there ought to be an apprehension about such certainty, some questioning of why it had to be inexorably so. But it was a questioning I could not handle, and what I felt most was the curious intensity of having seen it all unfold, myself somehow amid the scene as it swept past me. Somehow a pair of me, the one doing and the one seeing it done.

It was exactly that twinned mix—apprehension and interestedness—that I felt all during Ruth's startling time in our lives.

Now the awaited move, when we at last would put the ranch and its zone of combat behind us. Put them behind us, in fact, in a way as wondrous to me as it was unexpected, for Dad and Ruth faced toward White Sulphur Springs and undertook the last livelihood anyone could have predicted of either of them: they went into the cafe business.

The Grill, across the street from the Stockman, had come up for rent. It was the third and smallest eating place in a town which had not quite enough trade for two. There was the barest smidgin of reason to think of Ruth coping with such an enterprise; with her years of cooking for crews, she at least could handle a kitchen. But for Dad, the notion had all the logic of a bosun's mate stumping ashore to open up a candy shop. Yet somehow Dad and Ruth, this pair who had never been around a town business of any sort and who already were finding out that they flinted sparks off each other all too easily—somehow they talked one another into trying to run the Grill together, and somehow they turned out to have a knack for it.

The knack, of course, was nine-tenths hard work. *Those two took on that place like a house afire.* But when Dad sorted through his savvy, there was use there, too. From all the ranches behind him, he knew enough about purchasing provisions, and better yet, he knew the valley and its people. He put up new hours for the Grill. It would stay open until after the last saloon had closed.

There at the last of the night and the first hours of morning, the Grill found its customers: truckers on their runs through the pitchy dark, ranchers heading home from late business in Helena or Great Falls, some of the Rainbow crowd trying to sober up on black coffee and T-bone. Steaks and hashbrowns covered Ruth's stove, and Dad dealt platters of food until his arms ached. Saturday nights I was allowed to stay up as late as I wanted—on Dad's principle of fathering, that I might as well have a look at life sooner than later—and I looked forward to the pace of that last night of the week like a long, long parade coming past.

Just at dusk, ranch hands would begin to troop in for supper, minutes-old haircuts shining between their shirt collars and hat brims, because *Well, I gotta go in and get my ears lowered* was the standard excuse to come to town for a night of carousing. As the dark eased down and the war-whoops from the crowds in the Maverick and the Grand Central came oftener, the cafe would begin to receive the staggerers who had decided to forget the haircut after all and get right on with the drinking. They were a pie crowd, usually jabbing blearily at the fluffiest and most meringue-heaped possibilities in the countertop case. Sometime in mid-evening, Lloyd Robinson would arrive, suspiciously fingering down a coin for a cup of coffee and demanding to know if my freckles weren't from a cow's tail having swiped across me. Soon after him, as if the town's two prime bellies couldn't be long apart, it would be Nellie crashing in, chortling with delight and spinning a joke off the first item he spotted: *That jam jar, now—did you hear about the Swede at the breakfast table? 'Yiminey,' he says, 'I yoost learn to call it yam and now they tell me it's yelly.'*

Then if there was a dance in the hall behind the Rainbow, the night would crest with two tides of customers: one which filled the cafe as soon as the dance ended, and a second made up of those who had gone off to drink some more until the first wave cleared out. And at last, sometime after two in the morning, would come the phone call from Pete McCabe thirty yards across at the Stockman: *Save us three, Charlie.* Dad would put aside a trio of T-bone steaks, and before long, Pete and his night's pair of bar help would be straddling in to the counter and trading the night's news with Dad. A few hours before Sunday dawn, the Grill would close and we would step out the door into the emptied town.

A quieter flow of eaters presented themselves too, I was to notice—the town's oldtimers, the pensioners, the sheepherders and cowpokes hanging on from yesteryear. As I have told, the Stockman, where Pete McCabe was known to be the kind of a fellow who would set up a drink even when the pension check hadn't yet come to pay for it, drew most of these oldtimers, sometime in the night, sometime through the week. Now, over across the street, Dad was good for an emergency meal as well. How many times I heard one or another of them, joking so as not to seem begging, ask Dad for a meal *on account*—on account, that was, of being broke. Weeks and months and even years afterward, one or another of them might stop him on the street and say, *Charlie, here's that Grill money I've been owing you.*

Ruth, I think, never objected to those meals Dad would jot on the tab. They might fight over a spilled holder of toothpicks, but not that long apologetic rank of "accountants." Out on the valley ranches, she had seen in the crews clopping to her supper table the men who were growing too old for the work they had done all their lives, and soon too old for anything but those lame rounds of the saloons along Main Street.

Age was making that same wintry push on the one person Ruth seemed steadily to hold affection for, too. She had been raised by her grandmother—her family so poor and at war with itself it had shunted her off there—and regularly she went across the Big Belts to the next valley to see the old woman. Several times, on an afternoon off from the cafe, she took me on those visits.

Creased and heavy, stiff in the knees and going blind, the grandmother was the most ancient woman I had ever seen, and her house the shadowiest and most silent. The grandmother spent her days entirely in the dim kitchen, finding her way by habit through a thickening haze of cataract webs. When we stepped in past the black kitchen stove and the drab cabinets lining the walls, the grandmother would peer toward us and then begin to talk in a resigned murmur, eyes and legs giving way above and below a body not yet quite willing to die, and Ruth, listening, would be a different person, softer, younger, seeming to feel the grandmother's aches as her own.

But whatever Ruth took from those visits seemed to stop at our own doorsill. Time and again, she and Dad faced off, and then they would go full of silence for a day or more. Or worse, one would be silent and the other would claw on and on.

If nothing else set them at each other, there always was the argument about our small herd of cattle, which Dad had kept after all when we left the ranch and which he was pasturing now in the foothills of the Big Belts. He drove out each morning to pitch hay to the cattle, then came back to work in the cafe from mid-afternoon until closing. On weekends, I went with him to the cattle, and only then would hear out of him the few tiny snatches of music he knew, his absentminded sign of contentment. A forkful of alfalfa to the cows, then *But the squaws* ALONG *the Yu*KON . . . *are-good-enough-for-me;* a tuneless minute of whistling and looking out across the valley to the pinnacles of the Castles, then *When it's* SPRING*time in the* ROCK*ies* . . .

Whether or not Ruth knew he was out there singing and whistling amid the cows, she did suspect that Dad had not given up intentions of ranching. Dad suspected, just as rightly, that neither of them could keep up the day-and-night pace of the cafe work for long, and that our income soon was going to have to come from livestock again.

In the meantime, we had become town people, and I had the time to myself to roam White Sulphur. Once, in one of the off-balance tributes I would get used to in the valley, someone beside Dad in a saloon caught me studying up at him and blurted: *That kid is smarter than he knows what to do with.* Which was right enough, and yet I did know enough to keep my eyes moving through the town, reading whatever of it showed itself. The rememberings from that have lasted as a kind of casing which goes into place over the earlier odyssey with Dad through the saloons, a second and wider circle across undefined territory, and this time on my own.

The plainest fact I found, so plain that it seemed to me then it never could change, was that White Sulphur totally lived on livestock. All the places I liked best had the sounds and smells and feels which came one way or another from the herds and flocks out on the leathered slopes of grassland. In the creamery where Dad bought milk and butter for the cafe, the air hung so heavy with the dampness of processing that it was like walking against pillows, and everyone talked loudly out of the sides of their mouths to be heard over the rumble of churns. Nearby, the grain elevator took a noise like that and tripled it, the roaring clank of conveyors carrying off wheat and barley and oats somewhere into the high box of tower. At the railroad shipping pens, the noises came directly from the livestock. In their best of times sheep go through life in a near-panic, and their frenzied bleating as they were wrangled up the chutes into boxcars grew to a storm of sound. And the cattle, when they were pastured near the pens a day or so before shipping could be heard all across town—a constant choir of moaning, like wind haunting into ten thousand chimneys at once.

White Sulphur was as unlovely but interesting as the sounds of its livelihood. A teacher who had arrived just then to his first classroom job would remember to me: *The town didn't look too perky. It had been through the Depression and a world war, and obviously nobody had built anything or painted anything or cleaned anything for twenty years.*

Sited where the northern edge of the valley began to rumple into low hills—by an early-day entrepreneur who dreamed of getting rich from the puddles of mineral water bubbling there, and didn't—White Sulphur somehow had stretched itself awkwardly along the design of a very wide T. Main Street, the top of the T, ran east and west, with most of the town's houses banked up the low hills on either side of the business area at its eastern end. To the west lay the sulphur slough, the railroad and shipping pens, and the creamery and grain elevator. The highway, in its zipper-straight run up the valley, snapped in there like the leg of the T onto Main Street. Much of the countryside traffic, then, was aimed to this west end of town, while all the saloons and grocery stores and cafes—and the post office and the druggist and the doctor and the two lawyers, since it took two to fight out a court case—did business at the east end.

This gave White Sulphur an odd, strung-out pattern of life, as if the parts of the community had been pinned along a clothesline. But it also meant there was an openness to the town, plenty of space to see on to the next thing which might interest you. Even the school helped with this sense of open curiosity, because it had been built down near the leg of the T where two of the town's main attractions for a boy also had ended up—the county jail, and the sulphur slough.

Since the nine saloons downtown fueled a steady traffic of drunks, the jail was kept busy, and most schooldays we had a fine clear view of the ritual there. It was only a few dozen yards from the diamond where we played work-up softball to where the brick jail building perched atop a small embankment. Just in from the edge of this embankment, a wire clothesline had been looped between two fat posts. Right there, the prisoners often had a morning recess at the same time as ours. They were sent out to pin their bedding on the clothesline and beat some cleanliness into it—and, I suppose, to huff some of the alcohol out of themselves. Sheepherders who had come in from the mountains for their annual binge, the regular winos from the Grand Central who were tossed in jail every few months to dry out, once in a while a skinny scuffed-up cowboy from one of the Rankin ranches—there they would be, on the embankment before us like performers on a stage.

Most of the men I could recognize from my nights downtown with Dad. But one morning a single inmate came out, a slender man I didn't know but whose face I seemed to have seen before. The softball game stopped as we all puzzled at that strange familiar face. The instant before any of us figured it out, one of my classmates rushed to get his words into the air first: *Hey, that's my dad!* His face the replica of the man's, he looked pleadingly from one to another of us. Desperation knowing only bravado to call on, one more time he cried it—*That's my dad!*—before we faced around, shame fixed in the air, toward the next batter.

At the bottom of the slope from the school grounds, as if it had seeped down from the overflow off the prisoners' bedding, lay the sulphur slough which gave White Sulphur its name. On cold days, the slough steamed and steamed, thin fog puffs wisping up from the reeds, as if this was where the entire valley breathed. Any weather, the water stewed out an odor like rotten eggs. At the slough edge nearest the school stood a tiny gazebo, a rickety scrap from the town's days when it had tried to be a resort. Either as decoration or a roof against bird droppings, the gazebo sheltered a small hot spring. A corroding cup hung on one pillar of the gazebo, and if you dared to touch it, then you could dare the taste of the sulphur spring water.

One of my classmates—of course, Kirkwood—downed the water as if it were free lemonade. His grandfather, a nasty-faced character who indeed gave every sign that he might live forever, had convinced him that the stuff was a positive elixir for a person's insides. After Kirkwood had slurped down a cupful, I would reluctantly sip away. What bothered me even worse than the taste was the rancid look of the spring. The sulphur water had layered its minerals into a kind of putty on stones and clay and even the underwater strands of grass, and the spring always was coated with this sickly whitish curd, as if something poisonous had just died there. And yet, nowhere else had anything like this steaming place, and so the slough and its baleful water drew us.

White Sulphur had other lures I thought must be the only ones of their kind in the universe—the giant carcasses of buildings to be poked into. Late in the last century, when the town had figured it might grow, a few grandiose buildings had been put up, and they had not yet fallen down entirely. Near the sulphur slough stood the remains of the Springs Hotel, a long box of gingerbread-work and verandas which had been built for resort-goers who came to take the waters. I seem to remember that whatever was left of this building was so treacherous none of us would go out on its floor more than a few feet from the wall; you could fall through the sagging floorboards to some black awfulness below. Another awfulness clung to the Springs Hotel's past. The story was that someone had been killed diving into its swimming pool, that White Sulphur dwindled away from being a resort after that. The public death of that diver was epitaphed in the hotel's blind gape of windows and the broken spine of ridgepole. A boy stepped uneasily here, and stepped away not quite knowing what it was that brought him back and back.

Across town loomed a huger wreck, cheerier and much more inviting. This one was called the Old Auditorium—a sharp comedown from its original name, the Temple of Fun. It had been built in the 1890's by an earnest group of local businessmen—a magazine writer who happened through town described the type as *exerting every nerve to prosper*—who totally misjudged the town's need for a structure of that size. Probably there never had been enough people in the entire county to fill the place, even if they all had been herded in at gunpoint for culture's sake.

Built of brick, with a shingled dome rising from the middle of the roof like a howdah on the back of a great red elephant, and a forest of chimneys teetering unevenly around the edge, the temple had never been finished by its exhausted backers, although it was complete enough to use for school recitals and graduation ceremonies by the time the 1925 earthquake shook it onto the condemned list. A dozing dinosaur of a building, it had been collapsing little by little ever since the earthquake. Now the remains stood over us, roofless, ghostlike, magical as a wizard's abandoned castle.

I think it must have been not only the size and gape of the place, but the glacial spill of red brick that attracted me. Oddly, since in the early days White Sulphur had its own brickyard and a number of substantial buildings besides the Temple of Fun had been put up, the town had come through the years into a clapboard, take-it-or-leave-it appearance which made brick-built respectability seem very rare. And here was the largest stack of the reddest brick I could imagine. I could prowl in—windows and doors had vanished long since—and amid the clattering emptiness walk the old stage, study out from the dilapidated walls where rooms had been. Echoes flew back to me as if the auditorium had stored all the sounds from its prime years. It stood as a kind of cavern of history for a few of us, a place where you could go off into an expanse of both space and time.

One other large brick building graced White Sulphur, and if the old auditorium was a cave to be sought out, this next was a man-made mass you could not avoid. You came to it—the Sherman Hotel—as you walked up Main Street: three massive stories of brick and cornicework snouting out into the thoroughfare as firmly as a thumb crimping into a hose.

At the very start of White Sulphur's history there had been a dispute about where Main Street ought to run. The doctor who held the land at the west end of town banked too heavily on the notion that some judicious slough drainage and timber roadbedding would draw the route along his holdings. A rival laid out a plat to the east of him, complete with a 25-foot jog away from the direction of the slough and directly out into the path mapped out for Main Street. In some wink of confusion or bribery, the rival survey was accepted by the authorities, the town grew up along the misjointed plat lines, and for the next sixty years, the big brick hotel built at the boundary of the muddle squatted halfway into Main Street.

In the hotel lobby, a wide high window had been installed near the outer edge of this prowlike jut to take advantage of the outlook. Sitting there in a leather chair you could watch the cars come, straight as fence wire, until suddenly they had to angle off. Old men hobbled into the hotel to lobby-sit the afternoon hours away and watch the cars do their surprised swerve around them. It made a pastime, and the town didn't have many.

For some reason I can't summon back, once in those years Dad and I checked into the Sherman Hotel for a night. The room was worse than we had expected, and worse even than the hotel's run-down reputation. A bare lightbulb dangled over a battered bed; I think there was not even a dresser, nightstand, or chair. The bedsprings howled with rust. Sometime in the skreeking night, Dad said: *Call this rattletrap a hotel, do they? I've slept better in wet sagebrush.*

And yet, dismal as it was, the cumbersome hotel did some duty for the town. The teacher arriving to his job stepped from the bus there and went in to ask the clerk if there were lockers for his baggage for a day or two. *Just throw it there in the corner,* he was told. *But I'd like to lock it away, everything I own is in there. . . .* The clerk looked at him squarely for the first time: *Just throw it in the corner there, I said.* When the teacher came back in a day or so, all was in the corner, untouched.

One last landmark from those years, the gray stone house called the Castle. It speared up from the top of the hill behind the Stockman, a granite presence which seemed to have loomed there before the rest of the town was ever dreamed of. Actually, a man named Sherman had built it in the early 1890's, with bonanza money from a silver lode in the Castle Mountains. He had the granite blocks cut and sledded in by ox team from the mountains, and from a little distance, the three-story mansion with its round tower and sharp roof peaks looked like one of the sets of fantasy pinnacles which poke up all through that range. So in name and material and appearance, all three, old Sherman built for himself an eerie likeness of the Castles which had yielded up his fortune.

If the outside was a remindful whim, the inside of the Castle showed Sherman's new money doing some prancing. It was said he had spared nothing in expense—woodwork crafted of hardwoods from distant countries, crystal dangles on every chandelier, a huge water tank in the attic which sluiced water down to fill the bathtubs in an instant, a furnace which burned hard hot anthracite coal shipped all the way from Pennsylvania. All this was known only by rumor as I would circle past, because Sherman had been in his grave for twenty years and the Castle now stood with boards across its windows and swallows' mud nests clotted onto the fancy stonework.

Those were the relic faces of White Sulphur, the fading profiles of what the town had set out to be. Other features presented themselves to me, too, off the faces of the thousand people who lived in White Sulphur then, and a second thousand dotted out on the ranches from one far end of the county to another. Of all those twenty hundred living faces, the one clearest ever since has been our madman's.

What had torn apart Hendrik's brain—defect of birth, some stab of illness or accident—I have never known. But he hung everlastingly there at the edge of town life, gaping and leering. His parents, old and made older by the calamity which had ripped their son's mind, would bring Hendrik to town with them when they came for groceries. Slouched in their pickup or against the corner of the grocery, Hendrik grimaced out at us like a tethered dog whose mood a person could never be entirely sure of.

He was able to recognize friends of the family, such as Dad, and make child's talk to them—innocent words growled out of a strongman's body. And somewhere in the odds and ends of his mind he had come up with the certain way to draw people to him. He would gargle out loudly what could have been either plea or threat: *YOU god uh CIGuhREDD?*

No one would deny this pitiful spectre a cigarette, and Hendrik would puff away with a twisted squint of satisfaction, his eyes already glowering along the street for his next donor. Dad, who was uneasy around any affliction but was fond of Hendrik's family, always lit the cigarette carefully and said a few words, while I peeked up at the rough man. If he happened to look down at me, it was like being watched by the hot eye of a hawk. All through this time, I can pick out again and again that scene of poor clever lunatic Hendrik, and a town uneasy under his glare.

In that time I puzzled up into three other faces which were strange to me—the black faces of Rose Gordon, Taylor Gordon, and Bob Gordon. The Gordons, I know now, were one of the earliest and most diligent families of White Sulphur. The parents of Rose and Taylor and Bob had come in during the town's short heyday of mining wealth, and Mother Gordon had become the town's laundress: *Momma's back-yard looked like a four-mast schooner comin' in.* But to me, the three Gordons could have been newly set down from the farthest end of the world, where people were the color of night. They were very black—Rose in particular had a sheen dark as ink. Their faces were unlined, not crinkled at the corners of the eyes as Dad's and the other ranch men's were. And their voices chimed amid the burrs and twangs of everyone else downtown.

Taylor Gordon was a singer. Every so often he would perform at the high school auditorium, singing the spirituals he had heard from his mother as she worked at her wash tubs. His tenor voice could ripple like muscle, hold like a hawser across the notes: *Swiiing low, sweet chaaaariot. . . .* The strong, sweet sound had carried him to New York, where he sang in concert halls and on the radio and had been declared by a national magazine as "the latest rival to Paul Robeson." He also had gone through money as if he were tossing confetti into the streets of Harlem, and when the Depression hit, he promptly ended up back in the valley herding sheep.

But he brought with him New York stories such as no one in the valley had ever heard or dreamed of. Of his writer friend Carl Van Vechten: *He was a big Dutchman, he had very buck teeth, rabbit teeth like, and weighed about two hundred pounds, let's say, and was six feet tall. But he wasn't what they called a potbellied six. . . . He liked sometimes to wear a phantom red shirt, reddest red I ever saw. He wore rings, y'know, exotic rings, something that would stand out, or a bracelet, somethin' like that. Bein' a millionaire he could do those things. I remember one night we went to a party. Carl and I was dressed as in Harlem, dressed in kind of satire. Some man gave both of us sam hill. He said, 'You got somethin' to offer the world. You don't have to do anything out of the ordinary, just be yourselves.' Carl laughed and said, 'Well, can't we have a little FUN?'* Of a black man who Taylor said had a magic with words and deeds: *When everybody was broke, a lot of people would go to Father Divine and get the best meal in the world for thirty-five cents, see. And you'd be surprised—white, black, blue, green and the other, they'd eat in Father Divine's because you could get a meal you couldn't pay two dollars for downtown for thirty-five cents, including ice cream dessert. And he had 'em lined up, you'd thought a baseball game was goin' on.* Of how people in Harlem could tell where a man was from just by the scar on his face: *By the brand that was on him, y'see. They could tell where he'd been in a fight. If you were shootin' craps, you more or less would be bendin' down when you got cut and that way you'd get it across the forehead here. Whereas if you were playin' poker, you were more apt to be settin' up, then you'd be apt to get this one here across the cheek. Then if you were playin' what they called 'skin,' why you'd apt to get this other. So y'see, if a fella was cut here, he was from Greechyland, if he was cut this other way he was from Selma, Alabama, and so on and so on.*

Now, either Taylor or Bob owned the building the post office was in, and the pair of them lived on the second floor. Taylor came and went in a bold erect style, always with some new plan for singing in New York again or making a fortune from some gadget he had invented. He also took pride in being the one writing man the valley had ever had. Taylor was a talented storyteller—it was as if his voice put a rich gloss on anything it touched—and while he had been in New York singing at society parties, white writers such as Van Vechten urged him to make a manuscript of his stories of early-day White Sulphur. They steered him to a publisher and illustrator, and shepherded his guesswork grammar into print as a memoir with the title *Born to Be.*

The book with his name on it naturally impressed Taylor into thinking he could do another. This time there was no help, and no publisher. The failure worked on his mind for years; eventually he saw conspirators. The man who published his first book had become John Steinbeck's publisher as well, and for the rest of his life, Taylor told anyone who would listen that Steinbeck and the publisher had pirated his second book idea and made it into *The Grapes of Wrath.*

While Taylor built that phantom swindle in his mind, Bob Gordon crashed back and forth between street and room, a desperate drinker even by White Sulphur standards. I would see him sometimes when I went to the post office for the mail, off somewhere in his plodding stagger. I remember that he wore suspenders, one of the few men in town who did, and the straps made a slumping X across his big back as they slid down his shoulders. Brothers indeed, Taylor and Bob, in desperation as well as in skin, the one daydreaming of New York and second fame, the other fumbling for his next bottle of whiskey.

Rose Gordon lived apart from her brothers, both in place and behavior. She was the one in the family who had chosen to be courtly toward the white faces all around, and a time or two a week she came along Main Street, a plump dark fluff of a woman, with her constant greeting, *How do you do? And how are you today?* Rose had extreme faith in words and manners. The death of any old-timer would bring out her pen, and a long letter to the *Meagher County News* extolling the departed. She was especially fond of two groups in the valley's history, the Scots who had homesteaded in the Basin and elsewhere around the valley, and the Indians who had worn away before the tide of settlement.

Her passion for the Indians, fellow sufferers for the dusk of their skin, was understandable enough. *They were the first ladies of this land*, she would declare of the Indian women she had seen when she was a girl, and the saying of it announced that Rose Gordon knew ladyship from personal experience. But the transplanted Scots, my father's family and the others who had never seen black faces before and in all likelihood didn't care for them when they did? It was their talk. The lowlands burr, the throaty words which came out their mouths like low song, captivated Rose.

She was as entranced with the spoken word as Taylor was with the written, and the oration she had given when she was valedictorian of her high school class of five students in 1904—that oration given from a rostrum in the old auditorium, a large American flag fastened square and true along the back stage wall—had been the summit of her life. When I had become a grown man, she astonished me once by reciting word-for-word the climax of that oration sixty years before: *I gave my address on the progress of the Negro race. I ended, I said: 'The colored soldiers have earned the highest courage, and they won unstinted praises by their bravery, loyalty and fidelity. They have indeed been baptized into full citizenship by their bloodshed in defense of their country, and they have earned the protection of that honorable emblem, the Stars and Stripes!'*

While Rose held those words in her memory as if they were her only heirloom, other street voices plaided White Sulphur life for me as well. The twang which gritted out of Lloyd Robinson and the other Missourians: *You could of talked all day long and not said that . . . Seen anything of that long-geared geezer who was gonna break that gelding for me? . . . That Swede don't know enough to pound sand in a rat hole . . .* In June, mosquitoes would come in a haze off the Smith River, and the mosquito stories would start: *Bastards're so big this year they can stand flatfooted and drink out of a rainbarrel . . . saw one of 'em carry off a baby chick the other day . . . yah, I saw two of 'em pick up a lamb, one at each end . . .* Any time of year, the muttering against Rankin and his vast holdings in the valley: *That goddamn Rankin's so crooked he couldn't sleep in a roundhouse . . . so tight he squeaks . . . so mean the coyotes wouldn't eat him . . .* One rancher or another proud of a new woven-wire fence: *Horse-high, bull-strong, and hog-tight. . . .* Another, defending himself against the notion that his saddle horse was the color and quality of mud: *No, by God, she's more of a kind of tansy-gray, the color of a cat's paw . . .* Nellie in the Grill, shaking over early morning coffee: *I got lit up like a church last night . . . Went home and threw my hat in the door first. It didn't come back out, so I figured I was safe. . . .*

And always, always, the two voices which went at each other just above my head. *Ruth, where the hell you been? If you think you can just walk off and leave me with the cafe that way, you got another think coming . . . Mister, I didn't marry you to spend all my time in any damn cafe. Where I go is my business . . .* The look in my direction, then: *Better leave us alone, Ivan. . . .* But the voices would go on, through the walls, until one more silence set in between my father and my second mother.

The silences stretched tauter until a day sometime in the autumn of 1948, when the Grill and our town life came to an end. Dad and Ruth could agree on one thing: the tremendous hours of cafe work were grinding them down. They gave up the lease, and now bought a thousand head of sheep and arranged to winter them at a ranch on Battle Creek in the Sixteen country, not far from the Basin where Dad had grown up.

There seemed to be no middle ground in the marriage. Not having managed to make it work while under the stare of the entire town, now the two of them decided to try a winter truce out in what was the emptiest corner of the county, just as it had been when Peter and Annie Doig came there to homestead a half-century before and as it is whenever I return now to drive its narrow red-shale road. Gulch-and-sage land, spare, silent. Out there in the rimming hills beyond the valley, twenty-five miles from town, Dad and Ruth would have time alone to see whether their marriage ought to last. *Could* last.

And I began what would be a theme of my life, staying in town in the living arrangement we called *boarding out*. It meant that someone or other, friend or relative or simply whoever looked reliable, would be paid by Dad to provide me room-and-board during the weekdays of school. It reminds me now of a long visit, the in-between feeling of having the freedom to wander in and out but never quite garnering any space of your own. But I had some knack then for living at the edges of other people's existences, and in this first span of boarding out—with friends of Ruth, the Jordan family—I found a household which teemed in its comings-and-goings almost as the cafe had.

Indeed, *We call it the short-order house around here,* Helen Jordan said as deer season opened and a surge of her out-of-town relatives, armed like a guerrilla platoon, swept through. Ralph Jordan himself came and went at uneven hours of the day and night, black with coal dust and so weary he could hardly talk: he was fireman on the belching old locomotive called Sagebrush Annie which snailed down the branch-line from White Sulphur to the main railroad at Ringling. Ralph with a shovelful of coal perpetually in hand, Helen forever up to her wrists in bread dough or dishwater—the Jordans were an instructive couple about the labor that life could demand.

And under their busy roof, I was living for the first time with other children, their two sons and a daughter. The older boy, Curtis, thin and giggly, was my age, and we slept in the same bed and snickered in the dark at each other's jokes. Boarding out at the Jordans went smoothly enough, then, except at the end of each week when Dad was to arrive and take me to the Battle Creek ranch with him. Friday night after Friday night, he did not arrive.

Whatever Dad or Ruth or I had expected of this testing winter, the unlooked-for happened: the worst weather of thirty years blasted into the Sixteen country, and Dad and Ruth found themselves in contest not so much with each other now, but with the screaming white wilderness outside.

As bad winters are apt to do, this one of 1948–49 whipped in early and hard. Snow fell, drifted, crusted into gray crystal windrows, then fell and drifted and crusted gray again. Dad and his hired man pushed the sheep in from the pastures to a big shed at the ranch buildings. Nothing could root grass out of that solid snow. The county road began to block for weeks at a time. Winter was sealing the Sixteen country into long frozen months of aloneness, and I was cordoned from the life of Dad and Ruth there.

At last, on the sixth Friday night, long after I had given up hope again, Dad appeared. Even then he couldn't take me to the ranch with him; he had spent ten hours fighting his way through the snow, and there was the risk that the countryside would close off entirely again before he could bring me back to town Sunday night. *Tell ye what we'll do, Skavinsky. Talk to that teacher of yours and see if you can work ahead in your schoolwork. If she'll let you, I'll come in somehow next Friday and you can come spend a couple of weeks out at the ranch.*

All week, whenever the recess bell rang I stayed at my desk and flipped ahead in one text or another, piling up lesson sheets to hand to the bemused teacher. Before school was out on Friday, Dad came to the door of the classroom for me, cocking his grin about clacking in with snowy overshoes and a girth of sheepskin coat.

The highway down the valley was bare, a black dike above the snow, as he drove the pickup to the turnoff toward Battle Creek. Then the white drifts stretched in front of us like a wide storm-frothed lake whose waves had suddenly stopped motion to hang in billows and peaks where the wind had lashed them against the sky.

The very tops of fenceposts, old gray cedar heads with rounded snow caps, showed where the road was buried. Between the post tops, a set of ruts had been rammed and hacked by Dad and the few other ranchers who lived in the Sixteen country.

Dad drove into the sea of snow with big turns of the steering wheel, keeping the front wheels grooved in the ruts while the rear end of the pickup jittered back and forth spinning snow out behind us. Sometimes the pickup growled to a halt. We would climb out and shovel away heavy chunks like pieces of an igloo. Then Dad would back the pickup a few feet for a running start and bash into the ruts again. Once we went over a snowdrift on twin rows of planks another of the ranchers had laid for support, a bridge in midsea. Once we drove entirely over the top of a drift without planks at all.

Where the road led up to the low ridge near the old Jap Stewart ranch, we angled between cliffs of snow higher than the pickup. Near Battle Creek, with our headlights fingering past the dark into the white blankness, Dad swerved off the road entirely and sent the pickup butting through the smaller drifts in a hayfield. It had started to snow heavily, the wind out of the Basin snaking the flurries down to sift into the ruts. I watched the last miles roll up on the tiny numbers under the speedometer as Dad wrestled the wheel and began his soft Scots cussing: *Snow on a man, will ye? Damn-it-all-to-hell-anyway, git back in those ruts. Damn-such-weather. Hold on, son, there's a ditch here some-where . . .* The twenty-fifth mile, the last, we bucked down a long slope to the ranch with the heavy wet flakes flying at us like clouds of moths. Dad roared past the lighted windows of the ranch house and spun the pickup inside the shelter of the lambing shed. *Done!* he said out into the storm. *Done, damn ye!*

To my surprise, Battle Creek was not living up to its name, and Dad and Ruth were getting along less edgily there than they ever had. It may have been that there simply was so much cold-weather work to be done, feeding the sheep, carrying in firewood, melting snow for water because the pump had frozen, that they had little stamina left over for argument. Or perhaps they had decided that the winter had to be gotten through, there simply was no route away from one another until spring. Whatever accounted for it, I slipped into its bask and warmed for the days to come.

Each morning, Ruth stood at the window sipping from a white mug of coffee, watching as Dad and the hired man harnessed the team to the hay sled. Then, if Dad had said they needed her that day, she would pull on heavy clothing and go out and take the reins while the men forked hay off to the sheep. Dad helped her in the house, the two of them working better together at the meals and dishes than they had when they were feeding half the town in the Grill. The pair of them even joked about the icy journey to the out-house which started each day. Whoever went first, the other would demand to know whether the seat had been left good and warm. *It damn well ought to be,* the other would say, *half of my behind is still out on it.* Or: *Sure did, I left it smoking for you.*

The ranch house had been built with its living quarters on the second floor, well above the long snowdrifts which duned against the walls. A railed porch hung out over the snow the full length of the house, and from it the other ranch buildings were in view like a small anchored fleet seen from a ship's deck. The lambing shed, low and cloud-gray and enormously long, seemed to ride full-laden in the white wash of winter. Most of the time, the sheep were corralled on the far side of the shed, their bored bleats coming as far as the house if the wind was down. Not far from the lambing shed stood the barn, dark and bunched into itself, prowing up out of the stillness higher than anything else in sight. A few small sheds lay with their roofs disappearing in drifts, swamped by this cold ocean of a winter. Battle Creek flowed just beyond those sheds, but the only mark of it was a gray skin of ice.

In this snow world, Dad and his hired man skimmed back and forth on the hay sled, a low wide hayrack on a set of runners pulled by a team of plunging workhorses. I rode with the men, hanging tight to the frame of the hayrack prowing above where the horses' hooves chuffed into the snow. When the men talked, their puffs of breath clouded fatly out in front of their faces. Our noses trickled steadily. Dad put a mitten against my face often to see that my cheeks weren't being frostbitten.

The winter fought us again and again. Our dog crashed through the ice of Battle Creek, and the wind carried the sound of his barking away from the house. We found the shatter where he had tried to claw himself out before the creek froze him and then drowned him. A blizzard yammered against the back wall of the house for two days without stop. Outside the snow flew so thick it seemed there was no space left between the flakes in the air, just an endless crisscross of flecks the whiteness of goose down. When Dad and the hired man went to feed the sheep, they would disappear into the storm, swallowed, thirty feet from the window where Ruth and I watched.

An afternoon when the weather let up briefly, I climbed the slope behind the house, to where a long gully troughed toward Battle Creek. Snow had packed the gulch so full that I could sled down over its humps and dips for hundreds of feet at a time. Trying out routes, I flew off a four-foot shale bank and in the crash sliced my right knee on the end of a sled runner as if I had fallen against an axe blade.

That moment of recall is dipped in a hot red ooze. The bloody slash scared out my breath in a long *uhhhhh.* A clench ran through the inside of me, then the instant heat of tears burned below my eyes. The climb from the gulch was steep. Now the burning fell to my leg. Blood sopped out as I hobbled to the house with both hands clamped over my wound, and Ruth shook as she snipped away the heavy-stained pants leg. The cut, she quickly told me, did not live up to its first horrific gush; it was long but shallow and clean, and dressings easily took care of it. In a few days, I could swing my leg onto the hay sled and again ride with the men above the horses' white-frosted heels.

The two weeks passed in surges of that winter weather, like tides flowing in long and hard. On the last morning, no snow was falling, but Dad said so much had piled by then that we could get to town only by team and sled. Ruth said she wanted to go with us. Dad looked at her once and nodded.

Dad and the hired man lifted the rack off the hay boat and fixed a seat of planks onto the front pair of sled runners. Inside that seat, blankets piled thickly onto the heavy coats we wore, we sat buried in warmth, almost down in the snow as the horses tugged us along on the running bob. Harness buckles sang a *ching-tink, ching-tink* with every step of the horses. Dad slapped the reins against the team's rumps and headed us toward the hayfields along Battle Creek. The road would be no help to us, drift humped onto drift there by now. We would aim through meadows and bottomlands where the snow lay flatter.

The grayness stretching all around us baffled my eyes. Where I knew hills had to be, no hills showed. The sagebrush too had vanished, from a countryside forested with its clumps. One gray sheet over and under and around, the snow and overcast had fused land and sky together. Even our sleigh was gray and half-hidden, weathered ash moving like a pale shadow through ashen weather.

Dad headed the team by the tops of fenceposts, and where the snow had buried even them, by trying to pick out the thin besieged hedge of willows along the creek. I peeked out beside Ruth, the two fogs of our breath blowing back between us as the horses found footing to trot. More often, they lunged at the snow, breaking through halfway up their thick legs. Dad talked to the horses every little while: *Hup there, Luck, get your heft into it. . . . Pull a bit, damn ye, Bess . . . Up this rise, now, get yourself crackin' there . . .* Their ears would jab straight up when they felt the flat soft slap of the reins and heard Dad's voice, and they would pull faster and we would go through the snow as if the sled was a running creature carrying us on its back.

The twin cuts of our sled tracks, the only clear lines the snow had not yet had time to seize and hide, traced away farther and farther behind us. Except for the strides of the horses and Dad's words to them, the country was silent, held so under the weight of the snow. In my memory that day has become a set of instants somewhere between life and death, a kind of eclipse in which hours did not pass and sound did not echo, all color washed to a flannel sameness and distance swelling away beyond any counting of it. We went into that fog-world at one end of Battle Creek and long after came out at the other, but what happened in between was as measureless as a float through space. If it was any portion of existence at all, it did not belong to the three of us, but to that winter which had frozen all time but its own.

After that ghostly trip, I went back to my boarding family and Dad and Ruth went on with the struggle against the winter. It was another month or so before Dad arrived to take me to the ranch again. This time, we drove across the drifted world inside a plowed canyon, the slabs and mounds of frozen snow wrenched high as walls on either side of the thin route. *We've had a D-8 'dozer in here, the government sent it out when it looked like we were all gonna lose the livestock out here. I had to get a truckload of cottonseed cake sent in for the sheep, the hay's goin' so damn fast. They put the bumper of that truck right behind the 'dozer and even so it took 'em sixty-six hours to make it to the ranch and back, can ye feature that? That load of cottoncake is gonna cost us $2500 in transportation, but we had to have 'er.* I looked at him as if he'd said the moon was about to fall on us; $2500 sounded to me like all the money in the state of Montana. But Dad grinned and talked on: *You should of been out here to see all the snowplowin'. After they 'dozed out our haystacks, the crew was supposed to go up and 'doze out Jim Bill Keith's place. I was the guy that was showin' them the way, ridin' the front end of that Cat. Hell, I got us lost on the flats up here—same damn country I grew up in, ye know—and we 'dozed in a big circle before we knew what was goin' on. Plowed up a quarter of a mile of Jim Bill's fence and didn't even know it. Blizzardin', boy it's been ablowin' out here, son. They came out in one of those snow crawlers to change Cat crews—changed 'em with an airplane when they first started, but the weather got so bad they couldn't fly—so here they come now in one of these crawlers, and the guy* *drivin' is drunker'n eight hundred dollars. I thought he was gonna bring that damned crawler through the window of the house . . .* I laughed with him, but must have looked worried. He grinned again. *We're doin' okay in spite of it all. Haven't lost any sheep yet, and that high-priced cottoncake gives us plenty of feed. If this winter don't last into the summer, we're even gonna make some pretty good money on the deal.*

Then in the next weeks came an afternoon when Dad saddled a horse and plunged off through the below-zero weather to the neighboring Keith ranch. *He came up here wanting to borrow some cigarettes, and some whiskey.* Probably the truce with Ruth was wearing through by then. Dad idled in the kitchen, talking and drinking coffee with Mrs. Keith while waiting for Jim Bill and his hired man to come back from feeding their cattle. *I remember, yes, your dad had ridden up on a little sorrel horse and he was sitting in the kitchen with Flossie, and he kept looking out at this kind of a red knob out here on the hill. He looked and he looked, and pretty soon he jumped up and yelled: 'It's broke, it's broke!' and he ran outside. And that winter* was *broke. The hired man and I came riding home with our earflaps rolled up and our coats off, and our mittens stuck in the fork-hole of the saddle. Just like that.*

The chinook which had begun melting the snowdrifts even as Dad watched did signal the end of that ferocious winter, and somehow too it seemed to bring the end of the long storm within our household. Before, neither Dad nor Ruth had been able to snap off the marriage. Now they seemed in a contest to do it first, like a pair tugging at a stubborn wishbone.

Near the start of summer, Ruth announced she was leaving, this time for all time. Dad declared it the best idea he'd ever heard out of her. Alone with Ruth sometime in the swash and swirl of all this, I asked why she had to go. She gave me her tough grin, shook her head and said: *Your dad and me are never gonna get along together. We're done. We gave it our try.*

Why it was that the two of them had to endure that winter together before Ruth at last could go from Dad, I have never fathomed. Perhaps it was a final show of endurance against one another, some way to say *I can last at this as long as you can.* But that long since had been proved by both, and it is one of the strangenesses of this time that they had to go on and on with the proof of it. A last strangeness came over these years even after Ruth had vanished from us, and the divorce been handed down, one last unrelenting echo of it all. Dad no longer would even refer to Ruth by name. Instead, he took up something provided by one of the onlookers to our household's civil war. Naturally, the valley had not been able to resist choosing up sides in such a squabble, and a woman coming to Dad's defense reached for anything contemptible enough to call Ruth. At last she spluttered: *Why, that . . . that little flip!* For whatever reason, that Victorian blurt rang perfectly with Dad, put him in the right in all the arguments he was replaying in his mind. From the moment the surprising word got back to him, he would talk of Ruth only as *Flip, that damned Flip.*

Ruth went, and Flip stayed, one single poisoned word which was all that was left of two persons' misguess about one another. I have not seen Ruth for twenty years, nor spoken with her for twenty-five. But for a time after those few warring years with my father, her life straightened, perhaps like a piece of metal seethed in fire for the anvil. She married again, there was a son. And then calamity anew, that marriage in wreckage, and another after that, the town voice saying more than ever of her *She thinks everything should come in a cloud for her but she has hatefulness in herself,* until at last she had gone entirely, *disappeared somewhere out onto the Coast, nobody's cared to keep track of her.*

The son: I am curious about him. Was he taken by Ruth to see the grandmother blinking back age and blindness? Did Ruth stand with him, white mug of coffee in her hand, to watch snow sift on a winter's wind? But the curiosity at last stops there. When Dad and Ruth finally pulled apart, the one sentiment I could recognize within me—have recognized ever since—was relief that she had gone, and that the two of them could do no more harm to each other.

Once more Dad had to right our life, and this time he did it simply by letting the seasons work him up and down the valley. He went to one ranch as foreman of the haying crew, on to another to feed cattle during the winter, to a third for spring and the lambing season.

When school started and I could not be with him, he rented a cabin in White Sulphur and drove out to his ranch work in the morning and back at night. During the winter and in spring's busyness of lambing, I usually boarded with Nellie and his wife in their fine log house. Nellie's wife was a world of improvement from Ruth—a quiet approving woman, head up and handsome. In the pasture behind their house she raised palomino horses, flowing animals of a rich golden tan and with light blond manes of silk. The horses seemed to represent her independence, her declaration away from Nellie's life of drinking, and she seemed to think Dad was right in letting me be as free and roaming as I was. It occurs to me now that she would have given me her quiet approving smile if I had come home from a wandering to report that I'd just been down at the Grand Central watching a hayhand knife a sheepherder.

And after her season of calm, Dad began one for us together. When the summer of 1950 came, he bought a herd of cattle, and we moved them and ourselves to a cattle camp along Sixteenmile Creek.

There our life held a simpler pace than I could ever remember. The two of us lived in a small trailer house, the only persons from horizon to horizon and several miles beyond. Dad decided to teach me to shoot a single-shot .22 rifle, using as targets the tan gophers which every horseback man hated for the treacherous little burrows they dug. We shot by the hour, rode into the hills every few days to look at the cattle, caught trout in the creek, watched the Milwaukee Railroad trains clip past four times every day.

Then I had my eleventh birthday—five years since my mother had died—and it seemed to trigger a decision in Dad. Something had been working at him, a mist of despond and unsteady health which would take him off into himself for hours at a time. One evening in the first weeks after my birthday, after he had been silent most of the day, he told me a woman would be coming into our lives again.

His words rolled a new planet under our feet, so astonishing and unlikely was this prospect. Ruth had come and gone without much lasting effect, except for the scalded mood Dad showed whenever he had a reason to mention her. But the person he had in mind now cast a shadowline across everything ahead of us, stood forth as the one apparition I could not imagine into our way of life. My mother's mother.

In the night, in mid-dream, people who are entire strangers to one another sometimes will congregate atop my pillow. They file into my sleeping skull in perplexing medleys. A face from grade school may be twinned with one met a week ago on a rain-forest trail in the Olympic Mountains. A pair of friends I joked with yesterday now drift in arguing with an editor I worked for more than a thousand miles from here. How thin the brainwalls must be, so easily can acquaintanceships be struck up among these random residents of the dark.

Memory, the near-neighborhood of dream, is almost as casual in its hospitality. When I fix my sandwich lunch, in a quiet noon, I may find myself sitting down thirty years ago in the company of the erect old cowboy from Texas, Walter Badgett. Forever the same is the meal with Walter: fried mush with dark corn syrup, and bread which Walter first has toasted and then dried in the oven. When we bite, it shatters and crashes in our mouths, and the more we eat, the fuller our plates grow with the shrapnel of crumbs. After the last roaring bite, Walter sits back tall as two of the ten-year-old me and asks down: Well, reckon we can make it through till night now? *I step to the stove for tea, and come instead onto the battered blue-enamel coffee pot in a sheepherder's wagon, my father's voice saying* Ye could float your grandma's flat-iron on the Swede's coffee. *I walk back toward my typewriter, past a window framing the backyard fir trees. They are replaced by the wind-leaning jackpines of one Montana ridgeline or another. I glance higher for some hint of the weather, and the square of air broadens and broadens to become the blue expanse over Montana rangeland, so vast and vaulting that it rears, from the foundation-line of the plains horizon, to form the walls and roof of all of life's experience that my younger self could imagine, a single great house of sky.*

Now the mood moves on, the restless habit of dream and memory, and I come to myself in a landscape of coastal western-ness so different in time and place from that earlier one. Different, yet how readily acquainted.

LADY

Sitting up in a railroad coach seat for a day, a night, and another day, Bessie Ringer is jostled westward in the springtime of 1914. The Mississippi River lay several hundreds of miles behind, vaulted by a slim bridge which had made her flick scared glances down to the gliding water all the long way over. Minnesota had been crossed, and the Dakotas, where the homesteads of an earlier generation of journeyers nested in fat patches of turned earth. Rivers new and wild to her—the Little Missouri, the Yellowstone, the Powder—came looping widely beneath the roadbed, and now when the train made its wheezy stops in the middle of nowhere, the men who clomped aboard wore hats with swooping curled brims, and their women, she could not help but notice, looked leathered from the sun and wind. Where they stepped from, the arc of prairie flung straight and empty to the horizon, nothing could be imagined which might rule their lives except that sun, that wind. By the time, then, that her train was pushing out of the townless distances of eastern Montana, Bessie had come an entire world away from the pinched midwestern background she had been born into twenty years before. Come, what's more, for forever and with no regret ever said aloud. Her people back there were German stock, abrupt and gloomy as their family name—*Glun.* In the memories which stretched along the rails to the farmstead life in central Wisconsin's cut-over pine country, that name mocked itself into queer rhyme. It had happened because school dismayed Bessie, and in her unhappiness one day was caught whispering to the girl seated beside her. Picking up his pointer to threaten her, the teacher thundered it then: *Glun, Glun, don't have so much fun, or you'll have a swat of Jack Hickory's son!* At home, life was no less startling and strict under her burly mustached father: *I always remember my pa so stern. I was always scared of him.* Now train tracks, hour upon hour, were leaving *always* to the past, to the land falling away behind the West.

On Bessie's lap a daughter dozes in the train's cradling motion—my mother, Berneta, waking now and again to see the land flying and flying past her six-month-old eyes. She is plump and pretty, and with her full dark hair has begun to look like a small jolly version of a much older girl. A version, that would be, of Bessie herself not long before. On the wall by me is a studio portrait of Bessie when she had reached the age of sixteen or so, posed with the two Krebs sisters who were her best of friends. Out the oval window of photo, the sisters stare down the camera and any lookers beyond it, mouths straight as Bible lines. You would not tease with this pair, not dare their wrath without an open door behind you. They are iron and granite side by side, and are going to leave some bruises on the world. Beside them, Bessie's look is all the softer, the eyes more open and asking, her face wondering at life instead of taking it on chin first. She must have had much to wonder at, raised as such an apron-stringed girl, snugged all the more firmly into the family by the one lapse in her father's strictness. John Glun had brooded against a way of schooling which even for an instant could taunt a daughter of his, and after her third year, Bessie was not made to attend again. She spent the rest of her growing years entirely at home. That upbringing of choring for her mother and edging past her father's thunderhead temper left her unsure of herself, but guessing that the world must have something else to offer. *So that's the how of it,* she would say whenever some new turn of life had shown itself, and she seemed about to say it there to the camera eye. It is, all in all, an offering glance for the world, of which she might yet have had a strong gleam four years later as she held her prized daughter and watched the western Montana mountains begin to stand high ahead of the train.

Alongside Bessie, the train window shadowing his face close in beside hers, sits Thomas Abraham Ringer. Housepainter, handyman, wiry Irishman with a hatchet nose and a chin like an axe—last and least, husband. All three Glun children flew as quickly as they could from that narrow home, but Bessie went with one last disfavor from her father. He singled out for her this seldom-do-well Tom Ringer and bent her, at the age of 18, into marrying the man. *Gee gosh, a girl like I was who didn't know her own mind—I done it because my pa said it was my way to get by in the world.* Tom was twice her age, nearly as old as her father himself, and the one thing he had done exactly right in all his life until then had been not to take on a wife and a family. In fair charity—one-half of those who speak of Tom Ringer do give a rough affectionate forgiveness, while the other half call him something like a sour-minded reprobate—the knack of caring unswervingly for anyone beyond himself did not seem to be in this man. Alone, fussing a floorboard into place or stroking a paintbrush peevishly along a ceiling, that sharp face could simply prod all into tidiness and spear away whatever of life he did not want to see or hear. But being married was nothing like being alone, and there came the consequence which Bessie declared in the shortest and angriest of her verdicts on this husband. *Tom drank.*

It made a dubious marriage worse. The temper tamped inside Tom which he seemed to need to propel himself through life would turn ugly when whiskey touched it. *Darn his hide. He'd be going along perfectly fine, then there'd be a big blowup.* This, too: even when his wages didn't trickle away in saloons, they shrank and vanished some other way. All their married life, Tom and Bessie Ringer would live close to predicament. The one feat of finance they ever managed was this train trip, uprooting themselves half a continent westward to where a relative had homesteaded—a blind fingers-crossed jump to the strange high country of sage and silence.

At the town of Three Forks, they left the train. There the broad tilts of this new country suddenly tumbled three idling rivers into one another to greaten into the headwaters of the Missouri, and in every direction around, ranges of mountains hazed to a thin blue, as if behind smoke. *Mountains and mountains and mountains,* Bessie would remember.

The promise of a housepainter's job awaited Tom in this first town of the new life. But that job, or any other, wasn't to be had. What did present itself was the rumor of work at a small logging camp eastward in the Crazy Mountains. *See, Tom had been in the woods some back in Wisconsin. So we went off up there near Porcupine Creek in the Crazies, and Tom cut in the timber until winter come.*

Then, into the teeth of the mountain weather, Tom and Bessie and their tiny daughter climbed higher into the Crazies, to spend the winter cutting small trees for fence posts. Some thousands of feet higher than they had ever been in their Wisconsin lives, they set up a peaked photographer's tent in the dark pitch of forest, banked the outside walls with snow for warmth, fired up a long box stove which would be kept blazing all winter long, and whacked down timber from first light to last. *No, it wasn't so bad of a winter. We got by good, there was worlds of firewood.*

Through that timberland winter, isolated and snowbound, Bessie and Tom felled and unlimbed trees, then snaked the wood to a snow-packed skidway. She would clamber down the slope as Tom hitched their workhorse to the first pile of logs and looped the reins to the harness. The horse would plod down to her, the logs sledding long soft troughs behind in the snow. When Bessie unhitched the load, the horse would turn itself back up the mountain for the next load of work. That pattern of trudge was much like what lay ahead for Bessie herself, for if I am to read any beginnings at all in these lives which twine behind my own, my grandmother's knack for plowing head-down through all hardship surely begins here at the very first of these lean Montana years.

Then the kids' dad—she banished Tom to that in later times, his name never crossing her tongue if she could help it—*the kids' dad got us on at Moss Agate. The rancher ran a herd of cull milk cows there, and we milked all those cows and put up the hay on the place. We lived there, oh, a lot of years.*

Moss Agate was a small ranch at the southern reach of the Smith River valley, on an empty flat furred with sage and a few hackles of brush along the South Fork of the river, and walled in at every point of the horizon by buttes or foothills. The single vivid thing about the place lay in its name. The rock called moss agate is a daydreamer's stone, a smokey hardness with its trapped black shadow of fossil inside like a tree dancing to the wind or a sailing ship defying fog or whatever else you can imagine from it. Later, after my father had begun to court my mother, someone who saw him saddling for his weekly ride to Moss Agate asked if he was finding any prize agates in the hills there. *One,* he grinned. *She's about five feet tall, with black hair and blue eyes.*

On that ranch where dreams were trapped in rock, Bessie and Tom milked cows year after year, toiled to keep the few sun-browned ranch buildings from yawning into collapse, and plodded out their marriage. There was a new child now every few years—three boys in a row. Each summer, Bessie held the latest baby in her lap as she drove a team of horses hitched to the sulky-seated hay rake. *I wore bib overalls then in haying time. But silly thing, I'd run and put a dress on if I seen anybody coming.* Throughout the seasons, she rode horseback after strayed calves, fed hogs, raised chickens, gardened and canned, burned out the sage ticks which pincered onto the children, mucked out the tidal flow of manure-and-urine after the eternal cows. And all of it in a growing simmer against Tom.

I can watch her, in those Moss Agate years, being made over from almost all that she had been before: toughening, leathering, the salt of sweat going into her mind and heart. Even her body now defied the harsh life; the single luxury of that milking herd was dairy produce, and as her cooking feasted on the unending butter and cream, she broadened and squared.

But it was her look to the world that changed most, and in the few photos from about her thirtieth year, her tenth in Montana, a newcomer now gazes out from where the young bride had been—a flinchless newcomer who has firmed into what she will be all the rest of her life.

Her face now was strongest, almost mighty, at its center—the careful clasp of a mouth which seemed always ready to purse with no relenting, and the thick nose which has monumented itself all through the family line to her great-grandchildren. A brief ball of chin, a fine square span of forehead beneath neatly waved hair already gone gray and on its way to white. Blue eyes, paler and more flat in their declaring than, say, my father's mulling look.

She stood to the height my mother does in photograph—scant inches over five feet—but where my mother seemed a wand of a woman, this grandmother was an oak stump. Chunky as she had grown—at times weighing more than 150 pounds, and long since locked into an everlasting lost battle against her own pastries, snacks and second helpings—she somehow seemed stout without being overgirthed; steady without being stolid.

In this odd strong way, then, her very stockiness somehow made her appear taller than she really was, and a neighbor's memory at last explained: *The first time I remember seeing Bessie Ringer was at the Caukins schoolhouse, at a dance out there, and I just admired her so, she always carried herself so straight and dignified.*

Of course: so straight, and the dignity of that. For in both senses of the saying, Bessie Ringer was stiff-backed, with erect pride and the unbending notions to go with it. In a sense, the central ideas in her were lodged in place like the logs of a stockade: upright, sharply pointed, and as durable as they were wooden.

The first of her unattackable beliefs was family. This had started early, when my mother from her first breaths was seen to be an asthma victim and Bessie began to raise her with a special blend of love and fuss. It went on as each of her three boys arrived—musical Paul and mischievous

William and adept Wallace—and were given whatever sacrifices she could that they would be able to go through the schooling she had not, make it out into life whole and able. *We had to get by sometimes on a lick and a promise, but there's others didn't do as good as we managed, too.* That the family thinned off markedly at Tom's end of the table simply redoubled her affections elsewhere. It was as if his portion of her commitment had to be put to use somehow, and into the children it went.

Next came work. Bessie was uncomfortable with much depth of thinking—her slim school years and that tethered girlhood had robbed her mind there, and she knew it with regret—but doing came to her with lovely ease. She worked, that is to say, as some people sing; for the pleasure of it, the habit of it, the sense that life was asking it specially of her. *It gives me the willies,* she would recite, *to be sittin' just doin' nothin'.* In her own retelling and all told about her, I can find her at almost every relentless ranch task of those years: stacking hay, teamstering horses in dead winter, pulling calves from breech births, stringing barbed wire onto fencelines, threshing grain amid the itching storm of chaff, axing ice from the cattle's watering-holes. *She was a worker,* comes the valley's echo of her again and again. So much a worker, it may be, that items such as a wrong husband fell away behind the pace of task and chore.

Family, work—and the clinch across both of them, steadfastness. Life was to be lived out as it came. If it came hard, you bowed your neck a bit more and endured. So without thinking it through—not entirely knowing how to—she had set her mind not to be afraid of that spare weather-whipped land, that wan ranch life.

In this total rind of determination, Bessie was not like many of the valley women, or most of the men either. Down through the valley's history, such settlers had expected something of their work, and sooner or later uprooted themselves if it didn't come. Bessie only chored on. In her unschooled way, she was greatly more fearless about wresting a fresh life in Montana than my father's family had been. Those homesteaders newcoming to the Basin had allied themselves, formed a kind of trestle of relatives and fellow Scots. Compared with them, Bessie went along as alone and unaided as a tumbleweed.

Indeed, her stories of life at Moss Agate and a number of other hard-scrabble spots in the valley most often began with the aloneness: *The one time, I was alone by myself on the place—the kids' dad was off again somewhere—and it rained and it rained until the creek started to come up around the cattle in the corral. It kept coming and kept coming until I had to saddle our old roany horse and ride through to let those cows out. The water come up over my stirrups and of course that old roany made it his habit to stop dead whenever you tried to hurry him. But I got him through the water and tied one end of the rope to the pole gate and the other end to the saddle horn, and the cows could follow me out then. A person can do a lot of things like that when you're in a corner.*

But a corner of another sort was where Tom loomed in his private furies, and if steadfastness held her into the marriage and the ranch life, it did not overcome the pains of them. Gone to town for groceries, Tom might not return for days. When he did come back from such sprees, he arrived rasping at the way Bessie had done the ranch chores or was raising the children. *Gosh sakes, times you wouldn't know he was a man you'd ever met. Ornery old thing him, anyhow.* She began to fight back at him with silence, and she could be as grimly silent as oblivion.

Then the rancher who owned Moss Agate died, and passed from the valley with a storied funeral where the reek of whiskey oozed through the flower smells, and the tipsy pallbearers nearly dropped the coffin at the graveside. Whiskey had poisoned Bessie's life at Moss Agate, and now whiskey closed it. She and Tom and the four children moved to another ranch. That job lasted no time—it was in the deep of the Depression now—and soon they were in the tiny rail-line town of Ringling, in a ragtag house which at least put shelter atop their heads. Sometime then, Tom left Bessie alone again with the teetery household, and at last she broke the marriage.

She never bothered with a divorce. Going to law for something which she had ended in her own mind did not seem needed. But Tom—rather, *the kids' dad*—had passed from her as surely as if he had been tumbled into the grave with the whiskeyfied rancher.

That life done, Bessie was soon adrift. There was no income, and the last of the children were out of school and heading off on their own. In the Shields River Valley, near the Crazy Mountains where she had started in Montana twenty-five years before, she found a job as cook for an elderly farmer named Magnusson. He was prosperous but lonely, a widower, feeling old and trying to dilute his days with drink. When Bessie came, the drinking and the self-pity tapered away.

Old Magnusson came to rely entirely on her, and they became a familiar pair in the Shields River country, he driving her in his black pickup to a meeting of her women's club or off to the town of Wilsall for the week's groceries, she ruling in his kitchen and handling the farmyard chores for him.

Surely the sight of them constantly paired set tongues clanging—it took less than that—but they confounded the gossips considerably. No one ever managed to hear them call each other anything but *Mr. Magnusson* and *Mrs. Ringer* or to see them more than correctly cordial with one another, maintaining an austere arm's-length household it was all but impossible to read anything further into. Apparently suspicion fairly quickly was set aside, because Bessie became fast friends with some of the sternest neighboring wives and a well-regarded member of the Shields River community. Which left just one person on a moral high horse against her. My father.

The resentment between Dad and my grandmother must have circled in darkly from the past, all the way from his earliest courting of my mother. Lessons of lineage were not something Bessie Ringer ordinarily gave much thought to. But as she watched this only daughter, her first child and the ill one and the favored, being wooed by a showy young cowboy, surely her own too-young marriage to Tom Ringer came to mind, and probably too her mother's too-young marriage to the stern silent John Glun.

What was said there in the years of my father's courtship as Bessie tried to stave off the past's rhythm, I have never heard hinted. But the broad line of time tells much. It was only a few months before my mother's twenty-first birthday, when by law she would have been free of family consent, that she and my father were married, after six entire years of courtship.

From all that I can deduce, there was no open rift while my mother remained alive. My grandmother's sense of family likely stormed over past differences. In the marriage summer when my mother and father were herding sheep on Grass Mountain, Bessie would get on a saddlehorse at Ringling, ride half a day west across the sage prairie, and somehow search them out along the lengthy mountain slope. After overnight, she would saddle and ride off, to appear again in a few weeks as if having strolled across the street. If Dad was my mother's choice in life, so be it for Bessie. He had become Family, and she would become civil. And when I was born, her first grandchild and the sole one for a space of years, her visiting became heartier yet. *Oh, I used to come and stay with you while your folks was to a dance in Sixteen or Ringling. They had themselves a time there, and we had ourselves one to home, we did.*

But after my mother's death, something quickly hung in the air between my father and my grandmother, like the first blazing word of a secret and no more. She made a few uneasy visits to us at our first ranch in the valley. But she and Ruth were enemies almost at sight, and when Dad married Ruth, we abruptly were visited by my grandmother no more. Instead a reversal of sorts began, as if something were being acted out before angled sets of mirrors: Dad now encouraged me to go across town after school to visit my grandfather, Tom Ringer.

Allow this to my father, there was charity as well as defiance in this turnabout notion of his. At the time I was Tom Ringer's only grandchild, and dour as his life may have been, he showed an old man's gruff affection for me. He lived then in a small cabin across the street from the sulphur slough, and made his slow rounds uptown each day. *I remember he was quite worried about you,* my first-grade teacher would recall to me many years later, *in those months just after you had lost your mother. Whenever I'd meet him on the street, he'd inquire about how you were getting along.*

I think I did all too little to return his interest. He was by then into his seventies, a bent and gray-faced man with a colossal blade of nose, living lonely in a musty cabin, and I was not entirely sure where his life cornered onto mine. Grandparents in general seemed a difficult proposition. Those on Dad's side of the family, who sounded wondrously interesting in their Scottishness, long since were gone from the world, and here on my mother's side were this warring grandmother and this weary wraith of a grandfather. The only clear fact in it all seemed to be something Dad said: *It's hell on old Tom, left alone with himself.*

Beyond that visiting maneuver, Dad began to try to talk me—and himself—into forgetting Bessie Ringer. And at the same time, I suppose, to chant himself into a rightness about what he was doing, for along with all else borne in him since my mother's death, he had been living with twin fears. The first, that he would lose me, somehow be unable to keep me with him and raise me amid his zigzagging ranch life. Second and worse, that if he was forced to give me up, it would have to be to the mother-in-law he had been at spear-point with so much of the past.

It must have represented the last loss possible to his life: that his one son would be made a stranger to him. Dad tried to twine his other bereavement onto that one, as if he could knot together from the two a talisman of some sort: *Your mother would of wanted me to raise you instead of your grandma doing it, I can tell ye that. She said . . . she said just as much. She talked about it sometimes, after she'd had one of her bad spells. We always knew she might go during one of those spells—Christamighty, how she suffered with those. Times I would drive her to the hospital in Townsend thinking every breath was gonna be her last. She went through hell on this earth, your mother. And she never would want me to give you up, I'm-here-to-tell-you.*

Silence from him, then the next veer from fear to spite: *Hell, we'll get by somehow, son. We don't need that old woman running our lives. Look at her there, living with old Magnusson that way and never marrying him. She needs to run her own life more pert, I'd say.* Then this, the rest of the secret told. *She'd take you from me in a minute if she could. But there's no way on this green earth I'm gonna let her.*

But there was a way, and it came with a slow fierce sear inside him during our summer of 1950 at the cattle camp along Sixteenmile Creek. Dad began to suspect that he might be dying. For several years he had been contending with a fitful stomach ulcer; during Ruth's years it embered more often in him, and now had glowed itself into a steady burn. It became a rare day when he didn't throw up at least one meal. He lost weight, his nerves jumped. Everything the doctors prescribed seemed to make the stomach worse, and their obvious bafflement gave off the fear that this finally was more than an ulcer on a rampage.

For the first time, mortality was crowding Charlie Doig slowly enough that he could think it through, and across that charring summer it brought him to the greatest change of mind he could make. He needed someone in readiness to step into his place in my life. The readiest person on the face of the planet was the one who had loomed in his dark musings all this while.

My father had everything to gulp back, then, when he set out to make truce with this phantom grandmother of mine. I can hear, as if in a single clear echo, the pivoting of our lives right there: Dad beginning his desperate phone call in the lobby of the Sherman Hotel, spelling out her name in an embarrassed half-shout to the operator, staring miserably at the cars nosing off around the prow of the hotel as the long-distance line hummed and howled in his ear. Then: *Ah. Hullo, Bessie, This is Charlie. Charlie, Charlie Doig. No, Ivan's fine, fine, he's right here. Ah. Say, would ye gonna be home on Sunday? We could, ah, come over maybe and see ye. All right. All right, then. G'bye.*

The Magnusson farm, in the county south of us, lay in what we called the Norskie Country—a coverlet of farmed slopes and creek bottoms coming down along the watershed of the Shields River from the icy snaggled peaks of the Crazy Mountains. It was better growing country than our valley—lower, milder—and the Scandinavian immigrants were exactly the thrifty and stubborn people to make it pay. After her years at the sage flats of Moss Agate, my grandmother's job at Magnusson's must have seemed almost silken. As we drove to his farm, the furrowed fields were ruled straight and brown on one side of the road, the green flow of hayfields curving with the creek on the other.

Magnusson's house, brown as the plowed earth, came out like a rampart from the slope which led down into the creek's slim valley. As we went up the outside flight of stairs, a man and a woman stepped onto the lofty porch and looked down at us with curiosity. Magnusson proved to be a steady-eyed, stocky farmer in his seventies, with white eyebrows and a mustache stained considerably less than white. His rumbled accent came like a growl against Dad's burr, but he said we were welcome in his house always, then withdrew to the front room with his newspaper from Norway.

That left us with my grandmother, whom I barely remembered from three or so years before. She gave Dad a thin *Hello,* beamed down at me and said, *Where's a kiss for your gramma?* I pecked her cheek and husked a *Hello* as close as I could to the tone she had given Dad.

The three of us bunched ourselves at the table in the vast kitchen, which was where serious visiting was done in the coffee-habited Norskie Country. As she and I munched our way through a plate of cookies, Dad lit cigarettes nervously and between puffs chewed away at the inside of his cheek. In a fashion, he was courting this wary woman much as he had courted her daughter twenty years earlier, but with grimness instead of love. What was unspoken but being said more plainly than anything in his careful chat was this: *We need you. I may die soon. Ivan must have someone to raise him.*

How much the old rift between them was mended that Sunday, I do not know. I was too young to read the presence of the past, although I could sense it was somehow there in the kitchen with us. But rilesome as both of these figures could be about whatever might have happened in some yesterday, that first visit surely undid some of the anger just by not becoming a brawl.

I remember that at the late end of the afternoon I went out with her to feed the white geese in the farmyard, and that they hissed and flounced around us until her dog, Shep, came barking, delirious to have an excuse to scatter the bullies. *Shoo 'em, Shep!* I remember her encouraging in a kind of angry pleasure: *Shoo 'em good! Sic 'em out of here, the goshdarn old fools!* I remember too that by the time Dad and I left, I was calling her *Grandma.*

For his part, Dad had seemed not to know what to call his own mother-in-law. He avoided calling her anything at all during our kitchen stay. But from the bottom of the stairs, he finally said up to her: *G'bye to ye, Lady. We'll come again next Sunday.*

Almost every weekend after that we would make the long drive to Magnusson's to visit her. The bargain Dad needed was being forged. It would take effect sooner than even he dreamed, because one among us in that odd group was dying, all right, but it was not my father. It was Martin Magnusson.

Just before old Magnusson slumped into the series of hospital stays which saw him decline to death, Dad bluntly asked my grandmother further into his plan. The doctoring in Montana was not helping him; his stomach flamed more and more now, he felt himself growing weaker. He was going to a place in Minnesota called the Mayo Clinic, and he wanted not to go alone, to have me with him—and her. Would she come?

In a week, the three of us stepped up into the eastbound train at Ringling. I remember of the trip only that Dad wearily slept and slept, and that when Grandma drowsed with her head back against the coach seat, she sometimes snorted herself awake with a long *kkkhhh* of a snore, and that

I abandoned the pair of them to sit by the hour in the dome car and watch the worldscape of my first train journey.

At the destination in Minnesota, Dad hardly had the strength to carry a suitcase into the hotel where we would stay. He checked into the clinic, and immediately the doctors began days of tests on him. Grandma and I watched the people below from our hotel room far above the street, and spent time with Dad at the clinic whenever he was not in tests.

On the fourth day we were startled by a telegram for Grandma. Tom Ringer had died. His last torment of my grandmother was that she still felt something for him which made her want to return to Montana for his funeral. Dad agreed there was no choice, although it seemed to me there was all the choice in the world. She and I took the train back to Montana, leaving Dad to the doctors' solemn tests.

After the funeral, I went to stay again with Dad's brother Angus and his family, Grandma returned to Magnusson's farm. Several weeks dragged by before Dad followed us home to Montana, and when he came, he was a bony ghost with only a third of his stomach. That severe surgery was all that could keep him alive, the doctors had told him, and he would not be able to do any work for many months.

There the doctors had the matter backwards. Staying away from work, from knowing what ability was left in him, was what Charlie Doig could not do. Within a few weeks, he had hired on at a ranch at the western edge of the valley and there, pale and retching if he ate a spoonful too much at any mealtime, my father began slamming away at the job as he always had.

And he arranged a second matter, as much against the odds as the first. Grandma and I now were to live in Ringling, in the shambled small house where she had managed to put her own children through school and out into the world. From there I would ride the bus to school in White Sulphur Springs. That part of life changed little. But under a new roof with this restored woman called Lady and Grandma, almost all else did.

Ringling lay on the land, twenty miles to the south of White Sulphur Springs, as the imprint of what had been a town, like the yellowed outline on grass after a tent has been taken down. When the roadbed of the Milwaukee and St. Paul Railroad was diked through the site early in the century, a community—it was called Leader then—snappily built up around the depot: three hotels, several saloons, a lumber yard, stores, a two-story bank, a confectionery, even a newspaper office. When John Ringling's little railroad bumped down the valley from White Sulphur to link onto the Milwaukee and St. Paul main line, and the rumor followed that the headquarters of the great circus would be established there—surely the century's record for unlikelihood—the village was optimistically renamed Ringling. But before the end of the 1920's, the grandly adopted name was almost all that was left: many of the businesses had burned in a single wild night of flame. It was said, and more or less believed, that a Ku Klux Klan cross had blazed just before the lumber yard caught fire and spewed the embers that took half the town to the ground.

A few years later, another fire even less explainable than the first mopped up almost all of what was left. By the time Grandma and I moved there, Ringling stood as only a spattered circle of houses around several large weedy foundations. The adult population was about 50 persons, almost all of them undreamably old to me, and the livelihoods were a saloon, a gas station, a post office, Mike Ryan's store, the depot, and exactly through the middle of town, the railroad tracks which glinted and fled instantly in both directions.

Mornings, an eastbound passenger train tornadoed through, then came one tearing westward; afternoons, as people said, it was the same except opposite. My first days there I wondered about the travelers seen as tiny cutouts against the pullman windows—what they were saying when they looked out at us and our patchy, sprawled town-that-was-less-than-a-town. If they looked out.

These orange-and-black passenger trains whipped in and went off like kings and queens, potent and unfussed, on the dot. But freight trains banged around at all hours, and for a few weeks in autumn, Ringling made its own clamoring rail traffic as boxcars of sheep and cattle trundled back and forth from the loading pens at the edge of town. Otherwise, the town did almost nothing but doze, kept sleepily alive by the handful of people who lived there out of habit and the few ranchers who used it as their gas-and-mail point. The single wan tendril to its past was Mike Ryan's store, which I lost not a moment before visiting.

Mike Ryan was a very ancient man by then, near-blind, looming in his goggling spectacles and flat cap amid a dust-grayed avalanche of hardware, harness, stray dry goods, and stale groceries such as the bakery goods his cats liked to sleep on. The second words Mike spoke to you, after a broguey *Hello* and learning what it was you wanted, always were: *Now it's here if I can just find it.*

And it would be, for Mike Ryan's had been a perfect country store in its time, a vast overstocked bin of merchandise behind its high false front and under its roof with the yellow airplane signals painted hugely on. But now, as if the years were caving in on it, the enterprise was becoming more and more muddled, dim, musty. At times Mike himself would dim away into some reverie and would no longer see a person come in the door, and you could stand for moments, watched only by his brindle cats, and hear him breathe an old man's heavy resigned breathing.

Just as Mike Ryan's was the fading memory of a general store and Ringling itself the last scant bones of a town, Grandma's house turned out to be the shell of a place to live in. It counted up, all too rapidly, into a kitchen, living room and bedroom, each as narrow as a pullman car and about a third as long. The rooms had stood empty for more than ten years—empty of people, that is, for the flotsam of Grandma's earlier family leaned and teetered everywhere. Diving into the dusty boxes and dented metal suitcases, I came up with a boomerang sent by the son who had moved to Australia after the war, a lavender-enameled jewelry box which had been my mother's, albums of strange people in stiff clothes.

The place was stacked with dead time, and the first few days Grandma could not move in it without tears brimming her eyes. When at last she could, she called me into the bedroom and wordlessly began to dig down through the stacks and piles atop a low reddish wooden chest just larger than a seaman's trunk. As I watched, she propped the lid, looked down into the tumble of old clothes and ancient bedding inside, and snuffled. Then a quick honk into her handkerchief, and she began talking in a tone angrier than I had yet heard from her: *This here was your mother's hope chest. The kids' dad made it back at Moss Agate, when she first started going with Charlie. With your dad, I mean. He worked on this at nights for the longest time. See, he didn't have anything to make it from but some pieces of flooring, but he wanted her to have a hope chest of some kind. He did a good job with it. He could when he wanted to. It's sat here all these years. I want it to be yours now.* The back of my throat filled and tightened as she talked. I gulped, managed to say *All right*, and walked carefully from the room so as not to plunge from it.

Life with Grandma proved to be full of squalls of emotion of that sort. For one thing, she had a temper fused at least as short as Dad's. But where he would explode into words, she would go silent, lips clamped. If she could be persuaded to say anything, the words were short and snapped, displeasure corking each sentence, and you discovered you were better off to let her be wordless.

I know now that such silences came out of years of having no other defense: of being alone on a remote ranch, nowhere to go, no other person to unbend to, when a stormy husband went into his own black moods. But I did not understand it then, and found myself suddenly in a household which could change as if a cloud had zoomed across the sun.

The quickest annoyance I could cause was to look at her when she had her false teeth out for brushing, and after a time or two of blundering into that, I would veer off or turn my back if I saw it in prospect. There even was a way she could rile herself: as I had guessed on the train trip to Minnesota, Grandma was a thunderous snorer, and in the middle of the night was apt to snort herself awake and mutter irately about it.

But other of the unexpectednesses which kept tumbling out of her were entirely easy-tempered. To be doing something even when there was nothing to be done, Grandma sat at the kitchen table and played game after game of solitaire. When the cards continued to turn up wrong for her, she would cheat just once to try to get the game moving again, which I thought was balanced good sense. And whenever she won, the identical proclamation: *I got that game, boy. What do you think of that?*

Also, she was perpetually ready to go into a full-sail version of my childhood I had never heard before. When she had visited my father and mother so often in the first three or four years of my life, it had been she who spent many of the patient hours to teach me to read, the words fastening in my mind as I sat in her lap and watched her finger move along with her reading. And much else: *Oh, how you used to coax me to sing. 'Ah-AH-ah! SING, gramma!' you'd say. So I'd have to hold you in the rocker and sing by the hour. . . . 'Poor me,' you'd say when you didn't get your way, and you'd pooch out your lower lip so sad. . . . Lands, you used to scare me half to death, the way you ran down that hill at the Stewart Ranch. There was a big tree way up on the slope, and you'd take your dog up there and here the both of you would come, straight down. I used to hold my breath. . . .*

And back beyond all that, she had the news of how I'd arrived into the world: *You were born in Dr. McKay's hospital in White Sulphur, it's that building just up the hill from—oh, what's the name of that joint? Hmpf. The Stockman, just up the hill from the Stockman. When you were born, you had two great big warts right here in front of your ear, and your right foot splayed off like this, and you had the reddest hair. You were something grand to see, all right . . .*

Nor was that nearly all. At times she talked a small private language which must have come from those two islanded times of childhood, her own growing up on the Wisconsin farm and her children's years at Moss Agate. Words jigged and bellied and did strange turns then: *I'll have a sipe more of coffee, but if I eat another bite, I'll busticate. . . . Get the swatter and dead that fly for me, pretty please? . . . Hmpf, I been settin' so long my old behinder is stiff. . . .* Anything which lay lengthwise was *longways* to her; the stanchions of a milking barn were *stanchels,* the cows themselves were a word of my mother's as a child, *merseys.*

Her sayings too took their own route of declaring. That it was time to get a move on: *Well, this isn't buying the baby a shirt nor paying for the one he's got on.* Or to take a doubtful chance: *Here goes nothin' from nowhere.* Or when she did not understand something I read to her from one of my books: *Like the miser man's well, too deep for me, boy.* Or when she did understand: *I see, said the blind man to his deaf wife.* Neighbors were rapidly tagged with whatever they deserved: *She goes around lookin' like she's been drawed through a knothole backwards. . . . That pair is close as three in a bed with one kicked out . . . That tribe must never heard that patch beside patch is neighborly, but patch upon patch is beggarly.*

Each time the prairie wind swirled up her dress, there would be said: *Hmpf! Balloon ascension!* At least one meal of the day, she would pause between forkfuls and pronounce like a happy benediction: *I hear some folks say they get so tired of their own cooking. By gee, I never have.* And whenever something irked her, which was sufficiently often, she had her own style of not-quite cussing: *Gee gosh, god darn, gosh blast it. . . .*

And always the stories, such as the one of an early Moss Agate neighbor, a homesteader, who had a head huge and twisted as an ogre's. After a lifetime of despair over his own ugliness, the man began rethinking it all and soon before he died proudly willed his skull to medical science. As I shivered a bit at the tale, Grandma chuckled and said in her declaring style: *Headless man into heaven, think of that.*

To my surprise, dogs and cats fully counted into her conversations. Dad likely had not glanced in a cat's direction since the last time my mother had scratched Pete Olson's gray ears, and he spoke to dogs only to send them kiting off after strayed livestock. But Grandma communed with them all, especially all dogs. There had been one or another of them, generally named Shep, in her households ever since a huge woolly sheepdog back on her parents' Wisconsin farm, and the last of that name had moved to Ringling with us.

A fine white-and-tan with a hint of collie about him, Shep had gone old and as lazy as my grandmother would allow anything to be. He panted as he walked and spent most of life stretched under the kitchen table, where he filled all the space there was. Several times a day Grandma would shift her feet as she sat at the table playing solitaire, and there would be an explosion of pained howling and outraged sympathy: *Well, you shouldn't be there right under my feet, that's what you get! Serves you right, you aren't hurt, big baby. Come here, let me pet it, pretty please, that's all right, there you're all better now* . . .

Grandma's sure sign of good humor was to break into rough-house play with Shep or any other available dog, setting off wild barking and leaping which invariably ended with fresh bleeding scratches on her arms. By then, all the skin between wrist and elbow carried white nicks of scar, as if she had been lightly scored with a scalpel time after time. But that annoyed her less than the bathroom habits Shep and the others ungratefully put on display in front of her. Their natural post-sniffing and leg-lifting sent her into prompt fury: *Shep! Don't be so sappy! Get away from there, you darned fool!*

Cats too, aloof wayfarers that they were, did not manage to live up to her standard of expectation. Any that passed by, she fed as if they were famished but naughty orphans, scolding and huffing over them all the while she filled the dish with milk and bread: *What do you mean bumming around here? Why don't you stay to home where you've got good grub? I ought to let you go hungry, sappy old thing! Here, eat!* The only creatures in her world which got no affection with their scoldings were magpies. She hated their scavenging habits, and when she saw one making its black-and-white flash of glide in the air anywhere within range of her voice, she cut loose: *GIT! Git yourself out of here, god darned old thing, there's nothing gonna die here for you to peck on! Git! GIT!*

Grandma and I settled in, if living amid such salvoes could be called settling in, by somehow coaxing the tiny Ringling house to stretch and once more make way for people. When the single closet was full, we stashed boxes and suitcases under the bed and davenport as if ballasting the place. All the time we lived there, Grandma grumbled things in and out from under the bed, vowing someday she'd not have to do so. The ironing board went in with a tangle of fishpoles behind a door, my mound of paperback books covered the hopechest at the foot of the one bed.

My bed, for I learned at once that living with my grandmother always meant that she claimed the worst accommodations for herself, and the dreariest chores. This inside-out chivalry she must have formed in the Moss Agate years, when she found that she minded the drudgeries there less than did her edgy husband or my frail mother or her frisky sons and so took most of them upon herself. Beyond that, there simply was her assumption that if I was to be a special benefit, she would happily pay any price in chores.

Dad had been thoroughly right about one high matter: my grandmother did want me as a child to raise, the way a retired clipper captain might have yearned to make one last voyage down the trade winds under clouds of sail. Despite Dad's wariness of it, there had been little chance that she could have arrived in my life without his arranging it. Now that he had done so, here I was as the bonus child for her penchant about family—by several years the oldest of her grandchildren, and the shadow-son of her lost daughter. Everything in her said to treat me as a gift, and in terms of this new Ringling household it came out as her granting me the bed and the bedroom while she slept on the davenport in the living room, her climbing out first in the chilly mornings to light the kitchen stove with fuel oil and match, her doing every other task the place needed—until blessed common sense edged through and suggested that what might do me more good would be to have duties of my own. *How do you feel about that?* she offered cautiously. *I think it wouldn't hurt you none, do you?*

Unarguably it wouldn't, and I began then to take my turn at keeping the woodbox piled with firewood and the ashes emptied from the bottom of the kitchen range. But the main and everlasting chore was the water bucket, because the house had no well, and a neighborhood pump had gone rusty from years of disuse. The rain barrel at a corner of the house did the job for laundering clothes and a washtub bath apiece for us once a week. But every dipperful of the water for our daily use had to be pumped next door—I paced it at seventy steps in one of my earliest trudges—at the house of Grandma's long-time friends, Kate and Walter Badgett. And by unexpected fortune that perpetual bucketing carried with it something new and rich, for necessity's water was the least of what this ancient pair could add to our Ringling life.

There were enormities about the Badgetts which somehow seemed to bolster us simply by existing so near at hand. These began with size and age, and went on through manner. Side by side, the two weathered figures loomed like barn and silo. Kate was pillowed in fat, so wide that she seemed to wedge apart the arms of the huge easy chair where she spent her days. Atop that crate of a body was an owlish face, and a swift tongue that could operate Walter all day long and still have time to tell what the rest of Ringling was doing. On her desk by the front window which looked across the tracks to the gas station and post office-store, Kate kept her pair of binoculars. Who had come to town, for how long and maybe even what they bought—it all came up the magnifying tunnel of vision to Kate, then went out with new life, as if having added to itself while re-echoing through that bulk of body.

Then in some midsentence of hers, Walter would appear from one or another of his chores, in his pauseful way looming tall as a doorway, and nearly as still—a rangy silent sentinel with great hands hung on poles of arms. His face was more an eagle's than any other I have seen on a man: the spare lines of brow and cheek and the chisel of nose, somehow with the hint of a beak, and beneath it all, the mouth which turned down sharply at its corners not from mood but just the decades of pursing around a cusp of chewing tobacco.

Walter's eyes were a pale, flat, seen-it-all-before shade of blue. Once I heard someone tell of seeing him angry, which I never had. *He was tending bar for the day at the saloon there in Ringling, and one of Rankin's cowboys came in with a load on. He was helling around up and down the bar, and Walter told him, 'Better settle down a bit.' The Rankin man cussed him and said, 'Who the hell're you, old feller?' Walter came leaning across that bar, those blue eyes snapping sparks. 'I said you'd better settle down, or I'll settle you.' The Rankin man never said another word.*

Both coming onto eighty years old, the Badgetts were in the kind of outliving contest which very old couples sometimes seem to have, each aging only against the other instead of against time. Naturally, Kate was going to win, and she did, by nearly a decade. But at this point they both seemed as little changing as glaciers, and Walter in particular had slowed life to the exact amble he wanted. Midmornings, he would stroll to his woodpile halfway between his house and ours, and begin chopping with giant strokes: the axe easily high, then down in a slow arc, a *whunk!* as the wood blasted apart and spun away into the dirt. Walter would straighten, loose a long splatter of tobacco juice, study around town for anything to report to Kate, reach with one hand to set another piece of wood on the chopping block, then *whunk!* again.

Multiplying that woodpile, which would have kept half the county snug for a winter, spent his mornings. After lunch, he could be seen, in his slow angular stroll, headed for the post office to bring Kate the day's letters and any capturable gossip. Even his responses to her could come slow as a measuring now because he had a fitful mild deafness which gave him the excuse to answer an innocent uncomprehending *Hnnh?* while he mulled the latest of her constant orders.

Theirs was a household at once curt and cordial. Knock on the door, and Kate's voice boomed a single word like an empress's: *COME!* I was puzzled that she had the habit of calling other women only by their last names. Grandma always was simply *Ringer* to her. But Kate's brusqueness had a vast gap in it. Over the years she had ironed every thinkable vice out of Walter except for his habit of chewing tobacco; for that, he was permitted a coffee can behind the stove to spit in. Yet when she talked to him for any reason besides an order, the tongue that banged bluntly on every other life in town suddenly went soft and crooned, of all words, *Hubby*.

Walter had drifted north from Texas as a young cowboy, and I would learn from men who had worked with him in the valley that he was a storied man with horse and rope. The stories included the hint that he had departed Texas after a scrape against the law. Even here, Kate matched him: out of her background wafted the whisper that in Prohibition times she had been one of the area's most reliable vendors of bootleg whiskey.

In all their ways, then, these two serene old outlaws put forth a steadiness, a day-upon-day carol out of the valley's past, and for all I knew, out of the past of all the world.

Up the slope from our house, the other regular chimes in our Ringling life spoke weightier accents, graver outlooks. Mr. and Mrs. Brekke both had been born in Norway, and both come young to the new life in America: they met and married, found a small ranch beyond Ringling where they endured through to prosperity, and now, their family long grown, the pair of them lived at the top of the tiny town like gentlefolk quite surprised at their own new position of courtliness.

Each early afternoon, Mr. Brekke's serious singsong—*HEL-lo*—would sound on our porch, and he would hand in the mail he had brought from the post office, already backing away with a gentle smile from our thanks and invitations to come in for a moment. Mrs. Brekke did come, at least once a day either to our house or to the Badgetts', to hear the doings of the town with a steadily astonished *Ohh, myy!* Leaving, she invariably turned and urged: *Why don't you come up sometimes for ice cream and cake?*

The Brekkes owned the one house in all of Ringling that looked as if it truly had been built to live in rather than just to hold boards up off the ground. A white-fenced yard rulered neatly around it, framing half a dozen small tidy trees—the only ones in town—and a many-windowed sun porch which opened the entire front of the house. The first owners were a husband and wife who had been the local schoolteachers, a couple storied for their learning, and their books and a decade or so of magazines came to the Brekkes with the house. These I mined weekend after weekend, carrying home an armload of old issues of *National Geographic* and *Life* and *Collier's* and *Saturday Evening Post* at a time, reading them lying on my bed with the hot bedlamp at my ear. Mr. and Mrs. Brekke admired education almost as if it were a magic potion. When their own children were growing up and one or another would protest not knowing the answer to something, Mary Brekke had a single iron reply: *Well, you better learn!* Now they encouraged me into each new printed trove as soon as I had finished the last one—*Done with that batch?* Mr. Brekke would cry: *Come in for some more!* And Mrs. Brekke would cry after: *Then sit a minute for some ice cream and cake, can't you?*

The Brekke household's secondhand magazines and books became a second school for me, more imagination lit from it than from the one I rode the bus to in White Sulphur Springs each weekday. I read straight through whatever shone dark on the snowfield pages, a visit to Scintillating Siam lapping on into the swashbuckling of Horatio Hornblower, which likely took place back-to-back with a Clarence Budington Kelland shoot-out in the Arizona Territory. I read, that is to say, as an Eskimo who had never before seen a movie might watch the newsreel and then the cartoon and then the feature film without ever knowing to separate them in his mind, simply letting himself be taken with the habited flow of flashing images.

It all began adding up in my head in deposits which astonished Grandma. Her own information about the world was as spotty as mine was swirlish. She had been born when a man named Grover Cleveland was President. That she had no idea of this merely spoke her own unusual way of having been brought up. She was perplexed that there had been two Presidents named Roosevelt; Franklin Delano had served such a span in her adult life that she could easily believe he had been in the White House back at the turn of the century as well. The labor leader John L. Lewis and the boxing champion Joe Louis consistently mixed their names for her, and I was not at all surprised when she asked me if the Hemenway who intoned the news on the radio was the Hemingway whose books showed up now and then in my rummage from the Brekkes. She seemed entirely pleased with my knack for knowledge, and quickly learned to use it as a kind of utility, asking me to spell out stubborn words when she wrote a letter, to work out the balance in her checkbook, to comparison-shop the Monkey Ward and Sears, Roebuck mail-order catalogues for our items of clothing.

But lore ran both ways between us, and generally hers was more useful than mine, having come straight out of life instead of from printed pages. She recalled for me a pastime that her sons once tried, setting up a lemonade stand and taking turns to shout across town the advertising she taught them: *Lemonade, lemonade! Stirred by an old maid! With a spade!* I thought it over, but at last decided the business wasn't worth reviving; Ringling's population had plummeted so far that the only buying traffic I could foresee was Walter Badgett and Mr. Brekke. But another idea Grandma recalled had the right feel. The same enterprising sons had sent away for any free mailings they came across in magazines and, since Ringling had no street names, conjured for themselves whatever elaborate addresses they could think of. I got out paper and envelopes and set to work on the most current Brekke magazines. Quickly, offers for stamp collecting kits or pleas for me to get rich selling salve were pouring into the post office in care of *I. Clark Doig, 776 Sagebrush Acres* or *14 Jackrabbit Boulevard* or *801 Gopher Gulch* or whatever other elegancy I'd been able to dream up. Grandma much admired my gaudy mail; I much admired her for the lode of boy-raising behind it.

That exact lode, I began to find, came ready more and more as adolescence perked in me. Together, she and I pondered the pale frizz of hair taking over my upper lip. At the precise age when other boys were praying for some hint of whiskers, I badly wanted to be rid of that downy white shadow. Grandma of course had been through this—and apparently everything else—before. She came up with a salve called a depilatory which erased the fuzz, right enough, and felt as if my lip were being scorched away with it.

Impressed with her results, I asked if she knew anything to be done about my hair, which had a stubborn tendency to divide itself floppily on the exact top of my head, as if I had been bashed there with a cleaver. At once she dug out one of her discarded nylon stockings and snipped and sewed it into a snug skullcap. *We'll damp your hair down before you go to bed and you sleep with this over it, and we'll see how that does.* How it did was that within weeks her remedial yarmulka tamed the thatch into the pompadour I had worn out a lifetime of combs trying to achieve.

She was as handy with my other disquiets, such as the passion for baseball which had been brewing in me. The onset of this likely had come from Dad, who in his try-anything youth had played catcher for the Sixteen community team. *Did I tell ye the time we had a big Fourth of July game goin' while Jack Dempsey was fightin' Gibbons up in Shelby? Nineteen twenty-three that would have been. We were havin' a helluva game down there by Sixteen Creek, but somebody'd run down from the telegraph office at the end of every round and tell us what was happenin' with the fight, so it took us half the afternoon to play an inning or two. . . .* Then at World Series time in 1946, Dad had got tired of listening to his saloon chums mutter about the invincibility of the vaunted Boston Red Sox team and uncharacteristically began betting them that it wasn't so. He quickly had bets in every bar in town, and they added up to a couple of hundred dollars, undoubtedly the easiest money of his life, when the St. Louis Cardinals won for him.

Whether it was that windfall or some other encouragement—it may simply have been that Ringling was a perfect place to tinker at imagination, because so little else about the town was in working order any more—I had begun to daydream of myself as a shortstop or a pitcher, or maybe both, strolling across the infield to the mound every fourth day or so to fire fastballs. Now, all of a sudden, I had a teammate. Grandma tirelessly would toss a rubber ball for me to bat back and forth across Ringling's emptinesses. Our audience was Walter Badgett, launching his contemplative splatters of tobacco juice as he glanced over from his woodchopping. Once in a while the ball would bounce toward Walter, and he would pick it up and fling it back in a sweeping stiff-armed motion, like a weathered old catapult which still could crank up. Grandma and I went on with this even if it rained, playing catch inside the house by bouncing the ball between us the scant twenty feet from the kitchen door through the living room to my bedroom.

It comes as a continual surprise to me to realize that even here, where she first came into my life, my grandmother already was nearly sixty years old. Everything I can remember of this time has the tint of her ageless energy. All other entertainment failing, she was even willing to wrestle, and we would tussle stiff-armed against one another until we both giggled to a halt and she panted herself down into a chair saying *Whoof! Nosir, you're just too tough for your old gramma, I can't keep up with a wildcat like you.* And in half a minute, she would be up and in the kitchen, into the making of the next batch of bread or cinnamon rolls or butter cookies.

But one matter of that growing time of mine, not even her savvy and energy had come up against before. A bulge the size of a robin's egg appeared on my right leg, just below the kneecap. It was tender as a burn, and after some weeks of wincing almost to tears whenever the knee came against anything, I at last showed her the knot. She scowled. *Hmpf! We'll better get that looked at when your dad comes.*

The doctor in Livingston sat me on the end of a metal table, pressed the bump and watched me lift in pain. X-rays showed what he already knew: the knob of the long bone in my leg had cracked away, a hairline crevice now daggering through. The danger was, he told us, that this bone cap could be lifted further away by the pull of the large muscle across the kneecap—like the tugging power of a rope working across a pulley. To prevent that, I would have to keep the leg straight; have to bandage the knee constantly, keep pressure wrapped down onto the bone knob so that it would grow back into place. If I did not, there was a chance the leg would wither.

Medical science has changed its mind about that, and considers now that my fiery knee—the textbook term for the ailment is Schlatter's Disease—was not permanently afflicting and in time would have calcified its own fracture line. But I walked from the doctor's office then with only the understanding that I must drag my right leg stiff for a few years if I were not to drag it all my life.

I was miffed that Grandma could be so matter-of-fact about all this—*Wrap it snuglike and do what the doctor said and you'll get like new again*—and kept me at the chores we had agreed on, the water bucket sloshing maliciously now as I swung my leg along. The first several times, I made a stoic show of circling the yards of elastic bandage around my knee and into a tight crisscross over the bone knob. And then it became simply a groove of habit, and I became interested in how much I could ask of the mummied leg: I still could run, if in an odd stilty style; still could bat the ball thrown by Grandma, could wrestle her, could get on almost as before. My laming, it turned out, had happened in the best possible company—that which shrugged it off and silently told me I had better do the same.

Grandma and I went into our first winter together. A small window faced straight west just above the head of my bed. Mornings, as the first sounds of day scuffed outside, I had been able to sleepily lift myself on an elbow and see which of the town's cows or horses or sheep were munching past. Now this window also told the weather, even without my looking all the way out; mewls of wind came sneaking under the sash, and on genuine blizzard mornings the sill would have its own miniature snowscape, tiny sifts white as spilled sugar.

We learned at once that on blowy days our house leaked wind everywhere, like a weary little scow jetting water into itself the instant it touched the surface of the sea. Hardly knowing where to plug first, we would stuff a rag rug along the crack under the front door, pull the blinds down over the whistling windows, desperately fire up both the big square range in the kitchen and the little round stove in the living room, and hope for the storm to ease away promptly.

Shivery and caging as such blizzard weather was, it had to be admitted that Ringling looked much its best in a storm. The bald gaps between houses lost their starkness with windrows of snow gracefully coned between them. The very whiteness of a snowstorm came as a relief, a bright sudden paint over the worn town. Somehow, too, space danced itself along the wind into new distances. If we could not see the depot, a hundred fifty yards down the slope, the storm counted as a genuine shrouding blizzard, and we slogged around telling one another what a very devil of a bluster this was. Mr. Brekke looked like a general in winter camouflage when he handed our mail through the doorway now. Kate's binoculars could not cut the feathery swirl and find the news for the usual courier's gait of her tongue, so Grandma went over to play canasta with her by the hour to compensate. Walter's woodpile heaped under the whiteness like a buried haystack. The trip to the Badgetts' for water became a feat of walking with chin tucked into your coat and the filled water bucket tugging you off-balance as you broke through the drifts. Another trip had its hazards as well: Grandma and I joked about how far the outhouse—*the visit to old Mother Jones*—seemed to have wandered out onto the prairie since the blizzard whirled in. The only thing in the neighborhood which still seemed to be in place was Shep, and he was more firmly planted than ever. Throughout such weather, he could not be budged from under the kitchen table, and so was stepped on by Grandma ten times a day instead of his usual half dozen, his injured howls a mate-cry out into the keening of the blizzard.

Then when the snowfall and wind at last stopped, the world's one noise would be the scrushing sound of boots on silk-dry snow. In the fresh calm, wood smoke climbed straight up from chimneys, until it appeared as if the fat gray ribbons were dangling all the town's houses down into a bowl of snow. The comfortable cushioned silence would last until the first pickup truck began the fast *ratatatat* of its chained tires.

In this snow-scarfed weather as all other, once a week Dad would appear out of the night. The job he had taken after his operation was with a sheep rancher named McGrath at the Camas ranch, fifty miles from us on the far side of White Sulphur Springs. Dad intended to bide through there until summer, when he would have the contract to harvest the ranch's big hay crop. But he had come up with an idea further. The Camas might be a place for Grandma and me as well.

I would wake at once those nights he arrived, and come intent as a hiding fox. The open doorways leading from the kitchen to the living room and on into my bedroom were aligned, and a panel of light came thrusting through them all onto the foot of my bed, like a square flame from the charged talk which was beginning across the kitchen table.

The ritual I quickly knew by heart. Dad would ask if there might be a can of beer in the house, *just anything for a sip*. This was high risk, a step out onto the nearest swaying edge of Grandma's temper, but he always did it, as if answering some challenge. If Grandma pulled her mouth tight and her long dipping *No-o* came out, he was in fast trouble, no matter that he had fought blizzard roads across the night to spend time with her. But if not, if the moment came mellow enough in her, she would get out the beer for him and he would persuade her to take a tiny glass of it herself, the only alcohol she would touch. Letting my breath ease, I would curl closer toward the portal of light to hear what would come along it next.

That old heifer of a cook, by God I can't see why McGrath keeps her on. The meal she put on the table this noon I wouldn't make this dog here eat. Liver fried until you could use it for shoeleather, and a little dab of boiled spuds, and some store bread, and that was all. You can't keep a crew on grub like that, now can ye? Oh, the men aren't going to stand for it much more, they'll be asking for their checks. And Mrs. McGrath just sits there and lets her get by with it. McGrath is no better, he ought to know that a crew is only as content as its cooking. Funny damn way to run a ranch, or I'll put in with you. . . .

The notion sheened a bit more each time out of his talk. If the cook at the Camas were to be let go, if the job could be Grandma's . . . *There's a helluva big house there, plenty of room in the upstairs where I am for the three of us. Ivan would have to stay some place in White Sulphur for school a bit of the year, but weekends and the summer we'd be all together* . . .

A waiting. A beer bottle is set on the table, a small glass follows. This, oh so carefully: *What would ye think of the idea, Lady?* And Grandma, who has been offering only *hmpfs* until now: *I don't just know.* Waiting. *I suppose it would be good there.* Waiting. *For darn sure we could use the wages, and I'm plumb able to work.*

Invisible in my half-dark—it is the mystery of this time that no one ever caught on that I was a light sleeper and would hear anything said at any hour in that slim house—I would listen to Dad once more ease from his night of trying to talk the future around to his own route. *Well, we'll just have to watch our chance. I'll put it to McGrath in a minute if that cook is let go. And you can see then what you think* . . . The echo from Grandma: *Yes, we can see then* . . . His *good night,* hers. Then my father's body at bed edge. *Ivan. Ivan! Move across a bit, son, I'm home.* I sigh pretended sleep up at him, and heavily shift across the bed, away from the eyelet of light.

Winter at last brawled itself out, and spring basted Ringling in mud for some weeks. Near the start of summer, Dad brought about his notion. Grandma was offered the job as cook at the Camas ranch. *Golly gee, I don't suppose it ought to be turned down, only I hate to break up housekeeping here again.* . . . and break it up we instantly did, closing the house in Ringling, more boxes than ever stacked into it, saying our goodbyes and thanks to Kate and Walter and the Brekkes, driving with Dad in the pickup to the place where the three of us could be together, or at least less separate.

The ranch buildings stood out from behind the lofty line of cottonwoods on the west bank of Camas Creek, just at the base of the grassed ridges stairstepping up into the Big Belts. Nothing of the ranch seemed ever to have been thought into any order, the bunkhouse happening first along the road, its paint long vanished into a gray flecking scurf, next to it a small log shed with the wood dark and timestained and the chinking bright between the stacked roundnesses. Then squatted a blacksmith shop, a lower log shed which seemed to have pilfered out at nights and brought home countless scraps of iron, trinkets of harness, tosses of wire to make a great rusty nest around itself. Finally began an arc of an acre or two of battered machinery, auto carcasses and skewed reaper reels and generations of hay rakes and mowing machines.

Out of the clutter, looming up from the shaley roadway and backdropped by a yellow shale hillside, stood a high square grayish house, as if it were a giant crate absent-mindedly put down there. So overbig was this building that it could only be occupied, like a hotel, rather than lived in. The McGraths, even though one reach of room along almost the entire back of the house held only the long table where everyone on the ranch ate, had barely managed to habitate the first floor, and a central stairwell remorselessly marched on to another warren of rooms upstairs. Dad and I shared a corner bedroom up there, Grandma was given one across the stairwell, and the rest of the rooms either yawned empty or were crammed with stray boxes.

The Camas house was high-ceilinged and cold. Even on summer nights, the wind off the Big Belts slapped our corner room. It was chilly quarters in more ways than that, only a few clothes hung starkly in the closet, our underwear and socks in a dresser drawer, all else cached in the house at Ringling. We felt encamped rather than settled—Dad was still sizing up McGrath, deciding how far to cast us in with him—and the flow of life through the house did nothing to ease that feeling. Daylong there surged a restless tribal coming and going, the crew men trooping in for breakfast, the chore boy hauling in pails of milk and buckets of eggs, me wandering in and out chronically throughout the morning, McGrath and Dad coming in for a cup of coffee, the men trooping in for lunch, Grandma back and forth to the garden,

McGrath arriving with a hungover sheepherder he was delivering off to a sheep camp, me wandering some more, Mrs. McGrath off to give McGrath some message she had forgotten at lunch, the choreboy bucketing in more milk, more eggs, the men trooping in for supper . . . *People coming and going around here like chickens with their heads chopped off,* Grandma sometimes muttered, even as she herself, apron flapping, hustled down the storebin stairs for the twentieth time.

A different disorder went on during meals, when a dozen or twenty of us—it was one of Grandma's instant and justified grumbles that she never knew what the total was going to be—might be lined along the span of oilclothed table. McGrath had a small, stinging sense of humor, like a popper on the end of his whiplike temper. His one favorite story, guffawed mealtime after mealtime, was of the fellow he had seen fork in a mouthful of overhot potatoes, spit them into his hand, and hurl them back to his plate with the shriek: *Now blaze, damn you, blaze!* His other notion of fun was to single out one of the crew and fire questions about the day's work, delaying the man in his eating until everyone else had finished. Then McGrath would rear out of his chair and bray, *Well, let's go back to work. Andy, from the looks of your plate you must not've been hungry.*

Somehow McGrath's swagger had attracted a demure wife, half his size and a fraction his conceit. They whiffed past each other in life, McGrath in his steady gale of bluster and Mrs. McGrath eddying and zephyrlike. Her one mistake, which she made every week or so, was to try to edify the table talk above sheep ailments and butts of hay. Once she announced out of nowhere that she had just read in a magazine that every one of the sons of Franklin Delano Roosevelt was of strapping build, over six feet. McGrath looked at her, not unkindly but puzzled, and said: *What in the name of Bejesus H. Christ does that have to do with anything?*

What anything had to do with anything on the Camas often was not clear, beginning with McGrath himself. With his cask of chest, the even grander gut beneath, and a great boxy head jowled like a bulldog's, he always looked roundly out of place on foot. Saddle years had bowed his legs wide, and he toed along in cowboy boots as if hating each touch of the ground. But on horseback, the legs pegged down into the stirrups as if into a socket, his swell of chest looked right, the ugly head somehow went against the sky like the profile of a Comanche chief.

McGrath could flip a lasso onto anything his horse could catch up with, and whooped his own cheers when he did. Within weeks after the three of us at last were living at the Camas, one of McGrath's new sheepherders who hadn't sufficiently dried from a spell of boozing went out of his head and his clothes and ran off naked into the hills. McGrath grabbed a lariat from his pickup, heaved onto the herder's surprised nag, and joggled away in pursuit. *Dabbed it on him first throw, too,* he blared to us at the next mealtime. *Had him snubbed down for the doc in no time.*

Why this bred-in-the-bone ropehand had turned to sheep ranching, no one knew—although some made the guess that having been discovered searing his own brand on another party's cattle had something to do with it. On whatever wind of chance, McGrath had landed at the Camas and leased six thousand fat ewes to put on its grass.

He's quite the McGrath, Grandma said soon after we arrived, and did not mean it in admiration. From Dad's stories, it came as no surprise to see that McGrath ran the ranch as if showing the world a trick from under his hat. Decisions were all jangle and swash. At morning, everyone might be flung into fence mending as if every post on the ranch were going to crash over within the minute. By lunch, McGrath would have the entire crew ricocheting to some forgotten corner of the range to shove sheep onto fresh pasture. It was noticeable that McGrath had the clever bully's instinct about who to leave out of his loosely flung orders. Instead of his bluster, Dad and Grandma were favored with controlled grumbles of suggestion. Grandma of course met McGrath in kind, but Dad seemed more bemused. *Ye can tell this spread from half across the valley,* he declared as he watched the agitation. *It's the one with dust clouds going every direction at once.*

McGrath had quirks further. He let what looked like a rogue's gallery of the dog world roam the ranch—half a dozen mutts and slinkers whose one common characteristic was that they were almost useless around sheep. Shep had not survived his winter, the life gone from him one night as he lay in his peace beneath the kitchen table in Ringling; even Grandma admitted that it was fortunate he was not on hand to contend with this bullying pack.

McGrath's philosophy about his crew seemed the same as his notion about dogs. He hired some of the most hopeless of men, on the calculation that he could get by with paltry wages and yet harry them into doing the needed work. One of these apparitions, of course, was the herder he had had to lasso when the man pranced off into the trees naked and delirious. But more baffling yet, McGrath one day arrived from town with another herder who was lurching out of several weeks of cheap wine, and when he had sobered enough to wobble to the supper table, it began to become clear that our newcomer had barely enough English to pronounce that he was straight from Finland. All else came out in some beyond-Helsinki gabble as if he were chewing glass.

Can't savvy what the hell his name is, McGrath mused between the splutters. *We'll just call him Finnigan.*

Two of the crew had been with McGrath for years, beating along behind him through southern Montana from one leased ranch to the next. They had done so for so long that their names were hardly spoken separate on the Camas, simply splined into *Mickey-and-Rudy* as if they were twins. They were anything but.

Mickey had a froggy face and build, one cheek forever wadded with tobacco and lifting his vast mouth into a disgusted smirk, his wide low shoulders always half-hunched as if to ward off the next bluster from McGrath. No one could quite decipher why Mickey stayed on and on with McGrath, but it must have fed a habit of disgracing himself. By every instinct in him, Mickey was a bunkhouse lawyer, grouser, something just short of a saboteur. He could slouch through his work for McGrath, as much of it as he did, in a slow huff and speechify inside himself about the misery of it all. You could see his lips moving as he practiced his outrage. McGrath, for his part, cussed Mickey elaborately at least once a week, with practice nips in between, and put him on the dreariest jobs that came up. Hornlocked together, they showed never a sign of value for one another, and every sign of going on with their blood feud until apoplexy truced it for one or the other of them.

But Rudy, the other longtime hand, would listen sharply to each of McGrath's orders, say in great agreement *Right you are, Mac*—then with perfect deftness go off and do whatever task on the ranch he thought needed doing. As he marched off in his own directions, often with an irrigating shovel rifled on his shoulder, Rudy looked like a frontier trooper strayed from a Remington sketch: rod-straight backbone, all his striding motion from the waist down, noble white hair and a trimmed white mustache. Also, strange skills kept appearing from him. He could play the violin, and carve surprises from wood, and had built a tiny model cannon which could blast a ball bearing through a one-inch board. But the great startlement of this parade-ground knight was his eternal spitting of snuff juice. It squirted from him in abrupt brown blurts, punctuating his sentences, announcing a thought to come. Rudy was the one man on the ranch never beset by mosquitoes, and always claimed it was the snoose juice percolating through his bloodstream which kept them off.

When Dad hired on at the Camas, it had been with the contract that when summer came he would thread through the disorder of the place and get the ranch's rich hay crop harvested. Somehow a crew had to be held together through the months of mowing and raking and bucking and stacking of 150 butts of hay, some 1400 tons of it when at last all the fields had been sickled and combed clean—and Dad's reputation in the valley said he was a man to do it.

The first move he made was to turn down McGrath's offer to include Mickey-and-Rudy in the haying crew: *I'll have my own men, and I'll particularly not have that pair.* He next left word with the bartenders at the Stockman and the Pioneer. Out of their Saturday night throngs they sized men for him, he winnowed the candidates, and came back to the Camas one June evening with a complete haying crew of nine men.

By summer's end, nearly three months of tricky rain-delayed hay harvest behind him, Dad still had the same nine in the crew, man after man among them asking to come back for the season again next year. It was a matchless job of foremanning even for Dad, who perhaps had needed to prove skill to himself again after his desperate time of sickness.

Whatever accounted for the silken summer of haying, McGrath put it against his own slapbang style of crew being hired and more promptly fired, and made Dad an offer to stay on at the Camas as—what? Not foreman, exactly, because McGrath wanted to be able to catapult Mickey-and-Rudy and a few other hands around the ranch as he pleased. Not entirely the sheep boss either, although taking on a share of the camptending would be part of the job. Dad was to be *oh, hell, just generally in charge, Charlie, you know what's to be done on this spread.* The lambing shed and the haying season would be his to oversee, the hay once again on a valuable contract of dollars-per-ton; beyond that, Dad would have direction of any of the crew not being reined around at the moment by McGrath himself.

The fuzzed line of authority—entirely typical of McGrath—was a bothering notion, but the offered wage was good, particularly with the haying contract added. Also, Grandma would be kept on as cook. *Well, it's something to try,* Dad offered, and Grandma agreed. With what was beginning to seem our tendency for somewhat askew arrangements, we stayed on in the upstairs of the big house at the Camas.

In these earliest months at the ranch, my grandmother and my father gingerly began to put together something like a family life for us. The two of them being who they were, that life of course came at the elbow of hard work and had to pant as best it could to keep up. The one time of truce I could always count on was summer dusk. After her dawn-to-supper day of cooking and house chores and his as-long day of haying and handling the crew, Grandma would go with Dad to the hayfield and help him repair machinery for the morning—shave a drawknife along fresh pine poles to make teeth for the buckrake, plop beside the stacker arm to grip a wrench onto a bolthead for him, anything that needed doing on the downed equipment, all of it done with a certain declared calm between them.

Yet those level evenings hardly ever held the pleasure for me they ought to have, because Dad's style of mechanicking meanwhile would have started me gritting my teeth. He saw me, fair is fair, as his logical fetcher of tools during that repair work; my ailing knee excused me from all other work during the haying. What he did not see was that his notion of fetching had exactly the jittery, hoppity-skippety rhythm, or lack of it, which I rapidly was learning to dislike about ranch work. If I was sent to the pickup to dig out a boxhead wrench for him, the next moment I would be sent again to pick up the chisel which lay beside the wrench. Nor was there any outguessing him—always some further gizmo to send me trudging again, or worse, dogtrotting all the way to the blacksmith shop.

Six evenings might pass, then, with the pair of them gentled and me muttering behind my teeth, and on the seventh, the regular trip to White Sulphur Springs for groceries, and into real trouble.

This, as acute as if it is happening again now: this father of mine has parked the pickup in front of the grocery store and says, oh so much too offhandedly, *Well, ye don't need me to get the groceries, do ye? I'll step over to the Stockman for a minute.* At best, this grandmother of mine pushes out a level *Well, all right then,* as if being reasonable might just fetch him back that much sooner. At worst comes the flat snapped *I suppose,* which in truth means *Yes and you're going to overstay and I'm going to take you to war about it.*

All during the grocery shopping with Grandma, I half-hold my breath wondering if he will be back at the pickup by the time we get there. Every once in a while, surprise to us all, he is there, and the mood leaps up, the drive back to the Camas is full of chatter. Most often, he is missing. I look desperately toward the Stockman, hoping I can declare in triumph, *Here he comes now!* That hope snuffed, I go on to the next one as we climb into the pickup: maybe he will arrive before Grandma begins to mutter—no, too late, *Darn his hide anyway* she steams, *why doesn't he come?*

By every evidence in my memory, and in the words of everyone I have found who knew him well, my father cannot be called an unfeeling man. He tended opposite, fretful about a calamity on anyone he knew, trailing generosities I still happen onto in his wake: *Knowed your daddy since I landed into this country in '36, at shearing time at the Dogie. He staked me for my bedroll, I was so dead busted. Didn't have to do it neither, but he done 'er . . .* But with those waitings, he inflicted a pain as sharp on my grandmother's mind as any that can be conjured. She had had one relentless stint of waiting around in life for the saloons to let a man go, and she seethed at the idea of another, even if it amounted only to minutes of casual beer.

To Dad, that is exactly what it did amount to. The saloons and the men ranged on their barstools had been a heartbeat of him, and of the valley, all his grown life. A beer or two was simply a chaser for the mellow conversation. My own feelings were hopelessly mixed, tiered. I wanted Grandma not to be angry, even as I was more than half-angry at Dad myself. I thought up excuses for him: *Why shouldn't he have a breather to himself, see his friends? The world isn't gonna end over a few minutes of that.* I switched at once to the argument on our side: *The hell, why do we have to stew in this pickup while he guzzles beer in there?* It was frazzling, a crisscross of tensions cutting tight inside me. And everything would become worse, I knew, if Grandma gave her final fidget and sent me to get him: *Gee gods, see what he's doing in there.* If he wasn't ready pronto to leave the saloon, then I had the predicament of trudging back to try to tell her so—*Ah, he says he'll be along in just a minute*—or of hanging restlessly at his side until the spirit moved him, both of us now rooted in the Stockman while she simmered across the street.

When he finally came—all of this might have crackled for only twenty minutes or so—he generally would try an offhand *Ready to go?* She would give it back to him—*We been ready for ages*—and the silent battle would begin. Halfway to the ranch, one or the other might try to break it. But most often a trip which started in ice ended the same, and I would look aside out the window touching cold on my shoulder, wordlessly crying a kind of prayer that the mood would get no worse, damning in my head the one or the other of these chilly warriors. Or more often, the both.

Beneath it all was a hard unsaid truth we all knew. The three of us by then had been together long enough, and closely enough, that if my father and my grandmother parted ways, I now could have the choosing of which one I would live with—and I would choose at once to go with Dad again. I felt love for Grandma, she would bring me up more steadily and standardly than he could, in countless ways would make more sacrifices in her life for the sake of mine. In justice to us both—perhaps all three of us—she was the one to raise me less hazardously, if choice ought to be made. But I would never choose so.

By then, I had been shaped on the opposite side of the family from her, the side which indeed cared less for family than for friends and the valley's flow of life, and so suggested that if my ranchman father could not manage to be enough family for me, at least he was going to be a friend such as none other in the world. The side, too, which always had half a notion to hie off for opportunity rather than settle in for obstinacy.

In outlook and manner then—and I suppose in inner murmurations which I could not hear until much later—I had become more thoroughly Charlie Doig's son than I could ever become Bessie Ringer's grandson. It lay as a hammer of fact amid us that she knew all this, and that, a woman who long since had determined she was through putting up with bad bargains in life and longer since had earned that right, she could only accept these short-sided terms.

If, that is, she stayed on with Dad and me at all, now that his health had mended once more. It apparently became a guessing game in the valley whether she would. A town voice has reported: *There was some that said they didn't see how she could take over the daughter's husband, and the child too. But I said there was love there, that was the way of it.* It wasn't quite the way of it, for there still was all too little sign of love—or affection or admiration or much of any other warmth—shown between my father and my grandmother. They were, after all, an alliance, corded together only by the bloodline which knotted in me, and perhaps the best that could have been expected of them was the wary civility of allies. Some of the time, as in the aftermath of those trips to town, it took their most dogged efforts to muster that.

Yet the months added up, and the three of us remained under the same roof. Rather, Dad and Grandma remained under it, and I edged under on weekends, for when the school year began again, I once more had to board out in White Sulphur.

If it had occurred to me, over the next span of time I had all the grounds to demand of Dad just how this pieced-together family of ours was making my life any less unsettled. In the several years between my mother's death and Grandma's arrival, I had followed Dad through seven or eight places to live. In the year and a half after Grandma and I left Ringling, I ricocheted among half a dozen. Two of Grandma's sons and their families lived in White Sulphur, and whenever possible I boarded now with one or the other of them. But the sons themselves were in a period of changing jobs and homes, and in fast sequence here when I was twelve and thirteen years old, I hopscotched after them through households as various as they were numerous. One of the places was a tiny house which had its toilet in the cellar, reached by way of a trapdoor in the middle of the kitchen floor. Another was a looming old box which had seen its last paint a generation before. There even was a stint, apparently in some moment when everyone else was between households, back once more with Nellie and his wife, who didn't have the advantage of being relatives but at least stayed put.

The pattern to all this was jagged but constant: I would sleep on a couch in the living room of the moment, spend my day at school, roam town afterward as much as I wanted, come back to whichever house it happened to be—I once had a memory slip and returned to the one with the cellar toilet instead of the looming one across town—lose myself in a book or magazine until bedtime, dig the next morning's change of clothes from my suitcase behind the couch, and settle in for the night again. I found that everyone treated me fondly if a bit absentmindedly—as I had noticed at Jordans' during Dad and Ruth's winter of reconciliation, the boarding child is something like a stranded visitor that people get accustomed to half-seeing at the edges of their vision—and no one, least of all me, seemed to think there was much unusual about my alighting here and there casually as a roosting pullet.

Yet perhaps the unsettledness had more effect than I realized, for on weekends and in the summer I found myself islands of calm at the Camas ranch even amid the eddying energies of McGrath and his crew. It helped that this house too held shelves of books, as the Brekkes' had. Mrs. McGrath had learned that burrowing off somewhere to read could keep her aside from her husband's swooshes through the place. But when I borrowed from the shelves now, I found scenes never dreamed of in the Brekke books: *They killed him in Spangle Valley. They waited hidden among the rocks of Buffaloback Mountain and when he rode below they shot him out of the saddle . . . She was right down there at my feet, her eyes shining, her breasts trembling, drawn up in tight points, and pointing right up at me. She was down there and the breath was roaring in the back of my throat . . .*

When I had enough of printed roarings for the moment, the ranch could give me a silent place as well. For by greatest luck a silvered ship, high-hulled and pinging with emptiness, rode at the far end of the ranch buildings. A ship, at least, to my imaginings. In the years when the machine chomped broadly through grainfields, it was called a combine.

Now this dreadnought stood, in its tons of dulling metal and clusters of idle gearwheels, for me to climb into, all through: on careful hands and with my bandaged knee tensed straight behind me, over the floorful of threshing blades, past gearings fat with ancient grease which, when I touched through its dried crust, still came away slick in my hand; through pencil-thin rods of sunlight which drilled in around the gear housings and shaft ports; at last to the dark maw which fell away in shelves of teeth and gratings to the nose of the machine. The toes of my shoes clouted on sheet metal as I dodged under sets of spiky metal fingers and over driveshafts. When I stopped, the only sound was the ringing echo of my own listening. It was as if the old combine, the noisiest machine on earth in full shuddering gulp across a wheatfield, had gone quieter than anything else when it at last quit work.

Even the day's heat changed within its metal tunnels, flattened and spread into a cooking sensation which came from everywhere at once. I made a game of seeing how hot I could stand it in the dim shaft. When the searing metal was too much for me, I would climb, up and out, through a deft sliding panel in the machine's top and into the sheet metal grain-hopper which hung high over the side. This was the lookout spot, with baffling slippery angles which made me lodge my body across them and feel the tautness of watching, eyeing the ranch.

My mood there was to see everything as the edges of tomorrows, as if time were waiting in coiled shimmers behind the outline of whatever my watching picked out. The gasoline tank for the ranch machinery, with its round red face of metal which rang a deep *blung* when I hit a ball against it; that would be the vast green left field fence of Fenway Park if I grew up to be a baseball player. The meadows of wild hay splotched richly along Camas Creek, and the climbing slopes of grass: if I became a ranchman as Dad was, there would be such land mile upon mile. Grandma, on the way in from the garden with her apron held full of vegetables: she would magically become less sharp-edged and hard-mouthed, a Lady as steady in temper as in her fondnesses. Dad, arrived from the hayfield in the pickup and then into his hurrying stride to find some repairing piece of metal from the rusty muss around the blacksmith shop: the future magic would settle him into his best work, turn him from any provoking of Grandma. The clasped knee which began to twinge under me now: it would heal at once, and as quickly bear me out of growing up, into these glimpsed tomorrows.

What I gained from the machine's silences, Dad perhaps had found in the busyness of the ranch's chief chore—the raising of sheep. The Camas and its seasons were occupied by the gray thousands of them as if they were some daft race of dwarves, helpless and demanding, their long clown faces staring out in sad alarm from ruffs of wool. The bands summered in the mountains, plump targets for coyotes and bears and snagging branches; spent autumn in mown hayfields where they could do their best to topple into irrigation ditches or Camas Creek itself; wintered near the ranch buildings where in the nightly shed or corral they could try to huddle themselves into injury or suffocation. But it was the first fade of winter when the six thousand ewes drew the entire attention of Dad and everyone else on the ranch: springtime, and lambing time.

Lambing at the Camas stretched as one long steady emergency, like a war alert which never quite ignites into battle but keeps on demanding scurry and more scurry. No ritual more frantic exists anywhere in the rearing of animals, and McGrath hounded everyone around in their jobs to make it all the more skittish. The season would begin reasonably enough: in middle March, a lamb or two, tiny yellow sprawls of life, would appear suddenly amid the several thousand ewes. Dad, as what was called *day man,* would have had a helper or two readying the long low lambing shed on a knoll above Camas Creek. Inside it now stretched rows of boarded pens about four feet square, just large enough to hold a ewe and her lamb. Since the pens were so like small cross-barred jail cells, they were called *jugs,* and once in the jug, the first few lambs and their mothers were coddled and fussed over like the original customers of a seaside inn. But one day soon, half a dozen lambs are born; and the next day forty; then a hundred, one lamb or another starting its slow glistening dive from the womb into life wherever you looked now.

Then a sledge with half a dozen of the jug pens atop it and pulled by a team of horses would begin to shuttle—the *gutwagon,* named for the placenta and accompanying muss from the newly-delivered ewes. Because Mickey was the worst choice for it and McGrath wanted to miss no chance to harass him toward betterment, he was made the gutwagon driver. Like a duke dropped barefoot into a manure pile, Mickey would mince up to a fresh lamb, snatch it up and try half-heartedly to persuade the mother into one of the gutwagon jugs. When she wouldn't be lured, he would have to grab her by the wool and wrestle her in or, worse, try to snare her by the hind leg with a sheephook and snake her in backwards.

Mickey's dour mauling was only the ewe's first welcome to maternity. As the gutwagon was unloaded, Dad or one of his helpers would tip each ewe onto her rump and hold her there while her teats were worked to be sure that milk would flow for the lamb. Then she was strongarmed into one of the jugs, and her lamb put in after.

Sheep being sheep, not all ewes had the idea that they were supposed to be ready to mother their lambs. More than a few saw it all as a bad joke, sniffing the tiny animal as if he were something sour and then, often as not, would butt him flat in the straw and begin walking on him. *Damn ye,* Dad would erupt, *what the hell ye doin' to him? He's yours, old sister, just get used to the idea. Ivan, get in here and hold this goddamn pelter while I suckle the lamb.*

With the lamb bulging with milk and the ewe more or less bullied toward motherhood, Dad would send me for his paint tray. Then ewe and lamb were each stamped, in blotty digits about five inches high, with a number which showed that they belonged to each other. It also gave them a kind of selfhood, like hospital patients known by the traceries of their charts: *That 256 lamb has the drizzles. . . . That ornery damned 890 ewe still won't take her lamb . . . The 722 lamb is a goner, I'm gonna have to jacket a fresh one onto that ewe.*

Jacketing was a sleight-of-hand I watched with wonder each time, and I have discovered that my father was admired among sheepmen up and down the valley for his skill at it: *He was just pretty catty at that, the way he could get that ewe to take on a new lamb every time.* Put simply, jacketing was a ruse played on a ewe whose lamb had died. A substitute lamb quickly would be singled out, most likely from a set of twins. Sizing up the tottering newcomer, Dad would skin the dead lamb, and into the tiny pelt carefully snip four small leg holes and a head hole. Then the stand-in lamb would have the skin fitted onto it like a snug jacket on a poodle.

The next step of disguise was to cut out the dead lamb's liver and smear it several times across the jacket of pelt. In its borrowed and bedaubed skin, the new lamb then was presented to the ewe. She would sniff the baby impostor endlessly, distrustful but pulled by the blood-smell of her own. When in a few days she made up her dim sheep's mind to accept the lamb, Dad snipped away the jacket and recited his victory: *Mother him like hell now, don't ye? See what a helluva dandy lamb I got for ye, old sister? Who says I couldn't jacket day onto night if I wanted to, now-I-ask-ye?*

Recited. Yes, that is the word for this rhythmed period. Lambing was a season that recited itself with a clarity and cadence unlike any other in my past: . . . *nine'y-seven, nine'y-eight, nine'y-nine,* HUNNERD, IVAN! *one, two* . . . The numbers build in my head with the first warm morning of June, and before I can seat myself to write, are thrumming me into being again beside the gray-boarded corral as sheep plummet past. A fresh time, I am twelve years old, and piping back to McGrath: *a hundred!* More quickly than I can thumb down my jackknife twice to cut this first marking notch in the green willow stick, a dozen more ewes whirl out the corral gate beneath McGrath's counting hand. As he counts, McGrath flexes his right palm straight as a cleaver, chopping an inch of air as each sheep pellmells past him. His bulldog face moves a tiny nod at the same time, as if shaking each number out through the heavy lips onto the counted sheep. As always I am his tallyman, notching a stick to record every hundred ewes as McGrath singsongs the count to me. I know to stand soldier-still as I am now, against the corral and a dozen short steps from the gate where the sheep are squirting through, just near enough that McGrath can hear me echo his tally, know that it is marked . . . HUNNERD! . . . Again my jackknife—*a hundred!*—snicks softly, again a fresh tiny diamond of wood falls from the stick. Lambing is the one stint of work on a ranch that I entirely like. There is a constant doing about it, none of the usual jerky pace of idling one minute and rebuilding the world the next. A couple of times a day, all of the ewes in Dad's long lambing shed must be fed and watered. I help to carry pitchforkfuls of hay to put in the little feed rack of each jug, heft in a bucket of water to each ewe, wait while she noses the bucket suspiciously and at last drinks. Lambing's tasks are all necessities, one by one by one adding up to something. And the lambing shed itself seems a rare, rare place—a squatting wooden tunnel of a building which smells of damp manure and iodine and warm wool and alfalfa, a fog of odors. Then to come into the sunshine to drive small bunches of ewes and their week-old lambs toward pasture or, better still, to help when the oldest lambs get their docking. I am quicker in the catch pen than any of the men, snatching . . . HUNNERD! . . . snatching—*a hundred!*—a lamb from the bleating swirl of lambs. I pick up the caught lamb, clutch him to me with his slim back tight against my breastbone, hold both his right legs in a crossed grip in my right hand and both the left legs in my left, present him butt forward to the dockers, Dad and McGrath, waiting at the fence. McGrath reaches in between the legs, cuts the bag, squeezes the testicles up out of the cut, brings his mouth to them and nips the twin pale pouches out with his teeth, spits them to the ground. Dad steps in, knifes off the tail, swiftly daubs dark tarry disinfectant on the two oozing cuts. I turn the stunned—docked—lamb right side up, drop him gently outside the pen. Turn back to the swirl of lambs for another . . . HUNNERD! . . . Four notches—*a hundred!*—now. There must be ten when McGrath has finished counting, or sheep are lost. That will mean beating into the thick brush along Camas Creek and climbing into the coulees beyond the water, work which always runs slow and late. Worse, these are the final thousand ewes-with-lambs of the ranch's six thousand head, and the trail drive which will take them all to summer range must wait on the search. Worse again, McGrath is, as Grandma says it, *a crazy old thing* when he drives the ranch to look for lost sheep. Hurrying, he will aim the pickup across bogs which would swallow a train. Raging to have lost time, he fights free of the first bog and roars into the next. The story is told that when McGrath was a young cowboy, he rode his horse into a saloon in Greybull, Wyoming, and roped the mounted deer heads off the wall, scattering drinkers and poker players like pullets. Dad says McGrath still has a hellion streak in him . . . HUNNERD! . . . The notches begin—*a hundred!*—to be a design on the stick, a stepway of bright slots against the gray-green bark. I hear Mickey cursing a sheep which has broken from the back of the band. Oh, how Mickey dislikes lambing, detests sheep, despises himself for knowing no job but sheep ranching, hates us all for seeing his life's predicament. Mickey it is who behind

McGrath's back will sneer at him as *Little Jesus,* and who roared out to a Saturday night saloon crowd in White Sulphur that McGrath was a gutrobbing son-of-a-bitch to have to work for. I watch Mickey at the back of the sheep. He has the mean orange dog named Mike with him, a good match. The runaway ewe is being nipped savagely by Mike, to Mickey's encouragement. McGrath would blister Mickey with swearing if he saw the scene, but McGrath is too busy with his count. Mickey knows by instinct just when he can get away with anything . . . HUNNERD! . . . The soft snick—*a hundred!*—and the sixth groove from the willow peels away to the ground. These shards of wood, I notice, are the shape and size of the half moon at the base of my thumb nail. I look up from my hands and see, at the far end of the sheep opposite Mickey, Karl the Swede standing quietly and saying soft words to his sheepdog. Karl the Swede is a pleasant man and a good worker when drink isn't tormenting him. He will herd these sheep in the mountains all summer, if he can last the drought in himself. Lately to get his mind off whiskey he has spent his spare minutes chopping firewood, and his woodpile is nearly as long and high as a small shed. Oho: a ewe jumps some imagined terror as she goes through the gate, and McGrath steps back as she sails past his chest . . . HUNNERD! . . . I giggle—*a hundred!*—because she was a special ewe, a hundredth and flying like an acrobat as well. McGrath has kept the count steady with his chopping hand. When Dad does the count, he stands half-sideways to the river of sheep, his right hand low off his hip and barely flicking as each sheep passes. I have seen buyers, the men in gabardine suits and creamy Stetsons, with other habits—pointing just two fingers, or pushing the flat palm of a hand toward the sheep—as they count. The one trick everyone has is somehow to pump the end of an arm at each whizzing sheep, make the motion joggle a signal to the brain. McGrath says he knew an old-time sheepman who could count sheep as they poured abreast through a ten-foot gate. Could that be: could a person . . . HUNNERD! . . . keep such numbers—*a hundred!*—scampering clearly in his brain? The sheep plunge past McGrath only one or two at once, because Dad is working the corral gate in a rhythm which sluices them through smoothly. He watches too for lame or sick ewes, to be singled out later and put in the hospital herd. A black ewe blurs past, a marker sheep. Dad can glance across a band of sheep for its markers—a black ewe here, over there, one with a floppy ear, beyond, one with a Roman nose—and estimate closely whether the entire thousand ewes are there. The sheep don't look all alike to me, but neither do they look as separate as Dad sees them. Each ewe is different as a person to him, not even McGrath can sort them by eye that way . . . HUNNERD! . . . Now my yell—*a hundred!*—is louder, a signal to McGrath that we are near the end. Nine notches on the willow stick, a tight knot of ewes crowds the gate. If the count is right, no sheep lost, we will start trailing to the summer range in the Big Belts. A dozen miles a day, two days of trail. Moving the sheep is the piece of work I can do better than anybody else on the ranch. McGrath tries to take the sheep along in a bellowing brawl, setting the dogs on them every half-minute. Dad does better, but eventually he too is apt to grow exasperated and begin to overpush the sheep. But I can make a game of simply shadowing the animals, trying to sense ahead of their jittery veers, heading them off with a roaring *Hyaw!* or a tossed rock. Yet no matter who is at work behind them, sheep are the moodiest of creatures, one moment cruising down the road so promptly you can hardly keep up, the next moment refusing to budge at all. Which will it be this time, race or battle? . . . HUNNERD! . . . The tenth hundred ewe—*a hundred!*—gallops away as I press the knife for the next, last notch.

McGrath counts out the last straggle—*twen'y-two, twen'y-three, that's them*—and whirls to me. I nod and say, *a thousand and twenty-three,* counting with the knife blade my ten notches, then doing it once again as McGrath looks on and Dad steps close to watch. They are pleased: the count is right, lambing is at an end, the trailing can start. I grin across from the me of then to the me of now. Another time, we have finished spring, begun summer.

My talent for sheep and interest in them ended with lambing, but the herding season which began with summer swept me in anyway. If the meadows were too wet for haying, Dad would take a turn at camp tending, and we would drive off into the timbered slopes of the Dry Range with boxes of groceries, a full day to be spent chatting with the edgy herders and towing their wagons to fresh pasture. Or I might even go when McGrath himself did the tending, if he managed to find me for it. *You be careful riding with him,* Grandma inevitably warned, as if I could keep the pickup from careening off a cliff by putting my mind to it.

McGrath liked to have me along because I was quick at opening the several fenceline gates on the road into the mountains, and he liked such saving of moments. Also, sonless himself, he seemed interested to talk to a boy, although in his heavy way was not always sure how such a palaver was done. *Did I tell you of once I's workin' down at Greybull in Wyoming and seen a fella walk between a horse's hind legs? 'S a by-God fact. This geezer was a real horse hand, and it was hayin' time and he was a mower man, drivin' a real skittish team, a big roan and a gray. He's the only one in the crew could git a harness on 'em. Rained us out of hayin' a couple of days, and we all went to town and got good and howlin' drunk. The boss got us back out to the place, and this geezer is still Christamighty drunk and gits it in his head to show us how tame he's got this ornery roan horse. He had a fancy Stetson on, big wide brim on it out t' here. He tells us he's gonna get down on his knees, and he's gonna walk on his knees between that horse's hind legs with his big hat on. Show us how tame he's got that roan horse, see. So he goes down to the barn, everybody on the place followin' him. He starts going under the horse's tail down on his knees when the horse gives a Christamighty kick, catches that fancy hat and swipes it right off, sailed the damn thing plumb across the barn, see. That horse didn't miss his head a inch. So the guy is surprised as all hell, then he yells: WHOA, YOU BIG PINK SONOFABITCH, WHOA! Then you know, that goddamn horse just stood there and he goes right through his hind legs and out under his belly like he said he was gonna. Been you or me or anybody else, that horse'd have kicked him into the middle of next week, wouldn' you think? Hup, another gate for you . . .*

An hour or so of this and we would be at the first of the sheep camps, McGrath plunging the pickup off in a rough sweep for the herder and his band. What mood we would find when the herder at last showed himself, his saddlehorse and dog eyeing us with twice the interest he was, had always to be a gamble. In the eighty or so years that Meagher County had been one of the prime sheep areas of Montana, hundreds of sheepherders strode or rode its slopes of pasture, and they added up to something like a commonwealth of hermit gypsies.

Countless of them went through life trapped in their homeland language; it was a historic joke that the eastern end of the county originally had been populated entirely by Norwegian herders who knew but two words of English: *Martin Grande*, the name of their employer. Fairly or not, the numbers of Romanians who arrived as herders had a particular reputation for shunning any language but their own. Their chosen set of bywords was simply *no savvy*.

There exists the exasperated report of an early forest ranger who came upon a Romanian herder placidly spreading his sheep across an allotment of cattle range: *All I could get out of him was 'No savvy' until I applied a shot-loaded quirt. . . . it was surprising how quickly the incident got to all the Romanians in that district.*

McGrath had neither Norwegians nor Romanians on his slopes just then, but he did have the baffling Finnigan-from-Finland. While McGrath blared and chortled, Finnigan could only shake his head slowly as an ox and clack some gibberty mystery back to him. Karl the Swede was another uncertain talker, his shy throaty sentences so low they seemed to come out of his shirt collar instead of his mouth. Other herders had the language but not the inclination to do much with it. One I remember hated even to say *Hello* when we arrived at his camp; he would stand half-sideways with his eyes darting to the timber until gradually he would face around and at last begin to make sentences.

All in all, stepping out of the pickup at a herder's camp had some of the touchiness of coming ashore on a self-exile's island. I can think of only one of McGrath's herders who seemed entirely to thrive on the lonesome life—Louie, a tall soldierly man with a German accent. He owned a pair of tiny deft binoculars which snapped open like a case for eyeglasses, and spent his time peering for wildlife on the mountain slopes. *Yesterday a black bear come, up over there. I watched at him all morning.* But the others had the common herder's affliction, the mind sprung by the weight of the silences against it.

However slowly, and if it could be pried out at all, there generally would be news to be heard from the sheepherder: a coyote seen on a hillside, a ewe gone lame or ripped by a snag, a porcupine treed by his dogs as they suicidally tried to get their faces full of quills. Dad, if it was his turn at camp tending, would smoke and chat until the herder began talking, then only nod and ask enough to keep the flow coming. McGrath's style was to blurt at the herder until the man at last set off on some startled telling or another, the two of them steaming toward full exasperation. Then abruptly, an instant before the herder was ready to fling his job in McGrath's face, we would wheel away to move the sheepwagon to a new pasture site.

The sheepwagon could be seen to be a child of the prairie schooner. With its rounded canvas top and high spoked wheels, a first glance easily found it back amid the beadlike file of white-topped wagons westering through our history. But a sheepwagon always existed alone, remote as a drifting brig on the grass ocean. It was built for one man to bide through the narrow months in, and that single life only: in the mountain dawn or dusk, yellowed light from the kerosene lamp at a herder's wagon showed like one frail star fallen into the timber.

Inside the wagon with Dad or McGrath, it felt to me as if space, the very air, had changed, somehow tidied and tamped itself. I wanted to live in a sheepwagon, so much more interesting were they than the blank room back at the Camas. Nowhere else had the sense of deft shrinkage as if a house had been pulled in and pulled in until it came down just above your head and out past your fingertips. Storage bins doubled as places to sit, the table hinged daintily down from a wall when wanted, every built-in cabinet had a tiny firm clasp snugging its door. The bunk bed fit across the inmost end of the wagon as properly as a blade snicked into a jackknife. At the opposite end on a platform all its own sat the small square stove, usually with a pan of mulligan stew or a blue-enameled pot of sour tarry coffee waiting to be fired up one more time. Finally, to let the herder glance out more easily to the sheep, the wagon had a Dutch door; with its bottom half closed, I could lean out on it and feel as if far up on a lookout across this high pasture of summer.

In place, the wagon was a kind of ship's cabin for the herder, tidy, buttoned, comely. But during the move to the next site, it became only a floating bin. Everything loose had to be packed away in the wagon's nooks, then onto the floor was piled whatever firewood the herder had chopped, his coal oil can and likely a creamery can full of drinking water, his wash basin, the battered metal dish his dog ate out of, the gunny-sacked ration of oats for his horse, white sacks of salt for the sheep, and last of all, the small front steps for the doorway.

Because a sheepwagon sat so high on its running gear—the floor nearly chest high to a man on the ground—it towed across rough country with a staggering topheavy gait. A successful move of a sheepwagon was one that didn't topple the chimney pipe and leave it to be searched out of a few miles of roadside brush. At the new site, there was leveling to be done. A cup of water would be put on the table to see how the wagon tilted, then small holes were dug for the wheels to drop in, or a stout stick was shouldered under a corner of the wagon box to lift it into steadiness for another week.

Such, at least, was how a sheepwagon was properly moved. McGrath in his headlong way was apt to tow it as if dragging a tree stump. More often than not, he would forget to fasten the cabinet doors, and a flour can would fly out and explode snowily over everything, pots and pans then avalanching from the oven and likely a can of lard or jar of jam leaping in after.

Credit him, McGrath always seemed genuinely surprised to fling back the door and find the gooey wreckage. For a minute or so he would dab at it doubtfully, firing pots and pans back into the oven and kicking flour out the door in tiny puffs, then would snort *The hell with it, a sheep-herder's got more time than I do,* and off we would buck to the next sheepwagon move.

More than two years were spent on the Camas this way, the seasons milling into one another like the fitful sheep themselves. Dad and Grandma steadied the ranch with their work, but had less luck with each other. Ours remained a brink of a family, the two of them at sudden edge with each other, then calming again. When they came to take me to the Camas for the weekends with them, usually the mood seemed to me as chancy as among McGrath's wild sheep-herders. But as the third winter of this was about to begin, something vaster to judge came along. McGrath had made a proposition. He was going to give up the Camas for other ventures, and one of them was the lease of a small ranch two hundred miles to the north. He would put two thousand ewes on the place: would Dad run the ranch and the sheep for half the profit?

None of us had been to that far region of Montana, and naturally McGrath's prospects were as unpredictable as the country. But Dad was for going. He took me aside and talked out his reasoning: *Ivan, I think I'll take on those two bands of sheep for McGrath. He's a bearcat to work for, but the son-of-a-buck knows livestock and he knows how to turn money . . . I think it's a chance to take, going up north. But I don't know now, how do you feel about changing schools?*

Eight weeks earlier I had started high school in White Sulphur, with the classmates I had known since Dad and I came away from the mountains after my mother's death. The school, the town, the valley made all the lifestream I knew anything about. Yet when I put all this against Dad's words and the musing look on his face, the sum did not add up to as much as I expected. It may have been that I was more weary than I knew of the suitcase life of boarding out in White Sulphur, or that I was just now coming across a portion of restlessness inherited from Dad. Whatever was behind it, I swallowed and gave my father the answer he wanted, and apparently the one I secretly did too: *I feel okay about that.*

Grandma. She had lived in the valley for forty years now, nearly all her adult life. Her friends, her sons, her patterns of existence were there. The alliance between Dad and her had problems which showed no sign of easing. Whatever the ties of affection between her and me, I couldn't believe she could be talked into this total uprooting toward the north. *We'll just have to see about her,* Dad said. He rehearsed to me a dozen arguments he would put to her, and when the moment came simply fired out: *This damn valley has never got us much of anywhere, Lady. All either of us has to show for our lives here is a helluva pile of hard work. I say we ought to try out new country. Will ye come?*

She was silent a long while—but a thinking silence, not a perturbed one. At last: *All right then. When can we be gone and get it over and done with?*

The two of us watched, struck silent, as she honked into a handkerchief and then clouted pots and pans onto the counter for the next kitchen chore. She was truly corded to us now, and the fact came with a sense of wonder and relief—and somehow among them, a nudge of concern.

One shard of time repeats itself like the snow-helmets of mountains across each season of my memory. An edged piece of the day, that is, in the strictest sense—the high sun-point called noon.

It seems curious now that this one daily interval counted for so much. Daybreak did not, nor dusk; days arrived and went with an unnoticed ease then. But noon climbed up like a crier to a tower, and my father reckoned his life, and those of his ranch crews, and mine at his side, by its powers: After noon we'll just go and . . . Let's get shut of this by noon . . . Better noon up and get some grub, don't ye think? *And my grandmother, noon meaning to her the vast midday meal—we called it dinner, in full honor—to be arrayed along the sweep of table for a lambing crew or a shearing crew or a haying crew or whatever other kinds of crew might turn up from the world:* Ivan, pretty please, yammer the bell to call those good-for-nothin's in here. *Noon it was, too, when Taylor Gordon might be met on the street in White Sulphur, on the way to his cabin for his own dreaming meal and turning back at you to leave one last New York story or particle of philosophy:* Y'know, I've found in life that I'd rather make a fast dime than a slow buck. *Or when Harold Chadwick, straddled onto a counter stool in the Dupuyer cafe, might be coaxed to tell of hunting elk, when he was my age, with the ancient Métis mountain man Toussaint Salois:* He had his big old buffalo coat and could set by the campfire just as comfortable—the rest of us 'd be freezin' to death. *Even my mother, the one voice unknown from any of these years, can be almost-heard in some noontime, talking as she would have with my father as their morning's harvest of grouse sizzles on the campfire of their Grass Mountain herding site.*

For so potent a piece of time, noon was not exact at all. It never meant to us high twelve o'clock, any more than to the early English countryfolk who accounted their noon at three p.m., the ninth hour after sunrise. Noon meant instead the controlled curve of the day from morning into afternoon, where the beginning of labor crossed into the lessening of labor. A gradual but distinct passage, that is to say, which the sundial still could have expressed better than the clock. There would have been the advantage, too, that the blankness of the sundial on an overcast day would have said more truthfully how vague time became when clouds curded grayly over the valley and all work of the ranch was drenched out. Once or twice I can remember a two-day rain, which was all the rain we could imagine, and the loss of two working-noons in a row was befuddling, ominous, a dank eclipse. More than enough testimony, each time, that the sun's topmost moment of arch stood as a necessity in our world of ranchcraft.

NORTH

As the Irish fellow says, this place must be the back of the neck of the world. For once, my father's damnation of a ranch was underdone. He could have peppered in a few dozen of the Irish fellow's forlornest cusswords in justice to this one.

We had come the hours of distance north from the Smith River Valley and driven onto the ranch during the night. As Dad puzzled through the darkness along fainter and fainter scuffs of prairie road, our three styles of apprehension began to cloak in on us. Before we were halfway, Grandma demanded: *Gee gollies, aren't we never gonna get there?* Dad notched his chin ahead another full inch and choked the steering wheel as if it had betrayed him. I tried to stare shapes out of the blackness, but could find only an occasional jackrabbit racing in the net-edge of our headlights.

At last, Dad gave a start, began to brake the pickup down a sudden careen of slope, and the headlights fingered wildly onto a squat white building. *By gee, at last.* That was

Grandma; not a word out of Dad. *Where is the place, down in a hole like this?* More silence from him. As we stumbled from the pickup toward the house, the white walls too seemed to hold back from us in the dark, ghostly and telling nothing of themselves.

Daylight did all the telling we wanted. Testing doors, we found ourselves locked off from all but the back three rooms of the house—a small bedroom for Grandma, one hardly larger for Dad and me, and a high-ceilinged cavern of a kitchen. *McGrath's doings, I'll warrant you,* Grandma announced rightly: in haggling for the lease, he had euchred a point of some sort with the ranch-owning family by allowing them to store their belongings in the front portion of the house. From a keyhole I reported up to Dad and Grandma that furniture and boxes were piled all around a broad, bewindowed living room, with other rooms opening off as well. Plainly, the divvy of the house had dealt the larger share in there to dust and silence.

In alarm, we studied the ungainly little set of rooms left to us, and the single narrow envelope of view out the kitchen windows—to a dilapidating bunkhouse, the outhouse, and a bit of brown treeless slope ramping up to the benchland. Even Grandma couldn't come up with words for the situation, although the line of her lips said she was working on it.

She and I went out to peer in the windows of the denied rooms, as if we needed to confirm McGrath's treachery. I glanced around toward the silver-boarded sheepshed which squatted hugely across the yard from us. *At least,* I tried in what I thought was entirely grown-up sarcasm, *old McGrath got us a scad of room for the sheep.* But Grandma's attention had hit on the bleak bench of land rimming above us to the south, where the road curled in. She turned, and the same bench rimmed over us in the west. Another turn, and an identical flat lid of horizon to the north. She rotated to the last chance, the east, and was met with rimming benchland again, like the fourth lip of a vast square pit. *Hmpf. House in a hollow makes the weather follow,* she recited, slammed away into the back of the house, and wouldn't be spoken to for the rest of the morning.

Dad and I walked around the outbuildings. The sheepshed spread itself big beyond relief, bunkered along the base of a slope for a full forty yards, then elling off into the coulee for another forty, then closed around with a high board fence like a stockade. The one thing such expanse insured was endless walking for the day man—Dad—during lambing time. *Moose of a damn place,* he muttered now as if trying to shrink it.

Weathered and dour as a fortress, the sheepshed looked to have crouched on its site eternally. Every other building in the ranch yard, however, reared from open ground to open sky as though spilled into place, hard, only an eyeblink before. Nothing greater than a spear of grass backed the buildings—no brushy windbreak, no board fence, not even a pitying fluff of sage as the valley would have provided. As for trees, the entire sum of them on the 2500-acre ranch—two—hunched low at the front of the house, evidently trying to cower in out of the wind.

McGrath had told us that this leasehold—it was called the Jensen ranch—began as a homestead, which meant that people had lived here from at least forty years earlier. How had they never managed to make the place look less stark? From where we stood, a machine shed yawned with disuse on one side of us, a granary shed answered on the other. Between the pair bulked a barn built of notched logs, and its brown-gray mass only made the sheds look all the more cadaverous. Everything in sight—ground, barn, sheds, a rusting windmill—was slightly aslant, as if the impact of the giant sheepshed at the bottom of the yard had teetered the entire ranch toward it.

It was when Dad noticed that he hadn't yet found a place on the ranch where he could stand without one foot lower than the other that he pronounced the Irish fellow's lament on our new home. Then: *Aw the hell, Skavinsky, we might as well go see what the grass looks like.* The two of us—neither willing to risk a peace gesture in Grandma's direction yet—drove back up the long snout of benchland in front of the house.

We came up over the crest and were walled to a stop. The western skyline before us was filled high with a steel-blue army of mountains, drawn in battalions of peaks and reefs and gorges and crags as far along the entire rim of the earth as could be seen. Summit after summit bladed up thousands of feet as if charging into the air to strike first at storm and lightning, valleys and clefts chasmed wide as if split and hollowed by thunderblast upon thunderblast. Across the clear gape of distance, we could read where black-quilled forest wove in beneath cliffs and back among the plummet of canyons, we could make out the beds of scree crumbled and scattered beneath the marching shields of rimrock. The Smith River Valley had had mountain ranges all around. This high-set horizon twenty miles to our west thrust itself as if all those past ranges and twice their number more had been tumbled together and then armored with rimrock and icefield.

Off this carom-line of summits, we knew, the Continental Divide tipped rivers away to both the Pacific and the Atlantic. The shouldering might of what Dad and I were looking at seemed as if it could send those entire oceans too sloshing along routes of flow if the notion struck. Then as the pair of us stared and cleared our throats to one another, we began to see a thing more. Along these mastering mountains, all the hundred miles of gashing skyline in our sight, fresh snow was draping down.

Here was a thought. Dad and I had lived our lifetimes beneath weather-making mountains, none of which tusked up into storm clouds as mightily as this Sawtooth Range of the Rockies would. In front of us now loomed the reefline of the entire continent, where the surf of weather broke and came flooding across, and both of us knew what could be ahead when full winter poured down off these north peaks. Yet for the instant, to have come upon grandness anywhere near this spavined ranch, neither of us had the heart to care.

Down from the mountains as well, it turned out, this north country stretched as a land of steady expanse, of crisp-margined distances set long and straight on the earth. All the obliques of our valley life seemed to have been erased and redrawn here as ruler-edged plateaus of grassland, furrowed panels of grainfield, arrowing roads, creeks nosing quick and bright from the Rockies. The clean lines of this fresh landscape everywhere declared purpose and capacity, seemed to trumpet: *Here are the far bounds, all the extent anyone could need. Now live up to them.*

Dad stepped from the pickup, slid his hands into his hip pockets and studied the shards and shields of the Sawtooth Mountains and then the bold-edged distances north and south and east. *Dandy country,* he said, and turned to grin wide at me. *As the fellow says, just dandy fine. Let's go tackle that Lady situation.*

Dad by now had learned a considerable trove about how to handle Grandma—the remainder of his problem being that there seemed to be some dozens of troves yet to be figured out about her—and he had hit on what was needed to get her mind off the alarming ranch. *We got to figure some place for Ivan to stay for school, Lady. These roads are gonna be too much to drive every day when winter sets in this country. What do ye think we ought to do?*

The perpetual problem of basing me somewhere roused her. *Well, we ought to go into what's-its-name, Dupuyer, and see what's what, oughtn't we? Criminentlies, that seems to me how to do . . .* Now she looked Dad full in the face, acknowledging him with challenge. *Don't it to you?*

It did, and we drove the nine dirt miles north to Dupuyer, luckily a briefer route than the bramble of roads we had come in by from the south. We noticed, with no surprise, that the Jensen ranch looked like an elderly addled cousin of the trim ranches along the way. Then our dirt road at last sneaked itself to the highway, and down from a ridge—this north seemed to be all flat ridgeline where it wasn't iceberg mountains—Dupuyer lay tucked along a broad band of brush which marked its namesake creek.

Off from either side of the highway, which doubled for an instant as the main street, a few dozen houses and buildings lined away, like a Ringling which had been ordered to close in its ranks and paint itself up toward respectability. The first of the town's businesses we came to had one sign advertising it as a gas station, and another declaring it a cafe, as if the enterprise hadn't entirely been able to make up its mind and decided to take on both jobs. While Dad and I searched out someone to put gas in the pickup, Grandma marched into the cafe-sign side of the building and asked the woman behind the counter if she knew anyone who would board a high school boy.

The woman at once plunged into thought, her lips set barely open as if in a soundless whistle. This question from a stranger seemed to have taken her over entirely, until at last she had to shake her head and say, *No, just nobody comes to mind. I guess most people aren't willing to take in someone they don't know like that.* Grandma locked the woman with her steadfast look: *Well, how about you then?*

That clamping look and those words began my stay with the Chadwick family. Gertie, the woman of the cafe, said afterward that her agreement came as an out-of-the-clouds hunch which startled her as she said it; after all, she had not laid eyes on me yet. *But your grandma just had a way about her. I liked her right then, and figured I might like you.* We would learn in turn that Grandma had landed me with three people it was impossible not to cherish.

Gertie Chadwick herself was Dupuyer's touchstone. Short and square set, almost boxy—her parents had been stocky immigrants from Belgium, and the family line had gone even broader and more short-necked with her—she stubbed up just above the top of the cafe counter. But somehow there was the energy packed in her to run her enterprise as busily and fondly as if it were a boardinghouse table and the many dozens of customers each day made up the most interesting crew on earth.

She kept open for business 364½ days of the year. At Christmas, she would come downtown in the forenoon to feed the pensioned herders and widowers and others who took their every meal with her, then resolutely go home for the holiday afternoon. In day-by-day trade, travelers trooped in to her plentifully enough, as was guaranteed by Dupuyer's spot as the lone stopover of its sort amid a kinking seventy-five-mile stretch of the highway which led north to Glacier National Park and Canada. But Gertie's main service was to provide the community itself with brimming coffee cups and the daily victual of counter-stool chat to go with the brew.

Ranchers and farmers spilled in as they passed through town: *You fellows who've got winter wheat in will be able to be called Mister this fall . . . It'll be a beaner if I can get 'er harvested in this christly weather . . . They hailed out up across the Marias. Pounded the damned wheat flat to the ground . . . Looks like eighty-five-pound lambs up on the*

Reservation. Just a world of grass for 'em up there this year . . . Other hours, their wives made their call, on the way to buy groceries for a ranch crew or to fetch a machinery part needed in the grain harvest or just to trade news with one another. But the most precise and valued of Gertie's customers were her regulars, the lone men who bought meals from her by the month and arrived for them three times a day like figures marching across the face of an elaborate tower clock as certain hours are struck.

Since I took my meals side by side with them, the regulars eyed me briefly, learned that I was from a fending family and could see that I already was doing some of it for myself, and dealt me into their corps. A tiny ancient homesteader named Fred Groh at once told me of arriving in Dupuyer when he was my age, and at the break of spring hearing the thaw wind begin its roar down across the crags of the Rockies: *They told me it was the chinook, and I wondered what kind of animal that could be, to make a noise like that.* The gentle and gray postmaster John Wall eased in from across the street, puffing his pipe thoughtfully as he sparred jokes with Gertie. She upped the odds once by snipping a circle of cardboard and sliding it beneath the meat patty in his daily hamburger. As she turned back to the kitchen, he spotted the disc and slipped it out. Wordlessly he ate away as Gertie gnawed at her lip. At last the blurt from her: *Don't you notice anything about that hamburger at all?* He dabbed napkin to lips and gave me a slow wise wink: *No sir, Gertie, it tastes just like your hamburgers always do.* A gnome-faced man named Joe Smith mocked himself with little stories about his livelihood as a fur trapper, laughed with a *haw-haw-haw* which shook him all over, disappeared betweentimes to the traplines he had set along the creeks beneath the mountains. Gertie's husband Harold noticed my interest in this half-phantom—there was little

Harold did not notice—and began mumbling information: *That Joe, by the god, he can catch any beaver he wants to. How the hell he does it, I dunno. He'll go out there to a beaver dam and catch all the big ones, leave the little ones. These ranchers'll ask him to catch all them beaver, but huh-uh: he leaves them little ones for seed, by the god, for next year.*

Gertie herself must have heard innumerable times everything that was ever said around that counter, yet I noticed that she listened as readily as if every word was new to her and encouraged the talk with a rich open-mouthed chuckle which occupied her entirely, the way Grandma's question had done. This cafe of hers and its place in the life of Dupuyer, I quickly came to see, reflected exactly this new landlady of mine: plain to look at, hearty the day long, and years-deep in polished affections.

The polish swiped away at once when you stepped over the doorsill from the cafe into Harold Chadwick's service station. The place was a conglomerate of workshop and junk-yard, massed with mechanical gear and tools which seemed to have dropped down to catch their breath before seizing onto the next project. The rear of the station at any given time might house, amid the gasping hoods of cars, a de-motored tractor or an axleless truck or a grain combine towering like a freighter in dry dock.

Somewhere in the midst of it would be Harold himself, a tall black-handed wizard cobbling away at the community of machinery with deep pondering sighs. Luckily Harold's hands spoke for him, because listening to him otherwise you caught only those profound sighs, or a thin mutter which seemed to come mostly via his nose, or sheer silence. Soon after I began to board with the Chadwicks, a stint came when Gertie hired someone to run the cafe in the evenings, and so would feed us supper catch-as-catch-could at home, with Harold arriving to eat by himself whenever he found space between waiting repairs. Once after he made his wordless come and go, I went to the kitchen and joked to Gertie: *Harold must've been here for his supper, hmm? I heard the kitchen door slam twice.* She whooped with appreciation, and to my alarm retold the lines to Harold when he came home after closing. He looked across at me in surprise as I waited warily, and then gave me a great dark silent grin.

The Chadwicks had a son a few years older than I was—*Tommy Chad,* as the townspeople sometimes lilted about this boy-man. Tommy worked at the service station with his father, and had inherited the magic with machines. His mother's thick-set look had rebuilt itself on him—anvil shoulders and solid beams of arms, his neck a collar of heft, blocky power anywhere you looked—until he seemed almost a brother to the machinery under repair from his blunt, deft fingers. Tommy's mulling effort to make his head speak as well as his hands gave him a quiet watchfulness much like my own. Since each of us had been raised alone as best our families had been able to find time for us, and each had come out of it with a knack the other didn't—my diet of books, his touch for machinery—we appreciated each other by a kind of survivors' instinct, like a Brazilian and a Laplander somehow falling into step in the same forest.

Someone beside the pair of us as we forked down a meal at the cafe counter in comfortable silence turned and said: *You two don't have much to say for yourselves, do you?* Tommy gave it an instant, then: *No. Just enough.*

The three Chadwicks had a steadiness about them which carried out into their town. Dupuyer, unlike Ringling or White Sulphur Springs, seemed never to have had the least hesitation about its livelihood since the first wagonmaster wearily overnighted on the site sometime in the 1870's. In a dollar-counting meander between the horizon of mountains and the horizon of plains, the freighters' trail had marked itself northwestward through Montana from the steamboat landing at Fort Benton on the Missouri to the early Royal Canadian Mounted Police posts in Alberta. Even after the railroad speared crosscontinent to the north, the trail stayed busy as a capillary for mail and stage shipments out into the remote country edging the Rockies and their foothills. And all the while, the special site of plentiful grass and a constant creek was making itself into a merchandising settlement. The country rimming it to the west was found to be fine for sheep, and a local rancher named Oliver Goldsmith Cooper became president of the potent Montana Wool Growers Association. Before the turn of the century, a quarter million pounds of fleece were being shipped from the Dupuyer Creek ranches each year.

From then on, Dupuyer added little population, lost less: it somehow had found a spot of balance between the range hills and the farming plains, and the equilibrium set the town's mood. *Once a year, for about a week toward the end of winter, everybody gets at everybody else's throats,* Gertie explained to me. *Then the chinook comes and we all get along together for another year.*

One store, three gas stations, three saloons, the cafe, some few hundred feet of sidewalk, a few dozen houses, a couple of barns, several overtopping groves of cottonwoods, long winters, pushing winds, a hundred people, and a highway trenching it into halves. That was Dupuyer, entire and uncomplaining, and it won me in a week with its tidy life and the caress of its past. For the first time I could remember, I was living in a town which had a pace of life both useful and civil, and some deserved contentment with itself over that fact. With the Chadwicks, I was enfolded in a family which held warmths more constant than I was used to, even in the sunnier parts of the blizzard-and-thaw cycles of Dad, Grandma, myself. Even the Jensen ranch was proving less woebegone than expected in my weekends there with Dad and Grandma. The place was so basic after the pinwheel life of a big ranch such as the Camas that there was not much way to apply great effort to it, and Dad and Grandma were able to slacken their fierce work habits a bit. Beyond that, they too seemed to take pleasure from Dupuyer and the Chadwicks, to feel less edgy than any of us had for a long time. *Told ye this north country was worth a try,* Dad crowed. I agreed entirely for the first few weeks —and then plummeted into a time when I wished I were anywhere else on the continent.

The tripwire was in my new high school. Because Dupuyer had never reached the size to have its own high school, its handful of students jounced by bus to the larger town of Valier, twenty miles east across the farm plains. Unlike Dupuyer, which simply had sprigged up by a trailside, Valier had been grandly planted, as the headquarters town for an 80,000-acre irrigation project which had been ditched onto the prairie early in the century. Now the town had the somewhat nonplussed air of having built too much of itself for the size of its caretaking job. Empty blocks yawned away from, and sometimes through, its neighborhoods, and what had been allotted as a sizeable downtown held only a single thin street of businesses.

The high school too seemed to spread more than was called for, crouching broadly and determinedly across most of a block as if putting roots into the earth. Inside, the building flung itself open in the wide gaunt logic of a frontier fort—a vast central room like a parade ground, with students' desks soldiered into file, class by class, all across the center, and classrooms sentried regularly around the side walls. All in all, there seemed to be a grayish barracks-like feeling to the place, and I stepped in on my first morning with doubt crowding high in my throat.

By more luck than I could have prayed for, four of us arrived new to this school of a hundred students on the same mid-November day. Another of these newcomers rode the bus from Dupuyer with me—Carlton, who was a year or two older than I was, and boasted a gold tooth, black hair slicked back like an ebony skullcap, and girl-stories he began reciting as soon as he slipped into the seat beside me.

Your folks run sheep, huh? So'd the folks of my girlfriend last summer. She had to herd the goddamn things in this field, see, so they give her this Jeep and I'd motate out there, see, and get in with her and we'd get our clothes off and do it right there in that goddamn Jeep, see. Then we'd roar out after those goddamn sheep and round 'em in. Run right over the woolly bastards if they didn't move fast enough, see. . . .

I listened with interest. Anything about girls and the new white worlds of their breasts and the unknown gulch at the top of their thighs was an item to know. But Carlton's tale was boggling: I didn't know whether to be more astonished at the vision of a girl naked in a Jeep or at daring to run over a sheep. Disappointed in me as an audience, Carlton sidled off toward the back of the bus. In a minute, his murmurs were going again. . . . *do it right there* . . . *run right over the woolly bastards* . . .

With the lighthouse wink of that tooth and his insistent exploit, Carlton drew off attention in our first few days at Valier. But my camouflage of quiet faded quickly. Too many times each schoolday, I would look up and meet a set of cool gray eyes which could have outdrilled even Grandma's. The face around them was dark-browed, unadorned, and somehow both musing and ominous. Frances Carson Tidyman, who through a full generation had been scanning the students in her English classes as if they were muddy pebbles in a sluice box, had me under her steadiest focus.

What I already had begun to know about Mrs. Tidyman was as unsettling as her stare. She was the least likely presence to be found in a small farmtown school: a mysteriously spiced waft of booklore and speculative notions and astonishing languages and . . . oddnesses. It was circulated that she cared almost nothing for money—that she habitually turned down the salary raises due her to forestall a day when the school could not afford her, and that she paid in stores by asking what amount was needed, scrawling the sum into whatever counter checkbook the clerk happened to hand her, and forgetting the matter forever. In Valier, this quick blink of a system worked well enough. But in the county's main shopping town of Conrad, it left a patter of misbanked checks bouncing behind her, and her husband had at last to fund a bank account there solely to cover her offhand signatures.

As with finance, she seemed to declare, so with time and costume. They meant no more to her than that she eventually had to appear somewhere, with something on. This brought about her fame for occasionally gardening with her nightgown on, dark hair maned free and spilling to the waist—and of course, her flowers and vegetables encouraged to ally into whatever clumps and jumbles they would.

At school, she would arrive in dark plain dresses so alike that it could hardly be traced when she changed one for another; bunned her hair into a great black burl at the back of her neck; clopped from class to class in the severest of shoes. She was buxom, much like Grandma with a half more plumped on all around; her mounding in front and behind was very nearly more than the lackadaisical dresses wanted to contain. Leaning forward from the waist as she hurried about, she flew among us like a schooner's lusty figurehead prowing over a lazy sea.

The mind of Mrs. Tidyman was somewhat like that jostling garden of hers—sprigged here with the Greek and Roman myths she knew so entirely that she recited them to her children for bedtime stories, sprouting somewhere else with blood-red bouquets from Shakespeare, twining now into a tale such as having seen the cowboy artist Charlie Russell when she attended the university in Missoula: *In the midst of a sorority tea someone deposited him with us—dozens of fluffy girls, you understand, and he had been drinking for the ordeal—and then the utmost indignity, they took his hat from him and he had nothing to do with his hands, and sat helpless, imprisoned. . . .*

The foliage of her learning laced everywhere through the school. She taught all the English courses, first- and second-year Latin, occasionally a course in Spanish, directed the plays, advised for the yearbook and newspaper, and oversaw the library. It could not be imagined where she might exist except in the midst of all this. She had taken leave for enough years to have four sons, and afterward decided the absence had been a mistake. Chinese peasant women did it properly, she reasoned, giving birth to their babies in the fields and going right on with their toil.

That earliest watching I felt from this unprecedented woman, it turned out, was to see whether I was a thief. A few times a year, a school-wide set of vocabulary tests was given, every student then ranked against national statistics. The first test-time fell in the second week after I enrolled at Valier, and I attacked with joy. If there was one knack in me, it was to hold in mind any word I had ever seen, much the way Dad could identify any sheep from all others. When this first of the set of tests was scored, no one among the seniors, juniors or sophomores achieved better than a respectable 50. One of my classmates soared to a 60, well up in the national percentiles. My paper lofted off to an unscorable 75.

Before I had time to get the grin off my face, Mrs. Tidyman had asked me into the library, locked the door, and with as much tact as she could muster—somewhere close to none—wondered abruptly whether I had come across the answer sheet before the national test. Whatever denial I stammered to her—what nightmare was this, did I have to prove myself stupid before I would be trusted here?—she had a better one in the making. *All right. There are three more tests in the next three days, and I have the answer sheets secure. We'll just see how you score on them.*

Three times more I gapped everyone else in the school and shot out the top of all percentiles. I didn't know whether to be triumphant or apprehensive, but before I had much time for either, Mrs. Tidyman again was hauling me into the library, clicking the lock, eyeing me relentlessly. *You know, you really ought to take my Latin class next year. Latin will be an advantage for you in the use of English. And you should write for the school paper, there's good practice. And I want to know what you read. I have a houseful of books if you can't find enough here . . .*

I gulped the relief of being out from under Mrs. Tidyman's suspicion, and sat back to see what the gale of her approval would bring. In the classroom, each hour with her began like a conjuring, or a parody of one. She would clomp in and back herself onto a high stool behind a thin-legged lectern. At last secure in midair she would revolve toward the class, the entire billow of her far up over us, with the lectern-top before her as if commanded to hover there. Then her hand deep into her dress front, and out of that vault of bosom would come eyeglasses, tethered on a neck chain which still did not entirely stop her from losing them a few times each day; a balled handkerchief; a fountain pen, likely leaking; perhaps a fat ring of keys, or a shredding blizzard of notes to herself. Up would come her head from an unperturbed inventory of this rummage. A mild glare or a stern look of fondness—her shadings of expression could be baffling—fastened onto the last of the class to go quiet. With it might fall the entire total of her irony, the query *Do you mind if I begin now?*

At last supplied and delivered, she set at us. The day's assigned reading might be thumped open and launched into sheerly for the entrancement of hearing herself aloud: *'It was the best of times, it was the worst of times, it was the age of wisdom, it was the age of foolishness'—oh, people, can you hear those phrases ring against one another? . . .* If there was agony and tragedy, so much the richer fancy: *'As flies to wanton boys, are we to the gods; they kill us for their sport.' When I read the headline of an airplane crash, people, first I wish that no one I know was killed. Then that no one from Montana was killed. Then that no one from this country. Then that no one at all would have been killed —oh, people, the casual lightning bolts which come down on us . . .* She would escort Richard Cory and Miniver Cheevy to their poetic dooms one instant, bring Ivanhoe galloping in to the bleats of chivalry's trumpets the next. Now Lady Macbeth in gore, now Portia pleading against blood. In Latin class, Mrs. Tidyman never could have us read in Caesar's *Commentaries* without declaiming on Caesar the man; could not declaim on Caesar without sketching Roman society; could not sketch the Romans without embracing all the Mediterranean, on and on in a widening spiral of lore and enthusiasm, glasses flying in her hand and bosom wheeling above the lectern like turrets searching for new fields of gunnery.

But it was the grammar of English that exalted her most. Day after day we would troop to the blackboard to take apart sentences for her, phrases chalked to one another like scaffolding, being shown how a clause dovetailed here, an infinitive did the splicing there, the whole of it planed and beamed together as her pointer whapped through a reading of the revealed sentence. For her the language held holy force, and she shuddered at any squander of it. In what must have been her fullest spate of forgiveness, she once apologized about one of the townswomen: *Once you get used to her split infinitives, you'll find she's a very nice person.*

And so Mrs. Tidyman hovered at me from her heights of language, declaiming, diagramming, rhapsodizing, unabashedly giving favor to any of us who seemed rapt. I was more than rapt, held by her whirligig of language and learning as if I were a ball swung on a tether. *I bet she thinks she glommed onto something when you came to that school,* Grandma assessed after one of my reports about Mrs. Tidyman. *Maybe,* I said, as if I hadn't had the answer drilled into me by gray eyes.

Mrs. Tidyman, exhausting and exasperating and exhilarating, was one education new to hand in our northern move. Another introduced itself at the Jensen ranch on a weekend soon after we had settled in. Two plump men presented themselves at the door and asked *plees, to see the chentleman of the ranch.* Both were bearded, both wore black outer clothing over brilliant red shirts, and both stared as blinklessly into the kitchen as a pair of holidaying parsons who had lucked upon naked natives. Grandma shooed them off toward the sheepshed to find Dad, rammed the door shut and snicked a table knife into the jamb. *Who in Christmas do you suppose them two are?* I had no supposing to offer; they were as much apparition to me as to her. But when Dad came in for coffee, the pair clomped at his heels. *These fellows are Hoots,* he grinned. *They're our neighbors.*

Beyond the second ridgeline to the south of us, we discovered, lay a ranch colony of a hundred such Hutterites, a shy tranced people who gabbled among themselves in a German dialect and lived barracks-style according to their signals from God. Heaven told them an endless amount that we had never heard of, such as that when one of their men married he had to grow whiskers along his jawline to make the face-circle which represented a wedding ring, or that their women were proper only when swathed in long skirts, aprons and kerchiefs, like walking mounds of fresh laundry.

When we visited the colony to buy eggs or vegetables—the parsonly pair had come by to invite us to do so—we also found that the Hoots ran their ranch with a brisk orderliness which made the Jensen ranch seem even more woebegone. Each family was allotted a set of rooms with gleaming board floors and stern furniture. The small children waddled about like fat dolls in museum costumes, but the young men were hived off by themselves, several to a room, from their early teens until they married. The young women, rose-cheeked mysteries inside their hoods and curtains of ginghamware, stayed within the family until that marrying somehow managed to happen.

All the colony ate in a single great dining hall, the men and boys first, then the women and children after their superiors strode back to work. Hierarchy, it seemed, was their second religion. The Hoots doled work responsibilities as if they were the line officers of some farmerly regiment: one man was appointed the Cow Boss, another the Sheep Boss, a third the Vegetable Boss, on and on until every task was divvied out with its handle of duty and its claim on the colony's work force as needed. Perhaps having eyed other communal brethren toiling to stay with the old ways, the

Hoots also had made their decision about modern machinery: they would use every roaring horsepower of it they could get their hands on. The colony clattered with tractors, throbbed with helpful engines. A constant sight was a Hoot truckload of eggs speeding off to one town or another, a gaggle of black-clad young men in the back like crows hitching a ride.

All in all, the Hutterite system clicked out work like an assembly line. The Dupuyer people said the Hoots could thrive a hundred at a time on land where an ordinary family had starved out. They did not mean it as a compliment.

For the Hoots, we learned, had dark stains. The first scandal always recited about them was that they did not believe in serving in the army. Next, that Hoot colonies didn't pay taxes like the rest of us because they were church organizations. And beyond that, in muskier tones, their marrying habits. The Hoots, it seemed, intermarried cousin to cousin until an entire colony might have only two or three surnames in it, with the sinful clans further strung throughout colonies elsewhere in Montana and western Canada.

War, money and sex: whatever else you said of them, the Hutterites did not skirt the big topics of life. Dad, with his penchant for hard clean-edged work, liked the Hoots at once. As often as he could arrange it, some chore would take him to the colony, and the Sheep Boss would hail him —*Vell, Chollie! Vot's your business?*—and escort him into the dining hall, where one of the kerchiefed women brought him slices of bread or cake flat on the palm of her hand. There also might be a snifter of the fine sweet rhubarb wine produced by the colony, and manly grumbles with the Sheep Boss about the price of lambs and the prospects of grass. Grandma was less enchanted—the men ran the colony too high-handedly, *They parade around over there like they was somebody*—but eventually she too decided they were satisfactory neighbors. Certainly they were hard-working, and with her that nearly canceled out their quirks about soldiering and family line.

On the other hand, she made a perplexity for the Hoot men when they came to visit Dad, with her refusal to withdraw and leave the conversation to the males. Her abrupt verdicts of the world were beyond their ken—*Ach, vell, perhaps, Mizzus Ringer, perhaps, but yet*—and our rankly household must have been as mysterious to the Hutterites as their ordered family regiments were to us.

Yet Dad evidently was a sensible enough soul on any topic except women, and their nearest neighbor besides, so the Sheep Boss and a crony or two continued to come by and confide to him their worries about the younger Hoots, tender rabbits for the snares strewn by the modern world. Television was the newest and seemed the most treacherous. Harold Chadwick had sent off for a mail order course, scratched his chin briefly over the ream of diagrams, then wired up a picture tube which now flickered and snapped in the Dupuyer service station day and night. The elders recognized how spellbinding the fuzzed universe in the tube could be—Hoot youngsters were flocking in to gawk at Harold's miracle by the hour—but were stymied about how they could battle it. Still, one thing to be done was to stay as unsurprised as possible about the outside world's gray magic, and the Sheep Boss, showing how aweless he could be, began to tell Dad about his wife's fright when she glimpsed Dupuyer's startling television set. *Ho, she t'ot the vorld was going straight to*—here he noticed Grandma as usual listening sharply, and could not bring himself to say *to hell* in her presence. *Vas . . . vas going down!* he finished desperately, pushing his palms toward the brimfire below. Grandma eyed him with fresh suspicion of Hoot backwardness: *She took a look at a television and thought she was FALLING? Hmpf.*

The Hutterites gave Grandma something to mutter about, and she shortly solved for herself some of the ranch's yawning emptiness. McGrath had left us with a bonus of a few of his everlasting dog pack. Behind the bunkhouse door one evening, a small several-colored bitch apologetically gave birth. The pups were only two, but their mother's haphazard colors were passed on in fullest style. One came out with a coat of sheening black, ice-tipped at the tail and ruffed whiter yet at his chest and neck. The other was a snowfield with thaws of tan, the brockled markings romping up his sides and under his ears. Grandma at once claimed them both, pointing out to Dad that we'd had enough of McGrath's thuggish hounds and ought to train good sheep dogs of our own.

It was an argument he could not answer. I suggested we call the newcomers *McGrath* and *Jensen.* Grandma rapped out that she had never heard of such names for dogs—there was no answer to that either—and dubbed them *Tip* and *Spot.* From then on, these brothered dogs were to be the fourth and fifth members of our family, and to bring us rewards and woes almost as major as those we brought on each other.

Both, to Dad's discomfort, began to grow up with a stubbornness they seemed to imbibe straight from Grandma. Spot, winsome as his brockled coat, proved to be tirelessly happy and helpful. By every instinct in him, he was a superb sheep dog, eager, far-ranging, steady; he had a sense of what he was about to be commanded to do, and seemed to start his policing arc around a strayed ewe before your arm had quite come up to direct him. Tip was as tireless, but for him, that same straying sheep clicked in his mind as a target of opportunity: he was, brain and fang, a born biter.

Since Tip also was the fleetest dog any of us had ever seen—his black body sleek and whetted as a racehorse's, the white peak of his tail streaking flat behind him like the flare of a rocket—he constituted a lethal weapon. Dad and Grandma at last harangued and cuffed Tip into a rough civility, which put him in a mood of hurt astonishment that he should be veered from anything so natural as savaging a ewe. But for all efforts, sending Tip far around the sheep always remained chancy, like target-practicing near an ammunition dump, and the sheep learned to shy and stampede into retreat at the farthest sight of the black fury.

Spot watched his brother with curiosity—he knew just as deeply in his instincts that the sheep were never to be bitten—and loped his routes around the band like a guiding angel. But Spot too had the streak of insistence in him: his lust was for appreciation. From Grandma, he had reward in plenty, endless pettings and talkings-to and the freedom of the house. From Dad, quickly ablaze with having been jumped on fondly by Spot for the twentieth time in a day or having tripped across his doorway sprawl for the fortieth, he could not count on such affection, and it would seem to puzzle him briefly, his tongue out a corner of his mouth as he watched Dad's thwarting back. Then with a thankful look around the room, Spot would plop in the doorway again and wait for his next shift with the beloved sheep.

Dad and I thought we had become used to a life full of dogs when Grandma suddenly filled it more from another direction. From somewhere she now came up with a cat, a self-sufficient young gray tiger which she named—no advice asked or offered this time—*Kitten. All right, Lady,* Dad decreed, watching Kitten purr across his shins, *that'll be just about enough.*

In this first half-year of our new northern life, some surprises began to be shown by the Jensen ranch itself, basic and stark and drowsing as it seemed. The first was that the place had clay bogholes hidden like elephant traps in its grass. After a few plunges into those wallows and his cursing hikes to the Hoots for a tow, Dad traded the pickup in favor of a metal-cabbed Jeep. The next startlement came at lambing time, when snow clung and clung to the benchland slopes and the grass refused to green. Without the fresh grass, the ewes' milk was weak and their lambs came down with diarrhea. The pile of tiny carcasses outside the great shed began to grow by the hour.

Damn-it-all-to-hell, these lambs are all gonna drizzle themselves to death if we don't do something. Dad hurried a call to a veterinarian, and what we were to do was to spoon cod liver oil, for its vitamin D content, into every lamb.

Across a nightmare set of days—I stayed home from school for the crisis—we penned and caught and spoonfed each of the two thousand lambs. They survived, but we nearly didn't, thumbs aching from having forced two thousand stubborn mouths open for the medicine, backs bowed from two thousand reachings and liftings. As we grayly ate supper after the last handling of the last lamb, Grandma could barely mutter: *A sideways outfit this is, not even the grass wants to grow like it should . . .*

But there was pasture grass to come, months spilling with grass, as if a fifth season had been tanly matted into the middle of the year. Dad's decision to come north with McGrath had been keyed to this—the summer pasture for the sheep on the prairie of the Blackfeet Indian Reservation north of Dupuyer. *They say that Reservation is a bunchgrass country you can hardly believe. If I can't bring fat lambs in from grass like that, I've had my head off my shoulders for forty years.* The Jensen ranch was leased for only eight months of the year; from June through October, the grass months which would fatten the lambs for shipping, Dad and

Grandma and I would graze the sheep on a pasture allotment on the Reservation. We were about to see the prairie face of our northern life.

When the sheeps' hooves hit the road at the edge of the ranch on the last morning of May, 1954, we flung ourselves into three desperate days of trudging, yelling, dogging, cursing, fretting. Our Reservation range lay forty highway miles north from Dupuyer, and every step of it threatened to joggle loose the dim panic at the center of each sheep's brain. Pushing the skittery thousands of animals up the strange dike of pavement became a guerrilla struggle against every yapping farmyard dog, any blowing bit of paper—and worse, each and every auto that came along like a hippopotamus nosing among penguins.

Grandma would be seething against the motorists within the first half-mile: *God darn them, don't they have enough brains to even take themselves through a band of sheep?* Tourists stopping innocently in the middle of the band to ask why the lead sheep had a bell on and all the others didn't would find themselves fiercely invited to *git on through the sheep here, how would you like it if I laid down in your front yard and started asking you questions?*

We were to live for the summer in a much-traveled small trailer house which McGrath had flimflammed from somewhere; Dad had it in tow behind the Jeep—Kitten an indignant yowling passenger inside—and roved nervously with this worn-looking convoy in the wake of the sheep, jumping out to whoop stragglers down the highway and hustling around to catch any exhausted lambs which needed to be ferried in the Jeep for a time. I did whatever he couldn't get to, and as well panted off in endless arcing jogs around the sheep to flag down cars in blind spots on the road.

I had made, each for Grandma and for myself, a noisemaker called a *tin dog*—a ring of baling wire with half a dozen empty evaporated milk cans threaded on so that it could be shaken, tambourine-like, into a clattering din. Mile upon mile, with our ruckus behind them, the dubious ewes and their panicky lambs edged north.

Water decreed each day's push on the sheep. From the Jensen ranch, we had to make the 16 miles north to Birch Creek the first night, in order to bed the tired band where they could graze and drink. It meant funneling the sheep through Dupuyer at midmorning, the Chadwicks and other townfolk stepping out to give us a hand as the woolly sea of backs shied from gas pumps and parked cars and the thin neck of bridge across Dupuyer Creek; pushing on across a broad chocolate-and-gold bench of farmland; and then into the long tight trench of fenced lane, a full afternoon of battling traffic and time.

The only ones happy with the summer trail were Tip, who saw it as a feast of sly nips among the sheep, and Spot, who adoringly would begin to herd half the band up the highway by himself and to loll tonguey grins at us for appreciation. The pair of them had their grandest moment of the year here where the sheep had to be shoved like a vast ball of wool into the neck of a bottle. Time after time an exasperated ewe would prance out and, like a knight's charger for a single haughty instant, stamp a front hoof at the dogs in challenge. Then, it dawning on her that she was entirely helpless against the knife-toothed pair, she would whirl and waddle in panicked retreat. One of my chores was to try to keep Tip from tearing these bold ninnies to ribbons, and he regarded me with his puzzled hurt whenever I shouted him back in time. At last, after hours of working the tin dogs and the real dogs and ourselves—by sunset if we had been lucky—the sheep would spill off the highway to the graveled banks of Birch Creek.

The second day, the same straining push to water, this time a dozen highway miles to Badger Creek. In places the road now whipped into sudden curves, and I would spend most of this day flagging the coming cars in front of the sheep. We were on the Blackfeet Reservation now, and I passed my time between baffled tourists by wondering what our life here would be like. All I knew of Indians was that carloads of them whirled into Dupuyer most nights of the week. They had come for beer, would drink it in their cars, then drive off again in a lurching stutter of traffic. Every few weeks there would be slaughter, a beery pickup-load crashing off a highway curve and the limp bodies catapulted against cutbanks and along the barrow pit. The state highway department sternly put up a white cross wherever an auto victim died, and some curves on the highway here north of Dupuyer were beginning to look like little country graveyards. And I had read avidly what a Reservation correspondent named Weasel Necklace wrote in one of the region's weekly newspapers about the doings of his tribesmen: *Some of the people went to Conrad to do some shopping, and they all managed to come back through Dupuyer. From there they came home fighting and singing . . . Jesse Black Man was picked up at a ranch last week disturbing a home. And when police found him he was in a hay stack, with just his head covered. . . . Something wrong—Stoles Head Carrier has been staying home, he won't go to town. He does wrong when in town, and now has started to go wrong here . . .* The Blackfeet seemed to be a rambunctious people; I wondered what they thought of our white faces and gray sheep against the backcloth of their prairie past.

As we passed the accident crosses nearer and nearer to our Reservation lease, like silvered warnings along a route of pilgrimage, the landscape emptied and emptied until there was no hint of flowing water or tree cover. Then sometime beyond noon on the third day, a sudden earth-splitting trench of both: the Two Medicine, a middling green-banked river which somehow had found itself a gorge worthy of a cataract. We came behind the sheep down a long sharp skid of slope, looking below to high clumps of cottonwoods on the river bank, a few tribal houses, even what seemed to be an entire tiny ranch or two. Lazing east, the Two Medicine wound out of sight beneath a cliff face which banked about a hundred feet high, like a very old and eroded castle wall. We were told later that the site had been a buffalo jump, where the horseback Blackfeet stampeded the animals over the edge to death.

Then the final bridge of our route, across the mild flow of river, and the highway ramping up the facing canyon slope. The Two Medicine carved the southern boundary of our summer geography, our lease rimming off there at the fortress cliffs. And so, late in the third day, the sheep at last fan onto the summer pasture. We call in the disappointed dogs and let the band ease, graze, rest. Now for the next hundred days and more, the slow munch of the ewes and lambs across the ridges will be our pace of life.

A new country again: this Reservation land lay like long tan islands in a horizon-brimming tan ocean. Westward the Rockies jagged up as if they were the farthest rough edge of the world, but the other three directions flung themselves flat to grass, grass and grass. Eastering ridgelines such as the one we would live along ran from the base of the mountains tawny as lions' backs and crouched forward a bit toward the region's draining rivers, the Two Medicine in its plummet of gorge to our south and the Marias—a name I would hold on my tongue half the summer—beyond sight to the east.

Open and overawing as it was, this summer land somehow seemed tense, pulled taut and inward, with its contradictions. All this flatness and yet some purposeful tilts to it, our own ridge dropping after any few paces southward, slanting off to a sharp coulee which pitched deeper and darker, the single cut of line anywhere on the prairie, until it shot like a flume through the base of the cliffs above the Two Medicine. The sun wheeling so hot above the plain that sweat cooked from you even as you stood, yet on the crownline of the mountain horizon there might be white-gray snow clouds coldly billowing. A landscape which seemed to have nearly no water, and of water plentiful but unseen—for across our entire empire of pasture, there was a single tiny spurt of fresh water for us at a trickling spring near the ridge base, and for the sheep, dreg pools from the melt of winter's snowdrifts hidden in the bowl bottoms between every ridgeline.

Then the contradiction that answered my wondering about what it would be like living among the Blackfeet. We were amid them, all right, in the heart of the prairie which they had roved and ruled for generations, and there was to be scarcely an Indian in sight—nor anyone else, inhabitant or traveler—on our allotted grassland across the entire summer.

That left the question of how the three of us would live with ourselves. Almost before we had fanned the sheep onto the new grass of the Reservation and could begin to find out, McGrath arrived with another of his sudden projects. He had a contract to build several miles of fence on a ranch west of Great Falls, and Mickey-and-Rudy were at some other chore for him. He wanted Dad to subcontract the fencing from him.

It would be quick money, which we could use; Dad could easily finish the job in a few weeks. Dad turned to Grandma and me: *Can you pair handle these sheep for that time?* Not at all sure we could, we both echoed that we supposed so. Dad drove off with McGrath. Grandma and I stared down from the ridge to the four thousand grazing animals which now were our responsibility.

When we went down to take a closer look, we found that not all of them were grazing. A few were on their sides, legs stiff in the air, dead as stones. We looked at them in bafflement: they were some of the plumpest, best ewes in the entire band, the kind Dad called *dandiest*. Poison? There were no white-green blossoms of death camas in sight, and neither Grandma nor I could think of any other threat. Queasily, I snicked open my pocket knife. I had watched Dad skin the pelts from carcasses before, but never had done it myself.

By the time I had sliced and ripped the pelts from the dead sheep, Grandma was puffing back from a look at the far side of the band. *Gee gods, there's another one dead over there. I seen the trouble. They're getting themselves down to scratch.*

It dawned what this treeless, flowing grassland meant to us just then. There was not one upright particle on all these miles of range for a sheep to rub against, and an attack of ticks was beginning to make the ewes itch beneath their heavy fleeces. Of course it had been one of McGrath's economies that the sheep hadn't been sprayed for ticks as they were at the Camas: *Aw hell, in this country I don't think ticks will amount to anythin'*. Now the sheep were rolling themselves on the ground to scratch—a roll which easily carried them too far onto their deep-wooled backs to be able to get up again, and within minutes in the summer heat, their struggling would bloat them to death. We had the prospect of endless ballooned corpses around us.

I choked to Grandma: *What the hell are we gonna do?* She snapped: *I don't like to hear you say 'hell.'* Then: *We're gonna have to stay right with the sheep and turn 'em off their Godblasted backs.*

We spent every daylight hour of the next fourteen days patrolling the sheep. When we spotted the telltale kick of hooves in the air, I would run to the ewe, grab deep into her fleece and heave her over. She would wobble off, lopsidedly bulging with the bloat gas built up in her, but alive. Grandma used Spot and Tip. A ewe's redoubled panic as she looked along the ground and saw those eager jaws bulleting for her usually was enough to thrash her onto her feet.

But we could not be everywhere every moment, and so we lost sheep to themselves—one, sometimes two, a day, which I would skin out bitterly and carry the spongy pelt back to camp. We had lost about twenty when McGrath and Dad drove in one noontime.

McGrath was furious at the sight of the stack of pelts, each of them a few cents' remainder from one of his high-priced ewes. He found he was less furious than Grandma, who scorched him up, down and crosswise for not having sprayed the sheep for ticks.

Dad let it go on for a while—it was not often a person got to see McGrath take a torching of this sort—and at last broke in: *All right, all right, this isn't helping a thing. Let's get matters going again, why don't we? First thing, Mac, will you watch the sheep a couple hours while we go into town for grub? Lady's gonna have to do a helluva shopping by now.* McGrath saw no way to refuse, and Grandma and I sulked into the Jeep with Dad.

On the way into Browning we defended ourselves endlessly, until Dad at last settled us down by pointing out that the fencing money already was bolstering our bank account and that most of the loss of the ewes would come out of McGrath's end of the shares arrangement. *I know you did your level best with the sheep. I'd trust the both of you with 'em again in a minute.*

Grandma and I were improved by the time we drove back from Browning. We improved more when the Jeep growled down to the sheep and we spotted McGrath. He was up to his elbows in skinning a dead ewe. Unable to range fast and far enough on those brief bowed legs of his, he had lost three sheep on their backs while we were gone. A truce, never broken, came down over all mention of our stint of herding alone.

With Dad back on the scene, we settled into our slow summer, the trailer house towed back and forth along the ridge summit each week or so like a silver turtle creeping the horizon, the sheep nuzzling east or west on the prairie below as the grass led them. Separately, the lives of the three of us by now had touched down in dozens of random sites, but nothing out of the past of any one of us quite prepared a person for this flood of prairie. The Reservation country yielded two items: earth to navigate over, and the bunch-grass, sprouting like countless elfin quivers of white-tipped arrows, to nourish the sheep. All else of life had to be fetched, if it first could be found.

Every second or third evening, we bounced down the ridge in the Jeep to fill our water cans at the tiny trickle of a spring, and perhaps to have a swimming bath in the mud-banked reservoir below the spring. Fire fuel was scarcer than water. Not a twig of wood grew anywhere within sight, and we had to rove like horse thieves to find a collapsed shed or a driftwood pile along the Two Medicine.

There was a mockery here, because as we explored off across the empty spans of prairie, we again and again came across what seemed the eeriest of abundances: seagull flocks. Grandma and I had never seen them before, but Dad recognized their white soaring from his winter on the Pacific Coast: *Must be in here feedin' on grasshoppers.* Grandma, however, noted only that the gulls would scavenge a sheep carcass as avidly as magpies, and at once adopted them as the same sort of nemesis. She dubbed them *sharks,* and the

Reservation ridgelines began to ring with: *Git, GIT, you gosh darn sharks, nothin' dead around here for you good-for-nothings! . . .*

Our source of groceries was the Reservation headquarters town of Browning, some ten miles to the northwest. Going in for supplies once a week broke our monotony on the herding range, but replaced it with sour notions of the Reservation people. Whatever time of day we drove in, Browning always seemed a stunned place, snuffling in the dust from its chuckholed streets and bleary from booze or boredom or some worse affliction all its own.

The town's remnant of the Blackfeet nation seemed even more mauled than those who frequented Dupuyer—squinty leather-colored people, men with black braids dropping tiredly from under their cowboy hats, women so fat they seemed to waddle even standing still. These people dipped and veered along the sidewalks, entire families drunk by midday, cars racketing away with bodies spilled half out the windows.

Which was explainable enough: anyone who was industrious was out of sight somewhere earning a living, and to judge a people entirely by the Browning street scenes was as blinkered as walking into the non-Indian saloon crowds on a Saturday night in White Sulphur Springs or Dupuyer and declaring that no white person in the county could be capable of drawing a sober breath. Yet we did judge that way, and hard. When we met an Indian rancher at the eastern boundary of our lease land who was diligent and prosperous, Dad said: *Well, they can do some work if they want to, I guess. But most of them Browning bozoes ought to sign on for lessons from the Hoots.*

Since the Blackfeet never appeared out on their own landscape, we took advantage of the emptiness to become steady poachers, letting the pothole lakes feed us fresh meat.

Ducks and geese dabbled there all summer long, and our .22 rifle made a soft, quickly-gone *whinng* which couldn't be heard beyond the ridges. Dad and I had sharpshooting contests, trying to snick off the ducks' heads without touching the body meat. Spot, forever ready for trouble or help, instantly learned to retrieve; Grandma whooped orders and scoldings at him until he would deposit the birds to her gently as a feathery bouquet.

Life inside the trailer house was as cramped as life outside was unbounded. Our entire space was about twenty feet long and seven feet wide. Dad and I shared the bunk which went across one end; Grandma made her bed on the padded built-in bench which doubled as seating along one side of the table. Between the beds was walled a welter of tiny drawers, cabinets, closets, a cookstove, and the breadbox-sized battery radio on which Grandma listened to her soap operas in the mornings and Dad and I listened to the baseball broadcasts while the sheep were shaded down at midday.

The sun's heat hit the aluminum-painted roof of the trailer and went bowling off in dizzy wavers, but even so, the central part of the day inside our quarters was like being in a lidded stewpot. Time stretched and sagged. The dogs abandoned us and went to lie drooped and panting in the square of shade beneath the Jeep. When we weren't trying to doze through the hot hours, Dad and I read, Grandma either played solitaire or crocheted, periodically straightening her glasses in disgust and giving her commentary that *Wouldn't you just know, this thread keeps tangling itself six ways from Sunday.*

The one among us truly at ease with the drifting prairie life was Kitten, who instantly discovered himself to be a long-grass hunter. We would catch early-morning glimpses of him padding off through the ridgeline's shoetop-high veldt, an intent tiger the size and shade of a jackrabbit. To Grandma's agitation, Kitten always was away on a hunt whenever we moved the trailer house to a new site. Each time she would storm fretfully about his absence, each time Dad would declare, as if he knew everything about cats, *He'll turn up when he gets his fill of prowlin'*, and each time, that night or the next morning, Kitten would come purring in along the wheel tracks on the grass and leap casually into Grandma's lap.

But for the three of us cooped in the trailer house, this boundless northland—mockery again—seemed to be tightening and tightening our lives. The first weeks of July came, and the ewes were sheared by a Mexican crew who put up a canvas town amid the tan grass for two days and then vanished. The prairie hung even emptier once their musical jabber was gone. The land's tautness grew and grew into us until an afternoon in midsummer, when Dad got up from lunch to go look at the sheep.

He asked if I wanted to ride along. My nose sighted into a book, I said my usual *No, not unless you need me.* I recognize now that he did need me, in a way neither of us could have put to words then, but he said only no, he'd go alone, be back soon.

He came in the door an hour later pale and pawing his chin nervously. *What's got into you?* Grandma demanded. *Damn-it-to-hell,* he breathed: *I just almost shot a man.*

When he climbed into the Jeep to go, Dad as usual had taken his .30-30 hunting rifle with him. We had been warned in Browning that a dog pack was savaging sheep in the area, and *I want to be able to cut down on the bastards if they get into ours.* What caught his eye from the topmost lift of the ridgeline, however, was not a few dogs but an entire band of sheep, like a giant wedge aimed on a long ripping route all the way across our range. A band on the move of course was allowed to cross a person's range—a necessary code of the country—but these sheep were broadly flung and grazing, not being driven. It would take them three days to cross at their pace, and in that time they would scythe out our summer's best grass.

Dad drove down to the munching band, and pulled up near the herder and his dogs. *I said to old mister herder, 'these sheep are eatin' my prime range here, suppose ye can swing 'em nearer those north ridges and clear 'em out of here by tonight?' Big strappin' son-of-a-buck, he looks at me and says, 'I got a right to trail these sheep through here, I always have.' I says, 'Then why don't ye trail 'em?' Then he started cussin' and came right for me. He was set to drag me out and give me a good goin' over, he was.*

Startled, his hands still innocently on top of the steering wheel, Dad kicked the Jeep door open to show the .30-30 cradled across his lap. *That slowed the honyocker up some, you can just bet. He took a good look and backed off and put those dogs on the sheep and didn't stop until he was off our grass. But if he'd kept comin' at me there, I'd of had to pull the trigger on him . . .*

That day sobered us—Dad shoot someone? The deathly clap of the .30-30 shatter the prairie silence, blood spurt onto our lease grass?—as if we had been slapped from a trance. After that, I rode with Dad whenever he drove out to check on the sheep. Not the least of the lesson from the face-off was that if I had been with him instead of burrowed into a book, the two of us could have handled the charging herder without a rifle coming into it.

Grandma was subdued, on guard against herself from saying anything rilesome. Instead, one morning she came out with: *I just been thinking. I could take a turn looking at the sheep if I could drive the Jeep. Suppose you can learn me?* Apron flapping, this woman who had teamstered horses in weather and terrain most people wouldn't set foot into now strode out with Dad and me and settled nervously behind the first steering wheel of her life. Although she never would venture onto a road or be talked into trying for a driver's license—*I'm scared of that written part*—the Reservation's expanses after this regularly heard the sound of her grinding the Jeep along in low gear, bonused with the *beep!* of surprise as she brushed against the horn button every so often.

Dad made his own conciliation. He suggested that Grandma and I make a visit to White Sulphur Springs for a week. *I know you want to see your family there, Lady, you deserve to and I'll be all right alone here. I'll see there's no more funny business like that rifle affair. The two of you go.*

We did go, did our visiting. The Smith River Valley seemed to me to lay beneath narrower castled horizons now. Where was the expanse, the sense of living at the ridgeline of the entire continent, in any of this? Yet where in our summer trailer or in the Jensen house was any of the knit of the past which each of us, and Grandma most of all, still could feel from the valley?

I drove us north again wondering to myself how we were going to fend. If I wanted to look at our situation in its coldest light—and being a worrying youngster, I did—the three of us added up to a makeshift family who lived in half a house for two-thirds of a year and then trooped off onto the prairie to exist more oddly yet. It was nothing to recommend to the rest of society. But say this for ourselves, we still were together, after nearly four years of grimly cobbled truces between Dad and Grandma. And I found, as I mulled it, that a knack for cobbling was not a small thing from this thin-tempered pair.

I had another fret when we were back with Dad on the ridgeline and I rode with him to look at the sheep: *These lambs just don't look as big to me as the ones were at the*

Camas. Dad had a grinning answer for that: *They're not. But they're heavier. The grass is so crisp up here it packs a hard fat on 'em. They won't be roly-poly like the ones in the Smith River country, but they'll weigh like all hell when we ship 'em.*

He was right. On the late September weekend when we chuted the lambs into stock cars at a railroad siding north of our range, their poundage made it a festivity. McGrath broke into a crooked-toothed smile as he penciled the profit figures. Spot meanwhile outdid himself as a virtuoso among sheep-dogs. Even Tip, cruising along the outside of the shipping pens to grab bites of sheep whenever he saw the chance, seemed surprised to look up once and find his brother bounding atop the backs of a crammed knot of ewes to get to his next tactical position. I had heard that highest phrase of praise, *a dog that'll run on wool,* but never had seen it done until Spot performed. A railroad worker asked Dad who had trained the white-and-brown dog. *My mother-in-law right there,* Dad said with his admitting grin. *She's got him so he'll do everything but dance the schottische.* Grandma answered with a deeply pleased *hmpf!*

September also meant that I had to come off the Reservation for my second year at Valier, now with the notion beginning in me that I had better become more purposeful about what I studied. This did nothing to cure me of randomly reading whatever print I could lay my hands on, but it did get me over the delusion that I ever was going to be anything as exotic as a baseball player. I didn't even have a right knee that worked properly, although the doctor said I was in the last year of having to wrap the daily elastic pressure onto it.

When I tried to think of other choices of life ahead, ranching held itself up first. By now I knew much about livestock, especially sheep-raising, and Dad could teach me endlessly more. If that was where life was pointing with this fresh start in the north, our family chance at last to count up the profits that could lead to the buy of a ranch, there might be a logic behind it. I enrolled for the high school's vocational agriculture class. But I also chose Mrs. Tidyman's Latin class, and found I was at least as interested in the textbook version of Caesar's farmers—*Galba agricola est*—as I was in vo-ag's mechanized version.

The school had a new superintendent now, a silent large-headed man who seemed to have to spend his full time trying to look dignified. The effort went to doom at once when someone learned that his middle name was Eldo. As far as I could tell in the rest of my high school days, he showed never an idea about education except to patrol around it with *El-do, El-do* mocking off his measured footsteps. But I see now that his ambling route may have been lucky for any of us trying to learn, ignoring as it did whatever useful that Mrs. Tidyman and one or two others of the teachers resorted to in the classroom.

By second luck, I had arrived at Valier into an unusually self-steadying group of classmates. High school often is written of as a torchlit, raucous time, when friendships and enmities sear deepest. Perhaps because I had so much blaze elsewhere in my life, my high school class seems to me now, as then, a regiment of calm.

A dozen girls and ten boys, ours was the most equable population I had ever belonged to. Mrs. Tidyman could give out more uproar reading a paragraph of Dickens than the bunch of us might in a week. No one was particularly prettier or handsomer than those in the classes which had gone through before us, nor I think any more winsome or wicked; but several of us were more persevering than was usual, and a surprising number had more cleverness. I found, after Mrs. Tidyman's keelhauling examination of me when I first arrived, that I got along easily at the school. Clearly I was an odd commodity—my mind did tricks nobody else's did, nor did anyone else come out of anything like my sheep ranch–Reservation–Dupuyer cafe jumble of backdrop, nor were most of the other boys quite as stoic as I seemed about the subject of girls—yet none of these classmates seemed more than bemused by any of it. And I did contribute the point of pride that in those school-wide exams, I could be counted on to trounce everyone else in the school for us.

I went through the school year, then, to three steady pulses: days at classes in Valier, nights at the Chadwicks', weekends on the Jensen ranch with Dad and Grandma. Just once did this rhythmed northern life threaten to fly apart. In early December, out of nowhere, Grandma announced to us that she was going to spend Christmas with her sister in Wisconsin.

I had not been at the ranch while that decision brewed, but knew that there was little holiday flavor to it. *She'll get it out of her system this way,* Dad said, *and maybe then. . . .* And maybe then come back and tell us the trip had been so clarifying that she was going to keep on right out of our lives, yes, I could see all the *and maybe then.*

What the episode was all about, I never knew, nor did Dad seem to have any notion. Perhaps my grandmother simply reached a point where she had to make some test on life for herself, and certainly her turn was long overdue. We said an apprehensive goodbye to her at the bus station in Great Falls. She gave us a frosty farewell and marched aboard.

I had no idea how the ranch household could run without her. To my surprise, Dad housekept diligently. He cooked as heartily as she had—I had forgotten his stint in the White Sulphur cafe—and we lived in high style on venison steak and the rich milk gravy he made from the fry grease to layer over discs of fried potatoes. But the house echoed empty enough to boom lessons into us, and Christmas spluttered in and away as a wan day we were glad to see end. When Grandma arrived back in her promised two weeks, cheerful and full of scorn for Wisconsin—*Gee gosh, I forgot how dampish the winters come back there*—we were overfed and entirely eager to have her with us again.

The winter went in truce, then it was the lambing season again, the moment for another of the Jensen ranch's routine springtime calamities to conk us. A mid-May blizzard hit, and in a day and a night sealed the ranch in fat heavy snowdrifts. The Hoots came crashing across the benchland with a giant bulldozer and punched our way to the stranded bunches of sheep. We had some loss, but not nearly what it might have been, and at the start of summer we pushed the sheep north to the Reservation with the thought in our minds that this year's worst lay behind us.

But as soon as the Mexican crew finished shearing the sheep in the first few days of July, worry and edginess set in on Dad. The weather had an unaccountable chill—*Gee gods, is it gonna snow on us for the Fourth of July?* Grandma demanded of the sky—and with our shorn ewes we had on our hands a double thousand of the world's most undressed creatures, caught in only their paunchy yellow-white carcasses like hospital invalids with their gowns suddenly ripped away. Within a week, the sheep would be gray and hardy again, their next fat round sponge of fleece already beginning to cloak them. But for these first days, they stood naked, helpless to a storm. And dragging across the spire-line of the Rockies, black clouds, somehow sprung ahead from cold late autumn into July, were beginning to fray into rain.

Early on the second morning after shearing, Dad came back to the trailer house gnawing his lower lip. He had not turned the sheep out of the temporary corral where we were penning them these first uncomfortable nights. The nightmare prospect was that the band could panic in the corral and crush onto one another in suicidal piles. For certain, in a cold driving rain hundreds of trapped ewes would destroy themselves and their lambs that way. But the second worst threat was for a storm to maul into sheep loose for stampede on this unsheltered range, and this was the risk the swollen clouds were forcing on us now.

That weather's comin' in sure as hell. We're gonna have to hightail it for the brush on Two Medicine with these sheep. Lady, you'll have to work the dogs; dog the bejesus out of 'em. Ivan can run, he can get on the head end of the band and try push 'em toward that big coulee. I'll take the Jeep to round in the breakaways. The first blast of wind swayed the trailer. We piled out the doorway into the longest hours of our lives.

Before we could reach the corral, a sharp rain began to sting down. The mountains had vanished, and the gray which blotted them already was taking the ridgeline. Chill sifted into the air as the rain drilled through. Now a wind steadily sharpening the storm's attack. The sheep milled in the corral as if being stirred by a giant paddle, quickening and quickening. A stalled wave of them had begun to pack so tightly against the wooden gate that Dad and I together couldn't undo the wire that held it closed; the gate bowed, snapped apart against the tonnage of the hundreds of struggling bodies.

The pale shapes of the ewes rivered past us, slapped and spun us. Lambs dashed at their mothers' heels in blatting bewilderment. *Shoo 'em, Spot!* Grandma was shrilling. *Way 'round 'em there. Bite 'em good, Tip, God darn their crazy hides!* I ran the first sprint of endless running, crying *Hyaw! Hyaw!* as I tried to head the leaders. I heard the Jeep gunning as Dad set out after another runaway group.

What we faced, if we could not bring the band under control, was a rapid steady push toward the devastation of our sheep. The rain was pelting out of the north. As it spun the cold terrified sheep straight south before it, they were aimed like an avalanche to the cliffs which bladed up from the gorge of the Two Medicine. Countless of them could crash off there as the buffalo had in their fear-blind rush from the whooping Blackfeet. Only, our animals were being driven on to death by a clamor which could not be stilled—the howl of storm.

One way alone offered any chance to get the sheep safely down to the shelter of the river brush: try to funnel them along the bottom of the single big coulee which dived like a long trench across our range and out through the western base of the Two Medicine rimrocks. But to do it, we would have to fight the sheep west into the cleft of coulee, sideways along the punishing storm.

And so we fought, running, raging, hurling the dogs and ourselves at the waves of sheep, flogging with the gunny sacks we had grabbed off a corral post, shaking the wire rings of cans to a din, and steadily as the rain shot down on us, we lost ground. We were like skirmishers against a running army. We might bend the band slightly and gradually toward the coulee, but all the while their circling panic was carrying toward the cliffs now not more than a few thousand yards away. Only several minutes away for sheep running headlong. It was not yet midday, and grayness had clamped in on the ridgeline over us as if to rain for the rest of time.

We could do nothing right in the curtaining rain. I hurled my ring of cans to head off a breakaway ewe, and the wire circle fell neatly over her neck and sent her clattering crazily across the prairie at twice the speed. Minutes later, I tossed a rock as I had a thousand times to scare another ewe back into the band. The wet stone slipped in my hand, wobbled straight for the ewe and hit her exactly at the joint of the hind leg. Broken leg flapping as she struggled at the rear of the band, she haunted me everlastingly that day. I threw nothing more, tried and failed to make up for it with sack-flailing runs to turn the band. Grandma's voice was wearing to a croak. I saw the Jeep bounce into a badger hole so hard that Dad sat blinking for a minute to collect himself.

Now, slowly, wearily, some of the sheep began to stop running. They sank to the ground to die. Nothing could move them—kicking, lifting, even Tip's attacks. Exhausted and freezing, they jutted their necks flat along the ground, rolled their eyes, and did their dying. We abandoned these stragglers, humped white on the prairie behind us like small boulders left by a glacier, and fought on with the sheep still eddying across the grassland.

Then, for minutes, the rain eased away.

It left a sensation of acute, tingling emptiness, as in a blackened snagland after crownfire has hurtled through. Then Dad was roaring: *Give 'em hell now!* Grandma charged the southmost bulge of the sheep with the dogs, and Dad jounced the Jeep, horn button mashed down in a steady blare, into the head of the band where I was whooping myself hoarse. We rammed the animals a few hundred yards westward, close now to where the coulee shadowed darkest on the darkened land.

What achieved the last atom of push for us, there is no knowing—perhaps some instant of Spot's savvy or Tip's savagery, perhaps a whip of wind momentarily lashing around in our favor instead of against us. Perhaps only the force field of our desperation. Whatever levered them the last inches to the west, a trickling few sheep at the front of the sodden swirl at last were dodging into the coulee, and the main mass pressing blindly after them.

It cost us the rear hundreds of the band. When the rain bulleted harder again, a frenzied surge of ewes broke sideways around the dogs and spilled away from us like wheat out of a tipped sack. The rest of the sheep we held, barely, at the ground we had gained, and watched the breakaways scuttle across the rain-beaten grass toward the cliffs.

Now the battle in the coulee became one both to hurry and to hold back. The sheep trying to plunge ahead of the rain's flay still could pile themselves to destruction in the veers of the coulee's banked sides and had to be headed, beaten to a slower pace; the ones beginning to give up and drop had to be savaged into moving on. Dad abandoned the Jeep, came leaping down the coulee flank to join Grandma and me. The long white vee of sheep accordioned wildly down the coulee as we pushed and held, held and pushed.

None of the three of us said a word now, our voices long since given out. If the dogs yet barked as they knifed back and forth along the band, we did not notice. Silently Dad and Grandma and I flogged sheep with the damp gunnysacks as if they were a stubborn wall of flame and watched for the mouth of the coulee to inch out of the rain toward us.

We reached it in almost-dark, and the sheep spewed down beneath the juts of cliff to the river's sheltering brim of willows and cottonwoods. In a dozen hours, we had managed to flog 3500 desperate sheep a little more than four miles. A hundred or more carcasses spotted the prairie behind us, dozens more strewed the base of the cliffs which the runaway clump had avalanched toward. If this was victory—and we had to tell ourselves it was, for we could have lost nearly all the sheep in a pushing massacre off the Two Medicine cliffs—I knew I wanted no part of any worse day.

I remember that I looked back from the mouth of the coulee toward the dusky north ridges, still smoked with gray wisps of the storm. As much as at any one instant in my life, I can say: *here I was turned.*

How long such a moment had been in the making, I am the last to judge, because once made it seemed to have begun farther back than I could remember and yet to have happened like an eyeblink. Two decades later, readying to write about a man who had recently retired after decades of fame as a forestry scientist, I asked him in midinterview how he had found his way into his career. Until then he had been talking easily and in deft detail, but here he hesitated as if fretful. Finally, in no more words than this, he told me of simply deciding one afternoon, when he was a schoolboy plowing in his father's field in Indiana, that he would go off as soon as he could and become a chemist. Helpless to find any deeper decision back inside himself, he eyed me with both plea and challenge in his face.

But any questioning was gone from me, lost in the recognition that I had just heard so close a chord with my own unwordable instant. As soon as I could manage to do so after that July storm, over Grandma's dismayed protest and Dad's unspoken one, I left the Reservation to find myself a job for the rest of the summer—piling bales in the hayfields of a ranch south of Dupuyer. I had no steady idea about what I would do in life, but I intended now that it would not include more seasons of sheep on that vast gambling table of Blackfeet rangeland.

It startles me yet that I was the first, even as mildly and temporarily as I went about it, to declare my way out of our edgy alliance of a household. Dad nearly achieved it before I could, for the mauling the sheep had taken left its toll on him, too. What had been a year of certain profit now was going to be one more time of eking by, of hard and skillful work drawing small wage. Before I could leave for my hayfield job, a noontime spat built and built between Grandma and him, like the clouds boiling again on the peak-flames of the Rockies. At last he announced: *The hell with ye, I'm going into Browning.* She said in ice, *Go drinking beer, I suppose. You're damn right,* he said in fire, and flung off over the ridgeline in the Jeep. He was gone for the day, and then the night. When he came back the next noon, the extent of his plunge stunned us all, and we passed around it with as little said as possible. Erupting loose that way from whatever it was that held us together was not a thing we dared look at too closely, for within the past half year each of the three of us now had shown some such urge, and I would be off for the next several weeks across some boundary best known to my sixteen-year-old self.

When I went from the Reservation that midsummer to my first work as a hired hand, in effect I stepped across time to Dad's life at the same age, going off to try to earn from the very surroundings which had been so stingy to the larger household. But where under him the broad muscles of horses had rippled and become a way of life, beneath me machinery throbbed. In the hot weather of that year and the next ones to come, I learned to keep the pace of piling eighty-pound hay bales all day long onto a moving truck, of cocooning inside the roar and dust of tractors crawling across wheat fields, of steadying a grain truck beside a lurching combine to catch the harvested flow of gold. The north country opened and beckoned for me as the sage distances of the valley must have for Dad at my age. Clock hours changed, stretched, in that summer light: lunch happened whenever food arrived in the field, to be eaten gratefully in the shaded dust beneath a tractor or truck, supper came into the schedule when at last it was too dark to do anything else.

The Reservation's glacier of slow weeks was left to Dad and Grandma now, to fend with that and themselves however they could. In another of the unspoken but obstinate bargains our household ran on, I would help with the trailing of the sheep at the start of each summer, and with the first week or so of settling into the routine of the ridgeline. But then I would go. I could be expected to visit whenever I had a rare Sunday off from work, but all the other days of my summers were my own now—and I meant them to run full and swift.

I learned rapidly that I either had luck or had to make it. My second summer of hiring out, I heard of a job on a ranch somewhere far to the north of the Reservation, near a point on the Canadian boundary called Whiskey Gap. I asked Dad for the loan of the old Dodge car we had acquired and set off, fighting mud-greased roads and taking directions at any house I saw—few of those—until at last, fifty miles beyond Browning and within a glance of the Canadian border, I found the ranch. Dusk was going to dark, and no one answered my knock. I stepped out of my muddy shoes on the porch, walked in and went to sleep on the couch in the living room. In a few hours when the rancher came home and snapped on the light, his wife large-eyed behind him, I said my name and Dad's, and asked if I could have the job. Apparently as a reward for having found the place at all, I could.

The job was to drive a grain truck, and exactly at an impatient time in my growing up it fed me all the velocity and throttle-power I could ask for. The rancher's grown son, a lanky grinning man named Ron, drove one elderly red truck, I drove its mate. By gunning along the narrow graveled dike of road as fast as we dared, we could make one haul to the grain elevator at Cut Bank in the morning and another in the afternoon. There was a very long breakneck hill in the middle of the run which Ron and I traded jokes about. *I had the world moving on my last load,* he would drawl; *By the time I hit the bottom of that sonofabitch hill I must have been going a thousand miles an hour.*

Near the end of the summer, I was slamming my truck into higher gear on a flat stretch of the road when I saw a shallow trench of potholes ahead. With no traffic coming, I swerved at a slight angle across the holes to reduce the jolt. There was a bounce, and a second, and the horizon plunged away as a concussion crumpled the rear of the truck down into a howling tilting skid, dust fuming into the cab, metal screaming on gravel.

At last I sat, stopped, looking straight up into the air, gripping the steering wheel which now haloed above my face. I groped the door open and bailed for the road. The truck angled above me like a monstrous being with a broken lower back. I looked blankly toward where the rear wheels had to be, and there were none.

It took me long minutes amid the spilled wheat and strewn gravel to track out what had happened. The rear spring on one side of the truck, weakened from an old break, had snapped entirely when the wheels struck the potholes, and the following force of the other side hitting the depression wrenched away the truck's underbody, springs, axle, wheels and all.

When the rancher arrived and had a look, he said I was not to blame myself and it was time he bought a new truck anyway. I was behind a steering wheel for him again the next morning. When the chance came to spend a Sunday with Dad and Grandma, I showed them the newspaper clipping about my accident. *You were lucky that once,* Grandma said in judgment, as if I hadn't been thinking it every instant since. *I'm no example to talk,* Dad offered, *but no job is worth your neck.* The next summer, when I was working fields for a farmer near Dupuyer, I came in from the tractor one sunset to hear that a truck had been wrecked on the breakneck hill, killing its driver: Ron.

Now that I had gone across one line of decision in the summer of the storm-hit sheep, it began to dawn on me that I was edging across the next one. Ranching no longer seemed what I wanted. That clarifying idea, and likely Mrs. Tidyman's gale-force enthusiasm, pointed toward college. For Grandma, my first mention of it was the knell that one more person she had labored for would be on his way from her. But: *If that's the how of it for you, boy, you better do it.* Dad came around to the idea so rapidly and entirely that he began to think of it as his own. *By God, yes, you want to get into some other sort of living. Ranching is a hard go unless you inherit a hellish amount of land and have the health to work it. I never had those, and maybe you won't either.* One of his brothers had managed to send a son to college to become a pharmacist; Dad suggested that I think about the same. I didn't know what livelihood I wanted, but pharmacy didn't sound like it. Dad shrugged. *Do whatever it is ye want, son, and we'll back ye just as far as we can.*

Any backing to be drawn from a life divided between the Jensen ranch and the Reservation, I knew, was chancy. It became chancier a few days after I finished my next-to-last year of high school. The morning of our third spring gather of the sheep for the Reservation drive, we had edged the band onto the highway when Grandma missed Kitten's annual yowls from the trailer house: *The good-for-nothing, where's he got to?* Somehow Kitten had squirmed his way out, and Dad sent me back to the ranch in the Jeep to look for him. I found the cat in the yard there, and also a family who were moving into the house still warm from our leaving. *Got it leased for a couple of years,* they retorted when I demanded to know how long they would be there.

Even McGrath, seasoned conniver that he was, seemed shaken by the wordless withdrawal of the Jensen ranch from us. And Dad and Grandma now faced a Reservation summer with no point of return at its end.

The one thing plain in this new muddle was that the arrangement with McGrath was fractured. The three of us were agreed that we wanted no more of his risky ranches and jinxed sheep. Also, if the summer could be passed without catastrophe roaring in from the mountains or grabbing up out of the earth, this would at last be a year when we had made good money from the sheep and could afford some new start. *How about if we stay on until Mac can sell the ewes this fall?* Dad suggested. *Might take a month or so after the lambs are shipped, but we can tell him that's all, we're walking away from his damned sheep if he's not rid of them by then . . . Good enough,* I said. . . . *Hunky-dory by me,* Grandma said, *I won't shed tears over old McGrath. . . .*

It was this final herding season for Dad and Grandma that I spent on the trucking job near the Canadian border, and my exploded truck was not the only blast mark on our summer. I arrived to visit at the trailer house one Sunday to be told that Kitten had vanished several days before; Dad figured that an eagle had ended his stalking career. Another Sunday, as I stepped from the car only Spot pawed ecstatically up at me. *Where's Tip?* I asked quickly, and Grandma's face told me that there no longer was a Tip. Dad again gave me the details: the black dog at last had become the casualty of his chasing-and-biting habit, sneaking from camp to run with a dog pack on the range west along the Two Medicine. Dad had heard in Browning that the sheepmen came onto the dogs and shot several of them in their tracks; Tip had to have been among them. *He got what he was asking for . . .*

Grandma began and broke off in silent tears as Spot eyed around at us to choose one for his next fond nuzzle.

Only the sheep seemed immune from calamity that summer. The lambs fattened and fattened, and brought a top price at shipping time. McGrath next located stubblefields south of Dupuyer where the ewes could graze for a few weeks. That autumn's trailing of the sheep southward was our longest ever, nearly sixty miles. Dad and Grandma wearily waited in the trailer house amid the blond stubble for the sale of the sheep. A buyer was found, the ewes we had struggled over for a dozen seasons in the Jensen ranch–Reservation rhythm of years now vanished in a gray blatting stream into boxcars. On a day in early November of 1956, we drove north to Cut Bank to settle our finances with McGrath. Dodgy as ever, he was to meet us in a hotel room there.

I spent the trip dreaming of showdowns: *Give us our money or I'll break your ugly damn face.* I could all but hear the same battle breaking out in Grandma's mind: *God darn you ornery old cuss, we did all the work for three years and you think you're gonna keep the money in your dirty paws; you got another think coming. . . .* As we parked in front of the hotel, Dad said, *I want you two to wait here. I know how I'm going to handle this.* Half an hour later, he climbed in the car and showed us a check for our full share. McGrath had taken our calculations without a question, made out our amount and said only: *You people did a powerful amount of work for me.*

The one thing the three of us agreed on next was that we should not move away in this, my last year of high school. If there was any mooring in our lives now, it was my schooling. We moved into a small house in Dupuyer beyond the Chadwicks', a place with all its space in one expansive room, as if the walls of the trailer house had been pulled several times wider and longer. Again my paperback books teetered in stacks as they had in Ringling, again Grandma pulled out a daybed for herself each night. Spot strewed himself beneath our feet as amply as Shep ever had.

Weary of the steady life with the sheep—*Godamighty, Lady, do ye realize it's been nineteen months since either of us had a day off?* Dad ground out one evening—Dad and Grandma decided to wait until spring to look for their next work. When the ranches busied up then, a lambing man of his skills and a cook of hers would have no trouble finding jobs.

The leisure had its uses. Three years almost to the moment from when we had first seen the Sawtooth Mountains carving their canyons of stone into the sky edge, we at last had time to set foot in the range. On a crisp and bright deer-hunting day, Dad shot a fat young buck beneath one of the great rimfolds driven up into the blue; Tommy Chad and I skidded the carcass down through the scree and timber and we had meat for weeks to come. Grandma visited with Gertie at the cafe, and as we should have known it would, work came looking for her. Dupuyer lacked babysitters, especially babysitters with five raisings of children to their credit. Grandma began spending entire days with the small daughters of a family busy with travel, then evenings for other families. When a night came that two stints of work were offered her at once, she eyed Dad: *Why don't you take this other one, Charlie?* I looked at him for the fight to start. Instead he answered, *Yes, and why the hell don't I?*

Through the evenings of winter after that, the two of them regularly went babysitting several times a week. The notion at first embarrassed me; it didn't seem genuine work for grownups, especially for my top-hand father. But I began to see that they both enjoyed the change of task and scene. The household was easier to breathe in when we weren't crammed against each other every moment. The pair of them soon had more babysitting than they could handle, and I took some evenings of it myself. It was, I suppose, a way for Dupuyer to lend us a hand, and for us to lend one in turn, not the least of the town's graceful moments in our life.

In that last year of high school, 180 classroom days between me and the world, I began threshing for ways to go away to college. I did not know it, and it seemed least likely, but the one ally more I needed I met on the football field.

I had begun playing the autumn before, when my knee finally was declared healed. My season was brief that time: as if the quadrants of my body were going to take turns about this, my left hand was fractured in one of the first scrimmages. I suppose in the way Dad never had hesitated to swing back into a saddle after another of his near-destructions on horseback, it didn't occur to me not to try football again—although it did to Grandma, who loudly sounded her *Gee gosh, you be careful now.*

As it turned out, on the field at the first practice a new coach was waiting, a chunky, sharp-eyed man in his early twenties. His name was McCarthy; he had grown up in the smelter town of Anaconda and gone through a small Jesuit college on a football scholarship. He told me, without ever having seen me before, that I would be his fullback. Given Valier's small enrollment and the lack of heft among the seniors, he had decided simply to field the four quickest of us as running backs, like dice flipped across green felt. *You'll be the blocking back, since you're heftier than Butch or Vern or Glenn*—at 155 pounds I actually was only the least featherlike—*and we'll show these teams some footsteps.*

We did. Ours was the fastest backfield in the conference, and the most fitful. On the first play of the season we scored on an 89-yard run, and went on to lose the game. When we managed to mesh ourselves—something less than half the time—easy wins scatted onto our record. Other games, we simply whooshed up and down the field between the goal lines instead of across them, perpetually within a touchdown of stronger and more methodical teams and exasperating everyone except McCarthy, who seemed to enjoy our velocity for its own sake.

The season of football was one of the least useful and most purely pleasant things I had ever done, a time taken out from life simply to run and roll, like a colt discovering his gallop. Perhaps it was a reward for my willingness to be an atomweight fullback for him, perhaps he simply liked to see a person spin free and be off to somewhere: McCarthy out of the blue asked my college plans, listened to my vague notion that I guessed I would aim for science or engineering, and told me that I should think about journalism.

It may have been the first time I heard the word *journalism* spoken. But: *you've read more than any kid I've ever seen, and if you've been paying attention in there to the Last Duchess*—Mrs. Tidyman—*like I think you have, you've learned something about the language.*

Here was advice which could have come from nowhere else in my life. For all her interest in me, Mrs. Tidyman could not have brought herself to single out one direction from her whirling compass of learning, and no one else I knew had ever offered more than the vague encouragement that *with a head like that on your shoulders you ought to go on to college.*

Throughout the autumn and start of winter, I sent off applications to colleges and took exams in any scholarship competition I could find. Mrs. Tidyman thirty years before had gone away to Illinois for summer courses at Northwestern University; I automatically applied there. I read somewhere that rich universities such as Harvard and Princeton admitted a proportion of moneyless students; off went my paperwork. And to a dozen others, according to no plan but hope. No one seemed to know another method besides my own of flooding mail out across the map; no one in either line of my family had ever gone beyond high school, and even Mrs. Tidyman could not recall the last Valier student who had attended an out-of-state college.

Amid it all, Eldo stopped me in the assembly hall and said he wanted to see me in his office. When I stepped in, he picked up the latest of my scholarship applications and shook his wide head. *Ivan, all this isn't worth it. These eastern places you're applying to, a student from a school this size just doesn't have a chance. Make up your mind to go to the university at Missoula, and you won't let yourself in for disappointment.* He held the application toward me. *I don't feel I can put in any more of my time on these things.*

From then, I knew that I would go to one of the far universities if I had to walk there on my knees and murder to get in. Eldo was not a man for a goading strategy. In telling me that he was tired of the scholarship paperwork, he was simply reciting fact, and saying as well that he was weary of me and my beavering ambition. But writing me off was the one valuable thing he could have done for me. I went to my backers with his verdict. *That's very interesting,* Mrs. Tidyman said with deadly evenness; *I think you should apply and apply, and I'll write any recommendations you need. Goddamn-that-Eldo-to-hell,* Dad burred; *you go on and get one of those scholarships just to show that scissorbill.*

A winter of waiting, the babysitting winter. Then with the first of spring, a letter from Northwestern saying that I had been granted a four-year scholarship for full tuition. I had won that much. Now the question became how the rest of my victory could be afforded.

Dad and Grandma quickly went back to ranch work, now for a Two Medicine rancher named McTaggart. He was a high crag of a man, wintry, boulder-jawed, long-boned, who had been battling the northern plains for half a century and at last had edged far enough ahead of nature to own a ranch and a few thousand head of sheep. No one was deceived that McTaggart and Dad and Grandma made a ranch combination that could last long—*We'll be lucky if we can put up with his guff through lambing time,* Dad grumped—yet the three of them somehow went week after week without igniting.

When I visited from the Chadwicks' on weekends, McTaggart in the evenings would fix himself by the hour on a topic such as my going off to Northwestern and recite his history around it in a nervous, twining style. He too had gone to Chicago as a young man, he told, spending some months there when he worked for a buyer who dealt in Montana ranch horses. *We took 'em into Chicago to the 'yards for him. There was one bunch they wanted for lead horses for the race track. Them hot-blooded horses, you know, they got to lead 'em in—that fella with the white pants and the red jacket and big hat, you know, he leads 'em in on some gentle cow pony, might be a Apaloosy or somethin'. I had these nine, ten ponies headed out for Washington Park race track, then old Bill caught up to me, says Oh, I made a mistake, we unloaded 'em the wrong place, you gotta take 'em out to Arlington Park race track. So I just tailed them load of horses to one another and away*

I went down—there's a street, Halsted Street—went down that with them ponies about 35 miles to Arlington Heights. Had kids followin' me all the way. An' I made it, no trouble, they was gentle enough ponies. One of 'em I used to ride out here and he used to buck me off whenever he wanted, but back there he'd got on good behavior. First thing at the race track, he's so pretty, they give him a bath and put one of those muley saddles on, and I had to get on and ride him around the race track, show him off good and plenty. Oh, I been to Chicago, nnnhnnnn.

Dad said he could talk McTaggart into hiring me for the summer before I went to college. Grandma pointed out it would be our last time together *before you go off so awful far away*. But I still wanted my summer distance, and gave the one argument I thought was sure, that I could make more money at tractor work on a farm than on the ranch with them. *You never done any of that work before,* Grandma rallied. I said the unanswerable: *I'll learn.*

A few mornings after my graduation from high school, I hunkered atop the cleated treads of a Caterpillar tractor big as a locomotive and studied what seemed to be the control gadgetry for the entire solar system. With the farmer all but moving my hands through the patterns, I memorized the switchwork and the moves to start the Cat's rackety warming motor, the control levers inside the sheet-metal cab, then another battery of hydraulic levers to raise and lower the equipment being pulled behind the tractor. He rode with me a few rounds on the field, showing me the quick dance of brake-and-clutch to lurch the monster around corners, and said *She's all yours.*

I could see that the field corners were going to be the gantlet: the Cat had to be sharply angled in its turn, kinked back on its own path until it swiveled the wide harrow around behind it, instant calculation upon calculation to keep the roaring train of equipment from mangling itself. In my first hour, I kinked the tractor through a turn an instant too long. The cataract of steel tread caught the hitch of the harrow, bowed and twisted it to taffy.

I shut down the Cat and stood looking at the tangle. I could read the Latin of whatever Caesar's farmers had done, but would I ever decipher this gigantic equipment of my own? Sick with failure, I drove into Dupuyer with the crumpled hitch. The farmer scowled at it, then saw my face. *Well, don't get in an uproar over it. The kid I had last summer did this three times on his first day. Try not to beat his record. I'll forge 'er back into shape.* He did, and in the hundreds of hours of field work afterward that summer, I ran the tractor and its caravan of equipment as faultlessly as if on rails.

That set of summer months, an even twenty years ago as I come to write this, stands out as a season in dream. Shuddered throb of the Cat, curved tines of harrow digging by the battalion behind me, marching chocolate lines of worked field, cold flame-peaks spacing the western horizon —everything of each day was rhythm, pulse, pattern, and within such propulsion, like a space traveler sledding through orbit, I could cast myself free into every luster of my life to come. Four college years of reading *how many books can that be? dozens and scores and hundreds* perfect grades *Dad saying: you're right up there with the best of them in the world now* eyes of a girl inches away *Carlton says it is like losing your breath over and over* words of my own in print *how to begin? Montana today is a land of far fields uncommon people* a flow of money *Grandma: I never knew they pay wages like that* and then, then . . .

Then tugging of gravity, a letter in a long envelope. The last editorial I had written for the school paper had been noticed at the university in Missoula. The dean of journalism was asking if I would be interested in a scholarship there, and if he could come talk to me.

When I phoned Mrs. Tidyman from the cafe in Dupuyer, she told me the dean had been a Rhodes Scholar, an honor so vast I had heard of it. Early into the next week he drove to Dupuyer and was directed to where I was farming that day. Tall, trim, in white shirt and tie, he toed across the furrowed field to where I was pulling the armada of harrow behind the Caterpillar. As I stepped down from the Cat and dustily shook hands, he said, *What is this, a discer?* and I learned at once that Rhodes Scholars didn't know everything in the world. But he talked earnestly, seemed unbothered as he stood with the soft field dirt trickling into his lowcut shoes, and asked if I wanted, really, to be away from Montana.

For all the dreaming, that was the question somewhere in me, and his asking of it and the promise of a scholarship at Missoula made me rethink. One way and another, Dad and Grandma and I had survived much together. She now was sixty-four years old, and although she gave every evidence of enduring forever, I had begun to think of her age, and the sum that would go from my life when she did. Dad was fifty-seven, still a top hand but with his lifetime's worth of breakages in him.

Even beyond the two of them, there were the decades of effort of the other Doigs and Ringers, a weight of striving in these Montana hills and valleys and prairies which added up to the single great monument my family line would ever have. For me to go from this would be a reverse trek, in a sense, from the immigration which had borne my people into the high-mountain West. Yet they had sprung themselves free of the past when they felt they had to, and that was my own urge.

I took the decision to McTaggart's ranch the next weekend. Grandma brightened: *That'd be closer to home, if you went over to Missoula. Chicago is such a long old ways away*. Dad shook his head. *You got to do the deciding, Skavinsky. We'll-back-you-to-the-limit-whatever-place-you-go.*

The train to Chicago stood like an endless wall of windows. Each of the three of us snuffled in the September air, turned aside to swallow. Grandma's teary hug: as ever, she had talked herself around to the conviction that whatever I had made up my mind to do was the only thing, *you write us about it all and I'll do the like.* Dad's clamping handshake: in awe of all the education awaiting me, *You're away to a big place, son.*

Aboard, I had a minute of looking out the window to them, the one stout and erect and eternal as a pillar, the other handsome as glory under the perfect crimp of his stockman's hat. The train gave off sounds, and the depot platform rafted away behind me with the two of them.

Kin *and* clan. Son. Sire. *The* grand *calved on in* grandson, grandmother. *The words of all the ties of blood interest me, for they seem never quite deft enough, not entirely bold and guileful enough, to speak the mysterious strengths of lineage. I admit the marvel that such sounds are carried to us from the clangs and soughs of tongues now silent a millennium into the past, calling on and on, in their way, like pulses of light still traveling in from gone stars. But the offhand resonance of* bobolink *arrives that way too, and* sneeze *and* whicker *and* daisy *and thousandfold words more. What I miss in our special blood-words is a sense of recasting themselves for each generation, each fresh situation of kindredness. It seems somehow too meager that they should merely exist, plain packets of sound like any other, and not hold power to texture each new conformation with the bright exact tones that are yearned for.*

This example: here is a man and here a woman. In the coming light of one June morning, the same piece of life is axed away from each of them. Wounded hard, they go off to their private ways. Until at last the wifeless man offers across to the daughter-robbed woman. And I am the agreed barter between them.

Not even truth brought down to bone this way can begin to tell what I long to of the situation shared by my father and my grandmother and myself during the years I call from memory here. For my father had to be more than is coded in the standard six-letter sound of father, *he had also to be guardian-to-an-adrift-boy and as well, mate-who-was-not-a-husband to the daunting third figure of the household. In turn that figure, my loving thunder-tempered grandmother, who never had thought through roles of life but could don the most hazardous ones as automatically as her apron, had somehow to mother me without the usual claims to authority for it, and at the same time to treat with her son-in-law in terms which could not be like a wife's but seemed not much closer to any other description either. I believe that I inherited the clearest, most fortunate part in this, allowed simply to be myself-older-than-I-was, and to have the grant of a bolstered parent and the bonus of a redoubtable grandparent at my side as well. Yet even that lacks faithful wording: how can it be expressed that a boy's dreams of himself and his dream-versions of a threesome-against-life, yearnings so often drawn opposite each other in him, somehow were the same tuggings?*

And less explicable yet: the materialized fact that at last, whenever it had happened that they found the habit of being together counted more strongly with them than the natures pushing them apart, my grandmother and my father had become some union of life all their own, quite apart from the abrupt knot of bloodline they had made for my sake.

Memory is a kind of homesickness, and like homesickness, it falls short of the actualities on almost every count. In the end, I come to think of the wondrous writer Isak Dinesen when she was taken up in a biplane over the green resplendent highlands of Kenya and arrived back to earth to say, The language is short of words for the experiences of flying, and will have to invent new words with time. *So do I wait for the language of memory to come onto the exact tones of how the three of us, across our three generations and our separations of personality, became something-both-more-and-less-than-a-family and different from anything sheathed in any of the other phrases of kinship.*

IVORY

Dearest Ivan. Well dear time for another few lines to let you know that Dad and I are both fine. And hope you are to. And not working to hard with your studying. Is the weather good where you are. We are haveing Indian Summer but it gets cold nites. Dad and McTaggart are trucking hay here to the ranch. Old McTaggart is such a silly old thing about it he piles the bales way high. Yesterday the highway cop caught him at it and they had to unload bales off to the side of the road until the truck come down to legal wate. It took them 2 trips after that to get all those bales hauled what with the cop keeping his eye on them. Serves old McTaggart rite the silly old thing but I feel sorry for Dad haveing to handle the bales again. We're counting the weeks till you come home Christmas. Well dear guess this will be all for this time and I hope this finds you fine. So Bye with lots of love and kisses as ever Your loveing grandma.

The kitchen of the high-rise dormitory stretched away like a bazaar of sheened serving counters, long stoves, giant square refrigerators. Gertie's cafe could have been set down inside it in a dozen different places. A pair of mahogany-faced cooks rattled to each other in a language I could not even guess at. Two black women were dabbing lettuce leaves into hundreds of salad bowls. I walked on through to the white-tiled dishroom at the far end and stepped into warm cottony air. A bald man with skin the color of coffee with rich cream in it was blasting a jet of steaming water onto mounds of dirty plates. He turned, stuck out a dripping hand to be shaken: *Yo, you the new man? My name is Archie.* I said mine was Ivan. *Yo, Ivory. This here's what we do in here . . .*

Small tight penciling at the top of the quiz paper: *Please see me after class.* Above the words, like a cold half-moon hung over a battlefield, their reason: the grade of *D,* the first of my life. The history class went its hour with fear after fear sawing at the back of my mouth. *Godamighty, am I going to flunk out of here? . . . must have been a mistake, must. . . . what will I tell. . . . what could I have . . . how am I going to . . .* After eternity, the bell rang, the instructor walked me to his office. In a dozen steadying ways, he said a single thing: that memorized dates and facts would not carry me in college as they had in high school, I must think out essay answers now. When I at last stood to leave, his wide horn-rimmed glasses caught me like headlights. *Don't let it throw you, Mr. Doig. You'll do better here than you've started out.* Those first earthquake weeks of Northwestern, his was the one classroom voice to say such words to me. His course was the one I felt my way through to my first college grade of *A.*

Dearest Ivan. We are glad your getting squared away and that you like your board job fine. Thats a lot of dishes to wash every day and every day isn't it. Is the grub good there. I sure hope so. . . . We're glad your getting to know your journalism adviser Professer Baldwin he sounds like a lot of help to you. Dad thought it was a good joke that he thought you would show up at colege wearing a cowboy hat. Dad says to tell you we can get you a pair of bat wing shaps and a lariat rope if it will help your studies. . . . Your loveing grandma.

Trains began to calendar my life. In mid-September, the thirty-two hours eastward from Montana to Chicago. Three months and return west, now the prairies eider-white hour upon hour out the panning frame of window. The eastbound again, usually on the day after New Year's in glittering open-skied weather. The abrupt round trip in March, two and a half days' traveling to spend five or six days in Montana. And early June, the greenest journey west and the most unsettling, with its growing cargo of musings.

No time before or after in my life throbbed quite as those first-of-summer journeys did. *Trains cross the continent in a swirl of dust and thunder,* I would read at times from Thomas Wolfe, as if turning the manuscript pages of an oration as the words boomed from the orator himself—*the leaves fly down the tracks behind them: the great trains cleave through gulch and gulley, they rumble with spoked thunder on the bridges over the powerful brown wash of mighty rivers, they toil through hills, they skirt the rough brown stubble of shorn fields, they whip past empty stations in the little towns and their great stride pounds its even pulse across America.*

But: was the vital rhythm of this travel in pistons, or in the apparatus that was me? Even as my trains—Wolfe's trains—ate the distances of the middle-American prairie, I felt that I was hurtling separately, free of the given lines the machinery had to cling to. Already I had my habit of totaling up life, and in the train hours I could count the steps taken in the college year and those still to come: course upon course in writing and reporting, the adventuring into the Russian language as I had once followed Mrs. Tidyman into Latin, the immensities of history and literature. I knew nothing of an eventual destination except that it would be somewhere that I could work at writing; for now, the adding-up to get there held its own wonder.

The train hours were the enforced pause in time when all this marshalled in my mind. When I stepped down again to a Montana depot platform, Dad or Grandma would ask, as ever, *How was your trip?* I would begin one telling or another—*There was a herd of antelope, forty-fifty of them, on the flats a bit ago* or *We were held up a helluva time in Miles City waiting for a freight*—any answer but the private truth which said what a headlong striding time those journeys were.

When I returned to Montana in early June of 1958 for the summer between my first and second years at Northwestern, I came, for a change, into a season which was creamy with luck. Dad and Grandma still were at the McTaggart ranch, and as content for the moment as the pair of them were likely to be. I at once found a farming job, this time on the irrigated flatland near Valier. The farmer proved the easiest-going of men, interested in my college career and admiring me for it; the fields I worked sprung grain high and golden against the ripsaw-horizon of the Rockies; and a hailstorm, as we watched from the front window of the farmhouse like spectators at a race, went shaving past without touching a kernel of crop.

And the evening, a week or so before my nineteenth birthday, when I hurried to Valier to cash my first paycheck of the summer and then drove on, slower now, trying to think through the steps of the matter, north into the oil-field town of Shelby. Years of rumor had rough-sketched the location of the house for me, but I found I couldn't pick it from among several along a hilly street. Swallowing back the flutters which winged up from deepest in me, I veered downtown, singled out the busiest saloon. Inside, I sipped at a bottle of beer, nervously and intently watched the crowd along the bar. When a burly drinker clopped away toward the toilet, I swung off my bar stool after him.

He already was spraddled at the urinal trough, humming purposefully, when I joined him. He looked over at me cheerily: *Beer'll do it to you, don't it?* I gulped what I hoped was grinning agreement—*Sure slides through*—and faked around at the front of myself until he zipped and turned away. My zipping a fast echo of his, I spun after him: *Ah, say, I was wonderin' if you could tell me, ah, where the place up on the hill is. I don't know this town yet.*

Oh hell yeah, buddy, he began: *You take this street down to the corner 'n go left. . . .* I imprinted the directions on my brain like commandments as he mapped them in the air for me. . . . *'n when you get there, there'll be a black gal, kind of a maid, she'll let you in 'n ask who you want.* He paused like a clerk switching lists of inventory: *I ain't sayin' this is your first visit, but if it happens to be, ask for Estelle. She's got legs sweet as a preacher's dream, squeeze the last ounce right out o' you.* Estelle and her talent branded in atop the street directions.

Thanks-buddy-Jesus-thanks, I breathed out, as if tons had been swung off me, and tried to fumble a silver dollar into his hand. *Here, let me buy you a couple beers. . . .*

Naw, hell. He pushed the mid-air money back to me as if he were a croupier paying off. *Spend it up on the hill.*

Comin' through, Ivory, dishes comin' through! I snap myself away from watching the co-ed in the silken blouse choose her salad. *Let 'er come, Arch.* Grunting, Archie pushes rack after rack of dishes into the metal tunnel of machine between us. Soap is fogged on, cogs lurch the cargo into drenches of hot water; the last scald billows its dragon's-snort of steam around me. The first rack jostles from the machine, breathes heat from its eighteen dinner plates glistening upright in twin rows. *Do 'em pretty,* calls Mister Hurd behind me over the machine's watery roar. I fork my fingers, pull five plates at once with my right hand, four in my left, flip them together into a stack with a clattering riffle as if having shuffled a giant deck of cards made of china, pivot and slap the fat pile of dishware onto the cart behind me. My second grab empties the rack, I send it scooting along the floor until it noses to a stop inches from Archie's right knee, where he can put a hand down for it without looking.

More steam-wrapped racks, the swift double grab and flip again and again, the plate piles multiply as if uncoiling upward out of themselves. Across the dishroom at the sink where he washes the glassware, Mister Hurd is chanting a story, as much to himself as to Archie or me. He is a plump ball of a man, somewhere beyond middle age and as brown-black as rich farmland. Only weeks before, he rode by night bus from South Carolina, wife and children left behind until he can earn their way north as well, and Chicago comes as a giant wonder to him. *Tell you, I's in a big store this mornin' and I see the talles' man in my life. I's behind him and, tell you, I's lookin' at him right chere*—jabbing a thumb to his right buttock.

Archie eyes across at him, seems to make a decision, carefully sets his face innocent. *What you doin' lookin' at him there for anyhow, Mister Hurd? Yo, Ivory? What's he doin' lookin' at that man there, you think?*

I decide too, before I can know I have done so: *Tell you, Arch, he must just be seein' the sights all the time and all the time, hmm?* Mister Hurd giggles for minutes, so pleased at his first joshing in this vast new life.

Rank on rank along Sheridan Road past the Northwestern campus, deep-porched houses hung forth their sets of Greek initials, much as the vital gold pin of affiliation tendered itself out to the world on the angora jut of a pledge sister's sweater.

The university's preponderant "Greek system"—I never heard the words without the echo of the expression Dad and the valley men had for being deeply baffled: *It's Greek to me*—seemed to be meant to bin students into housefuls as alike themselves as could be achieved. It worked wonderfully; there were entire fraternities and sororities where everyone looked like a first cousin of everyone else. And the system's snugness paced itself on from there. Rush Week to Homecoming to winter proms to May Week and with keg parties and mixers betweentimes, residents of Greek Row could count on a college life as preciously tempoed as a cotillion.

By comparison, those of us in Latham House were like bandannaed gypsies grinning rudely beyond the terrace rail.

The first fact of Latham was that the university evidently had not been quite sure what to do with the property, or for that matter, with those of us who lived there as financial-aid students. The building was a glum and aged three-story duplex which hunched by itself at the edge of Evanston's downtown area, as if too life-weary to grope across the street to the actual campus. Where Latham's exterior didn't show several decades of urban soot, it had been blobbed with grayish paint. Inside, the same gravy-like cosmetic simply had tided across the doorsill and lapped on up every wall in sight.

Here the building's odd outer look of frailty and exhaustion quickly explained itself: a colossal incision, an air shaft some six feet across, all but sawed the place in half from back to front. Behind the thin streetside bay of facade, there were stitches of connection only at the front stairwell landing and at a passageway or two which bridged the halves of the house at its top floor. Except for these quick nips seaming it together, Latham House stood divided against itself like a decrepit frigate sprung open from stern to stem, or perhaps an ancient cliffdwelling cut apart by earthquake.

If Latham tottered as a single uncertain roof over two separate hives of rooms, it also sheltered some forty wildly distinct nooks of mind. Here is Votapek on his way to a concert career, coming in from each day's practice of Chopin to walk ritually to the ancient upright piano at the back of the house and tinkle the first bars of *Nola: DOO de doo DE doo de doo.* . . . Here, Benjamin holding constant stage in the front hall, now spieling Shakespeare, now doing his impersonation of Wrigley Field—arms arced wide to be the outfield fences, eyes bulging to capacity, out of his mouth the *hwaahhHH* sound of a crowd heard blocks away. The same again, this time in silence: his version of an open date on the baseball schedule. Then Zimmerman, standing atop one or another of the steam radiators like a penguin on a snowbank, hands forgotten in pockets as he mulls through the visualized pages of his philosophy texts.

All of this, and vastly more, came with the mesh of tensions brought by us inside the walls of Latham. On many of us, family hopes rode heavily, perhaps as the first ever to have made it to college, or as the one to step to success in the place of a dead brother or lost father, or simply to bear the lineage out of one or another crimped corner of American life. Several—the Votapeks, the Benjamins among us—already had the fervors of artistic performance cooking in them. Almost everyone was under the gun of the high grade-point average needed to keep scholarship funds arriving.

Such pressures gave Latham House a charged, ozone-like atmosphere, at once intense and giddy. Strange fevers came and went among us. I think of the year of intramural sports dedicated to losing. It was standing policy at Latham to scorn all campus activities; Homecoming alone rated a special gesture, usually rolls of toilet paper slung derisively out the front windows of the house. However, because a number of us had come from small high schools where we had been encouraged into sports, intramurals were the exception to the boycott. But we began to field Latham teams of such ferocious hopelessness—in tag football, a cursing match and then a brawl with the team from the Episcopal seminary; wholesale evictions in the first basketball game—that we decided to work on styles of forfeit.

Sometimes one or another of us—or better, the gaudiest stand-in we could recruit from the nearby delicatessen-cafe-hangout called the Hut—would go in street clothes to present himself single-handed to the other team. Other times nobody would go at all, but the intramurals office would be phoned to insist that the other team had arrived at the wrong place or the wrong time, and to demand that our chance to meet them—and forfeit—be rescheduled. We became phantom competitors in all available leagues, avidly posted the standings which showed us automatically winless. By the last of spring quarter, our softball zeroes daisy-chaining off the end of earlier forfeits, the Latham intramural program had perfected itself out of existence.

Latham House, if any single sum can be put to it, was a scuffed, restive, Aleutian-atoll of a place to spend one's college years—and every whit of it suited me. Friends from then tell me now, and the evidence of habit still is with me, that in the Latham gallery of behavior I was something of a machinelike student. I was asked a dozen times in my first two days at Latham whether I had just come out of military service, so much beyond an eighteen-year-old freshman did I look and behave. In the year I roomed with Zimmerman, stubby and even more baldish than I was beginning to be, the pair of us stood out like a pair of solemn veteran sergeants among green recruits. However gleefully I could join in epidemics such as the obliteration of intramurals, I was careful about what went on in my head on a regular basis. College—learning—was a job I recognized I could do well, and I did it: typing up my course notes and working on systems of underlining and outlining until I had private, handcrafted texts all my own; bearing down hardest where it counted most—the journalism curriculum, and history courses; chanting Russian verb declensions to myself as Archie plunged the rack-loads of dishes through the machine to me; and running a second, random-as-ever education for myself in offhand books alongside the coursework.

Northwestern was tagged at the time with the reputation of being a "country-club university"—an epithet as exotic to me as profanity from Mars; Greek Row was ridiculous, but not mandatory—yet it also had redoubts of famous professionalism in its schools of music, speech, and journalism. In the school of journalism I tapped luck one more time, drawing as my advisor a new faculty member named Ben Baldwin. A cherub-faced man with a passion for work, he had among the batch of students assigned to him a handful of us from the West, and recognized at once our small-town capacity for chores and perseverance. Again, as under Frances Tidyman's gaudy wing, I was given encouragement and answered with effort.

One thing further I gained from Latham House and Northwestern—a room of my own, the first of my life. Throughout Latham's welter of odd-angled walls and random hallways were a few leftover pouches of space which had been made into single rooms, and in my junior year I qualified for the Shoe, a tiny top-floor room nicknamed for its shoebox dimensions. There was barely space to edge into the Shoe between the cot crowded against one wall and the dresser against the other. The metal clothes closet for the room stood outside the door in the hallway, like a fat man thwarted by a narrow gate. My first act of occupancy was to congest the Shoe further: I saw the chance to swap its spindly desk for a huge, handsomely-shelved one down the hall. With the biggest accomplice I could recruit, I emptied the Shoe of all its furniture, dismantled as much of the pirated desk as I could, wedged the rest into the room and across the far wall, and reassembled the great piece to bulk there like an oak galleon in a bottle. Alone and thoroughly outfitted, I levered my grades up more, multiplied my reading. Across the shelves of my vast desk, Dinesen began to murmur beside Faulkner, Turgenev to tip hats with Wilder.

Dearest Ivan. Well dear we are done at McTaggarts. Dad gave him notice last nite that we'll stay on another week more. Then dear we are going back south to Ringling to live. Its so awful lonesome up here what with you gone away and no place of our own. The darned old days are longer than ever. Dad don't mind so much as he is with McTaggart or out and doing somewhere but he says he is willing to go we don't have anything here to hold us. So when you come home Christmas come on the train to Ringling. Can you cash in the one train ticket for the other. . . . Your loveing grandma.

Dearest Ivan. Just some lines to tell you we are counting the days till you come home for summer. I am at the Higgins ranch outside Ringling with Dad now. Cooking for the crew.

Dad says he can get you on the crew here for summer. That way we can be all together for a while again there is a place upstairs in the cookhouse here for you to sleep. The job will be haying mostly they put up a whole lot of hay. . . . Your loveing grandma.

Behind the bale stack, the pair of us sat waiting for the morning to inch on. Jeff swore steadily, like a sewer gurgling after a downpour: *sparrowheaded sonofabitch him anyhow. . . . 'll show the bastard, he can keep his goddamn stack fences and do the sonsabitches hisself. . . .* Jeff was burly, bright-nosed with decades of boozing, tobacco-stained at the corners of his mouth from the splatters he exploded to punctuate the cusswords. His forehead sloped back under his greasy hat, and his mind sloped off into hatreds and furies I could scarcely imagine. In the bunkhouse after breakfast, he had crossed tempers with the rancher as the day's work was doled out. It had been only an instant, Jeff going hard-mouthed as quickly as he had flared. Now, the two of us sent out together to fence haystacks, he had been in eruption all morning, in one spate sledgehammering posts into the ground as if he were a fence-building machine, in the next plopping behind the haystack to curse some more. *I know he's the world's bastard to work with,* Dad had said, *but he's an old hand on this place and if you say anything against him, there'll be hard feelings for all three of us. Stand the scissorbill if you can, will ye?* I thought back to my farming summers at Dupuyer and Valier, alone on a tractor with the north mountains to sight on over the silent rich pattern of fields, and began to count the time—July *suck-egg sonofabitch* August *never seen such a jangled-up spread* half of September *brain like a bedbug*—until I would step abroad the train toward Northwestern again.

o

Back from whatever chore had taken me into Ringling, I turned the ignition key to kill the motor of the pickup and stared with dread at the cookhouse. Then I stepped down and went in to say what had to be told. Dad quizzed me with a quick look. *It's Angus,* I said. *I heard it in town. His horse fell with him while he and the boys were working calves. They've got him at the hospital in White Sulphur.* My father whitened and whispered: *Just-like-Jim.* But there was to be a grim difference: this second brother of his to die off the back of a horse lay unconscious for more than two years before the last life went from him.

Each trip to and from Northwestern hinged into a mid-morning wait between trains in St. Paul. I made it a habit to leave Union Station and walk the neighborhood, nosing into a used-book store, dawdling over coffee in one half-awake cafe or another, and going at last back toward the depot along a hill street overlooking the Mississippi River, which I liked for its great fjordlike channel gouging through the city.

The coldest of these mornings, as I stood at the river overlook a last minute, a noise scuffed close behind me. I turned quickly to find two tan-skinned men tottering in broken shoes and wavery caps and dirt-stiffened blue jeans.

Buddy, the bigger and less drunk one began to recite, *you ever heard of Ira Hayes? Ira Hayes was Navajo like us. Come off the Gila River Res'vation. Wait, buddy. Listen. You know about Iwo Jima in that war? Sonuvabitch island there in that war? When they put that flag up there on that Iwo Jima, Ira Hayes was one of 'em. Know that, buddy? An' he come home, big hero. An' one morning they find him dead on the ground. Like that. Drowned in his own puke. Passed out, choked to death in his own puke, buddy. Muscatel got him. Helluva way for dying, buddy.* The second

Navajo wobbled, tried to firm himself somewhere between dignified listening and the threatening hunch of his mate. I used the interruption, put a silver dollar in the air before me as I had one other time. This time, it was shakily grabbed.

The pitcher's mound at Wrigley Field swelled from the infield grass like the back of a giant turtle swimming in a dark green sea—and atop it, I was throwing as teeterily as if the turtle had caught the hiccups. My stride awkward on the curved height, a pitch to Grant in the batter's box would fly high and away from him, then the next one explode off the dirt two feet in front of the plate.

Schulte, behind his camera tripod, began to look dismayed. The May morning was his—his idea to meet a course assignment in film-making with a quick reel of baseball instruction, his notion that because Grant and I knew something about baseball we would be his cast, his family connection with the management of the Chicago Cubs which ushered the trio of us into the empty stadium—and his film whirring away in frames of me firing baseballs to sky and earth.

I drew a pitcherly breath, looked up at the colossal shell of grandstand roof above us, its high straight lines fitted onto the sky above the green-and-buff geometry of the baseball field. Full of inhaled inspiration, I grinned into the giddy expanse of it all and got down to business, lobbing the ball now as tamely as if playing catch with a toddler. Grant cautiously timed the spongy throws and smashed ground hits which went whopping in huge easy bounces into the outfield. Encouraged, Schulte filmed busily: lob-*splak!*—whop, lob-*splak!*—whop.

What else do we show? he asked at last. *I've got to fill five minutes of reel.* I trotted to first base, poised myself a short three steps off the bag, broke for second with my left leg coming across to put me in full stride, splayed into a ragged hook slide. Twice more as Schulte shot. Then Grant fielded balls I rolled to him at shortstop, maneuvering massively as a skating bear to scoop into the caretended dirt and paw the ball across to an invisible first baseman. Each thrown ball gave off, an instant after expectation, a hard *whunk* as it ended its catchless throw against the grandstand, as if the geometric gravity which drew such heaves into a first baseman's glove had broken down.

Grant shortstopped on and on, his barrage of pellets thwacking against a cliff of wood. Then I jogged to the outfield and caught balls Grant lobbed high for me, the dotlike white satellite each time diving to me with surprising dazzle down the backdrop of thousands of vanished spectators. My throws, on a single bounce across home plate, skidded through to make the eerie delayed *whunk*, metallic now, against the foul screen.

At last Schulte doubtfully said he supposed he had filmed enough. Now, my wage in the bargain we had set. I carried a bucket of balls to home plate. Swinging a bat as hard as I could, I found I could mortar a ball to where the center fielder might stand and catch it with a casual saluting flip of his glove.

I walked from the plate, around the high bubble of pitcher's mound, to second base. Standing over the square wad of canvas, I tossed, slugged hard, and now one after another the balls flew away to arc out over the ivy-dressed outfield walls, dropping into the bleachers in wild clunking ricochets through the empty seats. I hit bucket after bucket of them until my hands began to wear raw.

Dearest folks. . . . Professor Baldwin has offered me a summer job here at college. I would be teaching and counseling in an institute they run here for high school students in-

terested in journalism. . . . It would be for five weeks, and I can earn more than I can at Higgins' all summer. But it would mean I won't be able to come home until middle of August . . .

Dear son. . . . If you want the summer job back there you ought to take it. Your Grandma and I will miss you and wish we could all be together again this summer, but it don't always work out that way. We will be happy to see you when you come home later on. . . . With love, Dad.

Early in my senior year, when I had begun to write fillers for a magazine in Milwaukee and when an article of mine was the only one by an undergraduate in the glossy new quarterly being published by the school of journalism, Holden, my closest friend in Latham, squinted toward me through his steady fog of cigarette smoke and said: *Damn you, Doig, you're just gonna be bigger than any of us, aren't you?* I thought that over, as I did everything, and faced my judgment on myself: *No, Thomas, not necessarily so.*

As if arguing against myself, in the spring of 1961 I finished up my intended four years at Northwestern by being awarded a scholarship for a year of graduate study. I bargained a military deferment out of my draft board, and set to work again at the school of journalism. A pair of messages markered my completion of that year. When the last pages of my thesis were handed back from their final reading by one of my research advisors, a note was clipped atop: *Around 1836 and 1837, people used to stand on the dock in New York and wait for the latest installment of the Pickwick Papers. With something of the same anticipation, I've waited for and read the chapters of your thesis.* The other arrived from Grandma: *Dearest Ivan. Well dear one I have sad news for you. Mrs Tidaman that you liked so much at Valier died a couple days ago. I'll send you the clipping out of the Gt Falls paper when I get my hands on it. Gertie says in her letter that Mrs Tidaman fell at school and broke her hip and died somehow of that. I'm sorry dear I know she was a wonderfull person to you. . . .*

At dawn, the pewter sky beginning to warm to blue above the Castles across the valley, Dad and I already were stepping from the Jeep at timberline on Grass Mountain. Grandma had climbed out of bed when we did, given us coffee and sweet rolls, made sandwiches out of her thick crisp-crusted bread, saw us out the door with: *Don't bring home more grouse than all of Ringling can eat.* Beside her on the porch Spot stood planted in astonishment and alarm that he wasn't being invited into the Jeep with us. Dad hesitated: *No, fella. Not today.*

September frost underfoot, a testing frost, the lightest dust of white on the broad bunchgrass crest of mountain. Dad handed me the single-shot .22, then the small box of bullets to put in my jacket pocket. I shook out a cartridge, barely longer than my thumbnail, clicked it into the breech. Carrying the light rifle underhand on the side of my body away from Dad, I started along the mountain slope beside him.

He had a hunter's voice, which could soften just enough not to carry far and yet be heard clearly. My own nosedived in and out of mutter as I answered him. He showed me herding sites remembered from three decades before, game trails angling up and across the summit like age-lines on a vast forehead, homestead splotches on the saged skirts of the valley far below us. In trade, I told him everything I knew of my half-year ahead, basic training at the Air Force base in San Antonio, a technical school probably elsewhere in

Texas for the rest of those months. The first grouse caught us both in midstep as it flailed like a hurled wad of gray leaves into the air in front of us.

That must've been one of yours, I said.

And who's carrying the gun along like a crowbar froze to his hand? As ready and free a laugh as I could ever remember from my father. *Ye could at least have throwed it at him.*

In minutes, I shot the next grouse before it could fly. I handed Dad the rifle: *Here, see if you learned anything from that.* I put the bird in the sack he held out to me, followed it seconds later with the one he shot from the top of a log fifty yards away. *I like to give mine a bit of a chance, ye see, instead of sneakin' up till I'm standin' on their tailfeathers.*

The rifle traded back and forth, we each missed shots, made more. At midmorning and four birds apiece, we knew the hunting was over, but kept walking the mountainside. *Right about over there, up over that little park ye see,* Dad pointed. *A time, there was a whole bunch, ten or twelve of us, ridin' back to the Basin from a dance at Deep Creek one night. Even Mrs. Christison, she was up in years, she was along with us. We got caught in a blizzard up here and all got lost off the road, the whole bunch of us goin' in a circle for about two hours. Finally we decided the best thing to do was just to sit down, wait and see if it'd clear up. We got off our horses—it wasn't cold; snowin' like sixty, but it was warm—and sat down on a bank there. After a while it let up and the moon come out so we could look around, and the whole damn lot of us were sittin' right square on the road.*

At early noon, we sat on a silvered log and ate our sandwiches dry.

Ye leave . . . when, day after tomorrow?

Yes.

Scared any of the plane ride?

Some. You know I'm like Grandma on that, leery about heights.

Unh-huh. His instant slant of grin. *As the fellow says, what if ye get up in that thing and it comes uncranked up there?*

Thanks a whole helluva lot for the idea.

I was up in one once, ye know. Nothin' to it.

Disbelief as if he'd said he'd once been to Afghanistan. *When the hell was that?*

When I was a punk kid about your age, at a rodeo or a fair or some kind of doin's. A guy had one of them planes with wings top and bottom, and he'd take ye up for a little ride. Angus and I bet each other five dollars about goin' up, and we're both so damn Scotch we didn't want to lose that money. I went first, I was the oldest. That guy turned that plane every which way, I'm here to tell ye. 'Well, how was it?' Angus says. 'If ye see my stomach up there,' I says, 'bring it back down with ye.'

You're a world of encouragement. I pitched a stone at a snag below us on the slope.

What about after this Air Force business? Are ye gonna be able to look for a job out here?

I faced around to him slowly, as if the motion hurt. *Dad, I don't think so. The jobs for me just aren't here. I think I'm pretty much gone from this country.*

I figured ye were. My father's straight, clean-lined face broke open in a tearful gulp, the wrenched gasp I had seen all the years ago in the weeks after my mother's death. I helplessly looked aside, swallowed, pulled at my lower lip with my teeth. I heard the breech of the .22 snick open, saw Dad palm the tiny cartridge out and finger it into the shell box. His face was steady and square again. *Don't say anything to your grandma yet. She'll miss ye enough these next months without knowin' beyond that.*

Listen up, you rainbows. . . . Still in civilian clothes after five days of basic training, I stood rigid with the others in the motley chow line, as if we were the arrest lineup in a precinct station. The first day's cropped haircut seemed to have put years on me for every hair it lopped off. I was being called *Old Man* in the barracks, as if I were an ancient Sioux chief. . . . *You will be marched to draw military issue at zero-eight-hundred hours in the morning. That's uniforms, garbageheads, and you smell like you need 'em. . . .* The San Antonio weather was blistering, end-of-September days which blazed hotter than Montana's July. Sweat had soaked in white stains across my shoes. . . . *Did I tell anybody in this here line to be at ease? Hah? Answer up, you bald dipstick. . . .*

October's fourth week, 1962. On Monday evening, 6 o'clock San Antonio time, someone in the barracks produced a portable radio; a dozen of us hunched in to listen to the presidential speech announcing a naval blockade of Cuba until the Russian missiles were taken from the island.

The next morning, even some of the training sergeants looked scared. Others looked ecstatic. On the rifle range, bothered with having to use a peep sight instead of the open sight I had grown up with, I shot worse than some of the recruits who had never touched a trigger before. A sergeant dressed down several of us with the most miserable scores: *The only way you yo-yos are gonna git yourselves a Cuban is by chunking the damn rifle at him.*

This day and the next, the rumors ran up and down the prism of possibility and off the ends. *Straight skinny on this:*

Cuba was going to be invaded. Troops on the far side of the base already were clambering into planes destined for Florida. *Got it from the First Sarge:* Evacuation was coming. We would be trucked—no, planed—no, marched—out of the giant missile bullseye that was Lackland Air Force Base. In the midst of the flustered reports, the base went to "condition three," the alert just short of war.

Thursday, on the obstacle course, a sergeant with a seamed face used our rest break *to fill in you people on this Cuba. What's happened now, see, is this United Nations general who's got a name about this long*—spreading his hands three feet apart to estimate the mysteries of U Thant—*is proposed a parlyuhment to consider the situation.* Pause. *Myself, I hope they consider in a quick hurry and go in and mow over them spics.*

Friday, as Khrushchev and Kennedy bargained everyone's fate, we were marched across the base for vaccinations. Showing off in front of a dozen other platoons, our drill sergeant gave us *by the right flank, MARCH!* and watched in horror as half of us ricocheted left. His bleated helpless fury was almost welcome; at least it seemed the safest behavior of the past five days.

We went into the weekend, and came out with the world undemolished. The powers-that-were had decided not to push their final buttons. For now.

After San Antonio, the training school in northern Texas was like a half-coma, full of skewed hours and uncertain seasons and dodgy behavior. A snowstorm lashed in from the south; after a lifetime of Montana's blizzards from west and north, I could not have been more surprised if the snow had flown up out of the ground or sideways out of trees. A barracks-mate from Houston came beside me as I looked out the window to the fat fresh snow: *Thet Yankee rain is startin' to pile up, ain't it?* An article adapted from my thesis was accepted by a scholarly quarterly; after lights-out one night, I corrected the proofs for it in the latrine. The Air Force had scanned my college degrees in journalism and slotted me to become a propeller repairman. We marched off to a hangar to class before dawn, stood blearily behind our desks for the first hour or so to stay awake. One lanky seventeen-year-old could doze standing up. *I'm real sorry, sir,* he offered with a yawn when caught for the third time of the morning. *You're sorry, all right,* the instructor said in wonder, *you're about the sorriest sumbitch I ever did see.* Each afternoon, we were adrift on the base. I found the base library, discovered that sergeants who would have stormed Iwo Jima with a cheese parer would not come near the place. In Grandma's Christmas package arrived a calendar from her son in Australia. I cut out the fine color photo of a wombat, pasted it inside my locker door, and explained to puzzled young enlistees from the South that the fuzzy creatures roamed the Montana hills, *just like you have possums. My daddy caught and tamed this one. We named him Grommet. Yup, Grommet the wombat.* Day and night, B-52's made their slow roar over us, seeming to hang in the air like orbiting battleships. I wondered by what miracle they were made to climb into flight; I had not yet found enough efficiency in the military to launch a silk handkerchief in a high wind. The months crept. By instinct, I hung at the edges of the system, dodged duties when I could and doubled down to endurance when I had to. I was not a good soldier, nor a poor one: I was the usual fuel of history's armies, the time-serving soldier.

Ringling dozed in its late-March bath of mud. Except that Mike Ryan's store stood hollow and socketed with broken windows, and that Dad had built a plank sidewalk from the doorway around to the woodhouse and outhouse, the town looked exactly as when Grandma and I had begun unstacking boxes there a dozen years before. I stood at the kitchen window, looking downslope to the two-toned depot—gray and a deeper gray—where I had stepped from the train an hour before. Spot nosed my ankle for the thirtieth time, plunged into comfortable collapse beneath the table. I said, too casually: *I think I'm going to take that Decatur job I looked at on the way back from Texas.*

Grandma: *Ohhh?* Her smallest siren of disapproval.

Now Dad: *Ye think so, son? What does something like that pay?* One hundred twelve dollars a week; more than half what he earned in a month at ranch work.

Grandma: *What'd you be doing there, then?* Writing editorials. *What are they, like Rose Gordon writes in the paper when anybody dies?* I tried to explain editorials. *Too deep for me, boy.*

Dad: *That's a better wage than you can get anywhere around here, that's for damn sure.*

Nothing said for a minute. Then Grandma: *How long of vacations do you get, to come home?*

Decatur was a city of 80,000 amid the dark wealth of soil which the glacial era had buttered across central Illinois. Fat fields of corn and soybeans surged from the earth and overspilled every horizon—relentlessly lush-green crops which seemed to me the agriculture of another planet—and Decatur had made itself the merchant city for the farming-sea which surrounded it. Large enough to have a beginning of urban manners and woes but insular enough to know it could never outcrowd bigger Springfield to its west or Champaign-Urbana to its east, the community was a good training stop for young climbers. The Caterpillar corporation seasoned executives at the tractor factory there before moving them on and up, fledgling store managers mastered inventories at the local Woolworth and Penney's as the step to grander merchandising, earnest not-quite-yet-middle-aged ministers polished their repertoires before being called east to higher pulpits. And the Lindsay-Schaub newspaper chain which had its headquarters in Decatur held a reputation for working its newcomers thoroughly but fairly, giving them a bit of leeway to show talent, then losing them to bigger publications.

Which was my quick career there exactly. Somewhere I had read of a newsman who liked to preen that he could write faster than anybody who was better and better than anybody who was faster, and that skimming waterbug pace was where I pointed myself in Decatur. Our editorial page staff of seven had endless call for our work—Lindsay-Schaub operated newspapers not only in Decatur but in the university towns all across central and southern Illinois, and the management saw itself in a sober, enlightened-gentry stance of responsibility—and after a few weeks I found that I could write four editorials a day, deft and unoffending skitters across Algeria-the Pentagon-civil rights-and-whatnot-other-issues of 1963 and early 1964, and still have time to do page layout, Sunday feature pieces, and study Dave Felts for lessons in Downstate elegance.

Before coming over to Decatur and ending up as editor of the editorial page, Dave had been a newspaperman in Springfield when Vachel Lindsay yet was writing and performing his poems there, and could be counted on for occasional ironic thumpy recitations from the old rhymester: *I brag and chant of Bryan, Bryan, Bryan/Candidate for president who sketched a silver Zion* . . . This and all else was said in apparent easy contentment, and out of the most dimming affliction a newspaperman could suffer: for years Dave had been fighting blindness, and with operation after operation pushed it back until he could work as zestfully as ever, bringing our sheafs of editorial copy up close to his dizzying glasses, bending interestedly close over his desk to nick out an occasional word with his editing pencil.

Not least because he had his own abundance, Dave liked style in a person; he kept on a shrine-shelf in his office the delicate martini glass of his predecessor, an offhand editorial wizard named Sam Tucker who was remembered for heading off to the backshop at each deadline, a dab of copy in one hand and scissors in the other, and by the time he arrived there would have snipped guest editorials from other papers until his own page filled exactly. My stock with Dave Felts shot up when he learned that I was carrying on a courtship in Chicago, 170 miles away: *One more grandeur of the big town, is she?*

I was convinced so. She was Carol Muller, whom I had met when we both worked in teaching-and-counseling jobs during summer journalism sessions at Northwestern a few years before. A trim, steady-eyed brunette of definite opinions and clean-edged talents, Carol now had traded in an East Coast newspaper job for a magazine editorship in a Chicago suburb. We re-met just as I had begun job-shopping beyond Decatur. I already was finding that I lacked instinct for the deep waters of newspapering. Amid the nightmare which began loosing itself in a November noon—the words *Kennedy* and *shot* seeping up from the hubbub of the lunch-place, the scrambling return to the newspaper building and the wire-service flood unrolling out of Dallas—I noticed that I was both exhilarated and sickened, neither of which seemed the most professional of responses. On a day-by-day basis, I savored more the Dave Felts announcement of a new pope—the face angled in my doorway in blinking search, *habemus papam* enunciated in somber Downstate flatness—than I did the weekend-wire-editor's shift which presented Paul VI in yards of words. Assessing myself, when jobs came open to me in New York and Washington newsrooms, I mulled briefly and would not make the step. What I did instead was to begin writing to magazine editors, and almost at once hit on an opening at The Rotarian--out of all the world, in Evanston, a few blocks from where I had entered Northwestern six years before.

I put first among the sheaf of writing samples asked for by The Rotarian editor what I had slammed out on the day of Dinah Washington's death: *The lady sang the blues. And lived them. . . .* That, I considered, would be something for a gentlemanly service-club magazine to start a decision on. Rapidly, I was flown in for an interview and hired. In mid-1964, a few days past my twenty-fifth birthday, I became an assistant editor of a magazine of 400,000 circulation.

One person alone was the greater audience than that. I spent hour upon hour with Carol, and saw her in my mind the rest of the time. Our backgrounds could not have been more different—she had grown up in a turreted New Jersey resort town which seemed to me as antique and daft as I imagined Lichtenstein must be—yet friends remarked how much we were like each other. Alike, it turned out, down to the deepest exactnesses—in having been wary of the commitments of mating, in surprising ourselves now with the quickness of emotion for each other, in deciding promptly to be married.

Two pairs of lives now, half a continent and a time-zone apart. Carol and I mail to Montana the bylined articles we turn out, Dad thrusts them onto all visitors and Grandma eventually jumbles them into one or another of her makeshift albums. While Carol and I leave our Evanston apartment each morning on her commute to the Together offices and mine to The Rotarian, Grandma is clearing away the dishes after the breakfast she has put on the long table at the

Higgins ranch. As I prop my feet on the desk to read manuscripts, Dad will be starting work in the calving shed, muttering his *he's-yours-ye-walleyed-old-sister* formula to make the cows mother their purebred calves. When I break for lunch, walking to whatever greenery I can think of to eat my sandwiches amid, Dad kicks off his overshoes at the cookhouse door, takes the cup of coffee Grandma is handing him, delivers his latest curses of *that-goddamn-geezer-of-a-Jeff*. As Carol works the phone to arrange the story assignment waiting for her in San Francisco or Atlanta, Grandma is setting the table for the ranch crew's lunch. As I dictate late-afternoon letters to authors, Grandma may be in her mid-afternoon round to gather the eggs, scolding Spot for his interest in a corral post. When I leave my office at the stroke of five, she has begun to cook supper for the ranch crew, the color of the sage hills has begun to deepen.

The four lives mix richly in Carol's first visit to Montana. The first night in the house in Ringling, Grandma departs at bedtime to spend the night at the Badgetts'; Dad takes her place on the living-room couch, Carol and I take his in the bed in the tiny bedroom. *Ah,* burrs my father's voice through the quiet to us, *as the fellow says, this is the place to be when night comes.*

We wake in the morning to a bell jangling close outside the window. Carol starts: *What's that?* I ponder for her benefit. *Mmm, could be sheep, or a goat. Or somebody's milk cow. Or a horse. Probably not a chicken, it'd have trouble dragging the bell around.* She looks out the window: *All right, it's a horse.* She gives me a grin of love and disbelief. It widens as the front door is clattered open, Spot explodes in and instantly has his head onto the bed-edge lolling rapturously up at us, Grandma cheerily is announcing: *Hi, you stay-a-beds in there getting up today?*

o

And in the next year, the set of decisions which lifted Carol and me westward: that we had had enough of the mountainless Midwest, and of midway-up-the-masthead jobs we could do with automatic skills. I had come to feel that if I was going to go through life as bookish as I was, I might as well bend with the inclination and become a professor. No sooner had I said so than Carol said: *Let's go do it.*

The University of Washington accepted me into graduate study. In the late summer of 1966, Carol and I arrived in Seattle, set out at once to walk its hills and shores and to explore into the mountain ranges scarped along the entire horizons east and west of the city. We were on new ground of the continent, and stretched gratefully to it. And then, as quick as this, we learned that now we were on another ground in life as well. My father had begun to die.

A story more out of memory, heard from my father a hundred times, and never enough:

It was along about 1935. Your mother and I were herdin' sheep just then at the old D.L. place. Jobs was scarce in those days. Ye had to take anything ye could get. Well, a damned bear got to comin' in to the ranch there, killin' sheep. Boy, he'd kill 'em right and left. He'd always wait till after the moon went down, till it got good and dark. All the neighbors, there'd be some of 'em there pretty near every night with me, to try get that bear, but we never could.

Your Uncle Paul, he came down there. The two of us were gonna spend the night in an old log barn there. The loft end of it was open, and we were gonna get old mister bear for sure. This bear now, he'd just kill his sheep and leave 'em lay, that's the way a bear does. They don't like fresh meat, they like it after it gets spoiled. So we got one of the first sheep he'd killed, up on the hill, and drug it down there, to bait him down there under that loft, ye see. We both swore we never slept a wink, but that night that bear ate the whole sheep within thirty feet of us, and we never knew it.

We went on not havin' any luck that way. Generally all we'd see would be the bear's eyes as he'd take off out of there in the dark. This one evening, Berneta—your mother, I mean—and me and the neighbor, Mrs. Christison, were sittin' there in the front room of the house. It had big windows, and the house sat up on a knoll, we could see down to where the sheep were bedded in just below. We didn't corral 'em, we didn't dare. That bear'd get into 'em and pile 'em up and kill half of 'em at once. So I heard the sheep bells aringin' and I looked out the window, and here comes the whole band, right towards the house. That bear was after 'em.

I grabbed the rifle—didn't have a very good rifle, either, just an old broken-down one I had loaded and sittin' there—and went back through the dining room through the kitchen and sneaked out the back door. I got out behind the bunkhouse. Then there's a creek there with heavy willows, I was gonna get on the edge of them and sneak around behind the bear. I thought I'd sure fix that boy this time.

I got about halfway to the brush and I looked up and here he had a sheep cut out right against the house wall. There's a pole fence come up and nailed right onto the corner of the house, and he was trying to catch this sheep in there. The radio was agoin', and your mother and Mrs. Christison were standin' there in the window just like that, watchin'.

I cut down on him with that old rifle, and he went WOOF! *I don't know if I hit him or not, but I changed his mind anyhow.*

Well, he either had to come toward me or go right back through the middle of the sheep, so here he comes toward me. He got, oh, about sixty feet from me, and he was gonna head around the edge of the sheep then. I cut down on him again, and I know I hit him that time. He let another WOOF! *out of him, and he was mad now. Here he comes. He had his old head turned sidewise. I could have counted his teeth there in the moonlight.*

I never give it a thought to run. Anyhow, he got up, oh, pretty close, I'd say about here to that window, six feet or so. I was tryin' to shoot him between the eyes. He had his head turned a little bit, and I got him right—you know the way a bear's head is, his ears are up towards the top of his head—I got him right the side of the ear there. The bullet went down through his neck and all the way into his lungs.

That took the WOOF! *out of him. Sat him back on his haunches, and he made a pass at me, and I ducked him as he come around or he'd of ripped me in four pieces. Just as he went by I jammed the gun against his ribs, right behind his shoulder there, and cut loose on him again.* WOOF! *he says again, and away he went.*

He had to go about thirty feet there till he hit a brand-new four-wire fence with cedar posts. He tore out about a hundred yards of that fence when he hit it.

He went across the creek into the brush, and boy, he was cuttin' up in there, groanin' and growlin' and tearin' up the brush. I looked up and here's Mrs. Christison and your mother, standing right on the bank above me. They'd been there all the time while I was shootin' at him. And one of 'em had a lantern. I don't know what they were gonna do with that lantern.

Mrs. Christison had this other old gun that was in the house. She says, You got any shells left?

I says, Yeah, I got some in my pocket—*that'd been the last shell I had in the gun when I put it again him there.*

Well, *she says, Mrs. Christison says,* let's go in and get him.

You can go in and get him, *I says,* I've had enough of him.

So we waited a little bit. It was all quieted down in the brush there, and I knew he's either dead or gone. So we went down the creek a little ways, there's a bridge there, and come up where the brush wasn't so thick.

He was layin' there in a heap of brush, dead.

I didn't get scared during it; never gave a thought to run when that bear was comin' at me. But I shook all night afterwards, after it was all over.

A hundred times told, and always that last lilt of wonder in his voice that he could have been both hunter and hunted.

ENDINGS

Split the tongue of the silence that beats in you when you first know that a parent is dying, and it will begin to recite everything unsaid across a lifetime. *Unsaid: that even in our most desperate time, when you were plunging into that wrongheaded marriage with Ruth and poisoning us away from the one you have come to call Lady, you somehow kept to the one great rightness as well—the constant clasp of keeping me at your side, whatever the place or the hour or the weather or the mood or task or venture. So swiftly did you have me grown beyond my years that neither of us entirely understood the happening of it, but knew it to be rare, a triumph and terribly needed . . . that it was you, in your burring troubadour's way of passing to me all you knew of the valley and the Basin, who enchanted into me such a love of language and story that it has become my lifework . . . that I know, if have never said, that as I stepped off from you to books and schools, you somehow saw yourself riding free from the Basin homestead and so had not a word for me but in praise, encouragement, proudness . . . that*

I know, and again could not speak it, how drastically you turned your own life for me, choking down pride as never before to speak the truce with Lady . . . know too that when you risked that truce time upon time, it was because you needed risk, needed somehow to sizzle ordinariness by dropping danger into it now and again . . . know, and could say least of all, the final fact of triumph that you and Lady had made your way to a cherishing of each other which went beyond family lineament.

Then the first and only words of this which would say themselves as they did now in my own voice: *Dad, we've got to find the doctoring for you.*

Late or soon, the siege of death-against-life must clamp itself around every family, and never the same for any two. I see now that ours had begun its queer quiet trenching some time before it could be recognized for all it was. There is this tremor, from the Christmas week of 1963, when Dad and Grandma came to spend the holiday with me in Decatur. Before their train trip back to Montana, I drove them north to Chicago for a weekend, at last to show them the Northwestern scenes—Latham House, the school of journalism, the cathedral-towered library, Lake Michigan lapping beside it all like an unexpected ocean—which had filled five years of letters to them.

Both of them were untiring sightseers, and the morning's saunter of the campus pleased us all, brought us proudly together in the accomplishment of having laddered me to such a place. We went next to our hotel in downtown Chicago, and in the snapping cold of the sunlit afternoon, a moment when I thought the city looked its ponderous best, I suggested we walk the surrounding blocks which offered the gaudy store windows of Michigan Avenue, the exotic bulk of the Art Institute, the skyline above the street canyons.

Grandma eyed everything with her mixture of suspicion and sharp interest, asking me explanations to why the sidewalks were so wide and the people so fast-paced. But Dad: I remember looking across at him in surprise, as if finding a stranger with us, when he suddenly said he had had enough, he felt short of breath.

On the way back to the hotel he had to stand and breathe deep time after time, the three of us a knot of concern in the grain of sidewalk traffic. Once he said, worry thick in his voice: *How-long-is-this-damned-block?*

But inside the warmth of the hotel, as I was set to call for a doctor, Dad's chest eased at once, he became himself and made a joke about Chicago being too cold for a sane man to walk around in anyway. And like him, not knowing what more to find in it—often enough through his life he had felt mild damp-weather discomforts in his lungs from the breakage of those horseback accidents and from his decades of heavy smoking—I wrote off the moment to the stabbing chill of the winter lakefront.

Then late in the next spring, weeks before I was to step into the editing job at The Rotarian, a bulletin from Grandma: *Dearest Ivan. Well dear one I have to write you that Dad isn't none too good. He is in the hospital in Gt. Falls they told him he has to quit smoking or else. I am here with him but he's so awful weak and coughing so. . . .*

Phone calls told me that he was not in danger at the moment. The hospitalization indeed was to begin easing him away from cigarettes and out of the coughing spells that were becoming chronic. When I hurried to Montana between the end of my old job and the beginning of the new, he told me the rest himself. Once out of the hospital and at home in Ringling, he had laid one fresh pack of cigarettes on the end table beside his easy chair. When he could no longer stand it, he smoked a cigarette. Some days only one, other days two, but never more than two. When the pack had emptied itself, he took that as the moment when he had finished with cigarettes for all time. *Hardest damn thing I ever did, ye know that? But I did'er.*

Dad's nerves jumped worse than ever now, which was saying much, and he looked like a thinner replica of himself. But his appetite was gaining and he felt he soon could be doing some part-time work. *Well, don't rush things,* I said, uneasy with myself for feeling there was more that ought to be said. Yet the doctors were finding nothing alarming, Dad seemed merely—if that word was right for any trouble beneath the breastbone—a man who had got in the habit of oversmoking and needed to be weaned from its eventual dangers.

This quick braid of times together, then, before it came clear that my father was in serious illness. I finger apart their pattern here because these are the moment-strands each of us will think of afterward and wonder, *Did I miss there some hint, some flicker of doubt or pain or incredulity, which told what was to come?* And the greater wondering beyond that: *If not, how can that skein of no apparent peril and the skein which followed it be portions of the same life?*

For now calamity began to make itself known as rapidly as if it had been invented entirely for Dad: a man who lived on his feet, he was finding himself more and more short of breath after each briefest stint of walking.

At first the doctors he saw suggested that he might have a kind of asthma. There was all the grief on earth in that verdict, with its convulsed echoes of my mother's agony. Yet Dad showed none of the wheezing attacks which so devastated her—his lung difficulty nagged less violently but more steadily—and the diagnosis shifted. It was sometime late in 1966, the year Carol and I had arced our lives to the Pacific Northwest, that a word neither he nor I had heard before was uttered to my father: emphysema.

In my mechanical way I read all I could find about the affliction, and each word more brought its own gloom. Emphysema, it emerged, could become a torture of the body beyond even my mother's suffering or the holocaust of cancer itself. As the honeycomb of air sacs in the lungs was destroyed by it, breathing would become forever more labored, a constant struggle against a sensation of suffocating. The act of breath would deliver less and less oxygen to the bloodstream, overload the heart into harsher and harsher pumping. Until the recent past, emphysema usually had been confused with asthma or bronchitis, and it had the worst of those ailments—an increasing wheeze, congestion—as well as its own cycle of deterioration in the deeps of heart and lung.

Somehow through the null medical words—*generalized overdistension, difficulty of exhalation, excess mucus*—I came to picture the disaster happening in my father's lungs as a pattern like the splotched burning of a sagebrush fire. Perhaps it was the years of blue haze drifting up from his cigarettes that made me think so of smolder and slow flame-lick. For whatever reason, the image came to me of the black turf such a fire spreads in its steady searing fan across the land, and the thought too that there would be no grass-bright greening in this fire's wake as time passed. Only char and more char.

And the role those words and that image spoke for me: For the dozen years since I had faced away from a storm-blasted band of sheep on the Blackfeet Reservation, this father of mine and this grandmother of mine unveeringly had shown me that they assumed I knew for myself what I was doing in life—which was a tremendous assumption. Then too, by the books and schooling I piled up, I was granted to be the authority on the world outside Montana.

If I happened to be on the scene when Grandma was writing one of her letters to her son in Australia, she still would ask me, as she had when I was eleven, how to spell some Down Under mystery such as *kangaroo;* if I had told her *q-y-n-g-u-r-u,* she would have thought it odd of the Aussies but certified correct because I had said it. When I wrote an article about rodeo and put in a few lines about Dad's own bronc-stomping days, he passed the marvel around to friends until the magazine wore out: *That kid of mine can write, if I do say so myself,* unarguably saying so. Beyond that, there was my becalmed temperament, amid the pair of theirs which swayed and whanged.

It all said that now I must truly become the authority in the family, this time on a matter beyond all of us. Here was the turn of time, sooner by a decade than I ever could have imagined, when I must become father to my own father, and I feared the matter, and wrestled it, and began to do it.

I sent along to Montana the levelest words I could draw from what the medical journals and texts said of emphysema, and the two conclusions which I said demanded doing: winnow until we had the most expert diagnosis and advice we could find about this mystery licking its way inside Dad, and move him from the blizzardy isolation of Ringling nearer to medical care.

The second of these, Dad himself took on as if snapped from a spell. Almost overnight he found and bought a small frame house in White Sulphur. Ungrand as it was, and carrying a sheaf of deeds which showed that it long had been a quick way-station for a procession of souls who couldn't afford better at the moment, the house nonetheless improved on the Ringling shanty in size and warmth and all else.

Grandma was uneasy about the move: *Don't we get by good enough as we are? Gee gosh, at our age, buyin' another house and all.* . . . I was the one to woo her from that. Carol said once: *If you told her you were going to run an opium den, she would come around onto the side of opium dens.* As promptly as I had Grandma persuaded out of Ringling, she flung into tidying and flower-bedding the new site. A month after she and Dad moved in, it looked as if the pair of them had lived there from time out of mind.

Yet one of them was not going to live any time at all unless care for emphysema could be found, and the next piece of persuasion was to keep Dad from throwing himself under surgical knives. An operation he had heard of was claimed to lift the sensation of heavy breathing; already the pushing effort needed to make his lungs work was dismaying him. *I'm not sure I've got anything to lose by trying that out, Ivan.*

By phone and letter, I found doctor after doctor against the surgery. Guardedly, carefully, I brought Dad around from the idea of the operation and to agreeing that he would come to Seattle to be examined at a highly reputed clinic as quickly as I could arrange it. In his mind, I believe, glinted the hope that he could somehow be rescued into wholeness again as he had been on the operating table at the Mayo Clinic sixteen years before. In mine was simply the vague medical prayer that the emphysema could be slowed, eased; I desperately wanted him not to be savaged into the worst of what the disease could inflict.

He was scheduled for several days of tests at the clinic. The first morning, I noticed Grandma putting on her best shoes and said to her without thinking: *I can stay with him down there, it'll be a long day.* The iron tone I had heard so many times: *I might just as well be there as setting around here like a bump on a log.*

Each day and all day, the pair of us lobby-sat. I thumbed magazines, and tried without showing it to watch her beside me. She kept her eyes on the waiting patients, studying the ones who could hardly puff their way across the room to the reception desk, who sat hunched with their chests swelling in and out for each windy breath, who toddled into the waiting elevator with a nurse balancing them at an elbow.

When Dad appeared, there was the relief, a quick lifting in the both of us, of seeing that he was so much sturdier than the others, his ranchman's stride almost too bold among the gaspy shuffles. And again we would set off with him, up or down the identical floors of the clinic to the next probing test.

Often he would come back to the reception area in surprise: *That wasn't so bad, they just had me lay down under some machine. Could of had a nap except it was so damn cold.* But other times, he arrived pale and grim and taut. *They gave me one of those damn barium deals, and I heaved it right back up.* Grandma would give her resentful *Hmpf!* against the clinic's dosing such torment into anyone, and I would try to talk him calm, keep him seated with us until the whiteness went from that handsome uneasy face. Then the three of us would move through the clinic once more, like a search party off to the next lair of apparatus for Dad to patrol into for us.

Eventually the tests were finished and adjudged. Dad and I waited in the doctor's office; this day Grandma had not wanted to come, had said I should be alone with him. The slim room was as neutral and toneless as if we were the first visitors ever to have been sent into it, like newcomers into a vacuum chamber. But outside the one thin window and below the clinic's roothold on its hill, the towers of the city marched to the dockside, and then the blue of Puget Sound pooled, rimming far off at a shore of timber and glacier-whetted peaks. My father, my one closest pulse back into time, sat looking at the towers and the blue and the stabbing mountains. Finally he said, in the worrying burr I had heard fret over vanished sheep and surprise blizzards and much else: *I'm just afraid of what he's gonna say, Skavinsky.*

But the doctor spoke some surprise, more texture of hope in his words at least than I had been able to allow myself. Of course—the harshest first—the diagnosis was confirmed as emphysema. Yes, Dad's life would be more labored. Several times a day he would have to breathe deep into his lungs a medicine misted out of a machine. He would have to walk only in short stints, learn to pace himself.

The doctor paused, went on. If possible, Dad should move to a lower altitude. Sea-level would be best, and the drier the climate the better. Dad: *No, it isn't possible. I'm too far along in life for that.*

The doctor nodded as if he had known what that answer would be, went on with his medical judgments. Dad's heart as yet showed little damage, not yet the expected overwork caused by emphysematous lungs; it pounded in him as strongly as that of a man half his age. His lung capacity still was considerable. His general health was remarkable for a person who had gone through his batterings.

Grandma demanded the news as quickly as we arrived home. I watched Dad to see how he would deliver it, how drastically the prospect of a hobbled life was going to veer him. He gave his cocked grin. *This doctor now, I don't know about him. If I was in as good a shape as he says I am, I wouldn't be sick atall.*

But when Dad and Grandma returned to Montana, his lungs soon enough gave trouble. He did learn to struggle more successfully with the emphysema, walk some uncertain line between too much activity and incapacity. But emphysema now brought an ally, bronchial infection which hit Dad again and again in the chill of the valley's autumn and winter. Now there were hospital stays for him, time upon time the 45-mile trip out of the valley and across the Big Belts to the hospital in Townsend.

A pattern began, like codes spoken by a people in war. Dad would suffer a new infection in his lungs. By telephone from Seattle, I would try to gauge how severe it was. If Grandma guardedly said, *He's just none too good,* in all likelihood he was ill enough to be hospitalized again. I would say *You'd better let me talk to him,* now hating the long moments it took for him to creep to the phone. *Hullo, son, how are ye?* How am I. Leave that unanswerable, begin my questions, calming, gentling. *God, Ivan, I don't know what I better do.* Now persuade him around to going to the hospital, tell him I will get free for a week to help out when he comes home.

At last from him, *All right, son, whatever you say.* Whatever I say. I could say all in the world except the magic we needed: that if he did this certain thing, his lungs would heal, he would not gasp for every atom of air. He would not die this most grudging of deaths.

Yet it was not a time of steady gloom. I think that is the true grief of it—that the four of us could glimpse the richness of life available if the haunting gape in Dad's lungs did not return again and again. The one pastime-without-exertion left to Dad was trout fishing, and the valley, in its style of either withholding ruthlessly or proffering something wondrous, provided him with a friend who would wet lines with him from daybreak to midnight if he wanted.

A railroad worker retired from tending the tracks which coiled between Ringling and Sixteen, Leo was a thick slab of a man whom it was uproarious to think of in the nickname of that job, a *gandy dancer.* Something—rumor said it had been a gassing on a World War One battlefield, although I counted years and couldn't find him old enough—

had erased every hair on his head, including eyebrows. Out of that blank ball of head came a high crackling voice and an Oklahoma accent; when he and Dad were out on a creek or lake, the vicinity jangled with Leo's sentences, as if broadcasts were shrilling in from some rim of space.

For his part, Dad accepted with wryness his reliance on Leo—*I'm wind-broke as an old nag, but that Oklahoman gets me to wherever there's a fish, don't think he doesn't.* Once Carol and I went with the pair of them to a favored lake, and as we hiked the hilltops circling their fishing water, Leo's voice racketed along with us as if he were at our elbows instead of half a mile below, Dad's murmur came in like a far purl of stream. I hold that exact scene like a photo, Dad and his bald bear of a friend in the yellow rubber raft at the lake's center, a cone of color in the dusky retina of water, while Carol and I listen to the steady crackle of fishing talk and grin down over the tassel-tops of sage.

In that first year or two of affliction, there were times even apart from his fishing outings with Leo when Dad could find periods of almost-unforced breathing. Seated in his big living-room chair in the White Sulphur house, his flat back and level shoulders square against the fabric, he could recline and talk with only a hinting rise-and-fall of his chest, as if he had just rapidly walked a block or so.

I'll tell ye a time, he might begin then if the nudge of encouragement came from me, or more likely from Carol's presence, for he found this new daughter-in-law a dazzling bonus to the family. *I was ridin' out here for the Dogie, and I happened to look up into a little park there in the Castles and saw a bunch of elk going across. I counted five of them. As the Dutch fellow says, as many as the thumbs on the end of mine hand. So I thought, well, this ridin' can go to hell for a little while, I'll just see about those elk. . . .*

Dad no longer could work at all, except to do the smallest repairs around the house, but the loss of that fifty-year habit of effort seemed to dismay him less than I had thought it would. He spent time reading, watching Grandma as she fussed at flowerbeds until she had a moat of color around almost all the house, somehow making himself fit so mild a routine of life.

But in other ways, surprising disquiets might break out of him now. Never a very political man and hardly a sympathizer with the strange long-haired counterculture which had begun to prance before him on the living-room television set, Dad was furious and bitter about the clubbings at the 1968 Democratic National Convention in Chicago: *Godamighty, I thought this was a country where the police weren't supposed to beat up on people.* The war in Vietnam worked confusions on him. He wanted not to see his country lose a war, and yet *What the hell is it we want over there anyway?* It was as if with sickness fastened into his own chest, he saw any sickness of the nation all the more sharply.

Time was carving fast at one in that Montana household, and hardly at all on the other. In her oaken way, Grandma went on now as if age didn't apply to her. At the start of the summer of 1968, when Carol and I had come to White Sulphur for Grandma's seventy-fifth birthday, Dad declared: *If I ever reach seventy-five, she'll still be up and pushing me around in a wheelchair.*

Even now, she was bolstering his life in dozens of ways, tending, nursing, scolding, puzzled by whatever had taloned into Dad's lungs but automatically ready to do all that his situation demanded. And almost as if she had the impulse to push back against the grayness settling over Dad's life, she now began to turn out vivid quiltwork.

Through her years of crocheting, Dad and I loyally had made encouraging and admiring noises, and I often marveled that she could follow the tiniest intricacies of pattern. But I had never cared much for the frilly doilies and lacy tablecloths that flew from her needle, regarding them as something like her everlasting games of solitaire, played in thread. But the quilting flamed away any opinions of that sort. What Grandma turned out now, in the living room as Dad watched from his haven of chair, danced with brilliant colors—snipped-and-sewn diamonds of ragwork marching and playing and jostling like a meld of rainbows, or some resplendent field of tiny flags from all the universe. To come out of our ungaudy family, this was an absolute eruption of bright art, and I blinked in wonder at this gray-haired woman I thought I knew so entirely. For her part, Grandma simply produced each quilt, demanded *Now then, isn't that pretty?* and gave it to Carol and me or someone in her sons' families. When we all had quilts galore, she began selling them, and there are valley households now with half a dozen blazing in their rooms.

And across seven hundred miles, in Seattle, Carol and I settled to our own changed life. Carol rapidly had maneuvered from one job to the next, and always up; within a year after our arrival, she had a professorship, teaching journalism at a community college. I was making my expedition through three solid years of reading and seminar work to the professorship of my own—one slog-step to the next, the only way I have ever known to get a thing done.

Along with that trudged the decisions needed for Dad. The dying of a parent is a time without answers, only anguished guesses, and I wished that I were an older and wiser guesser, able to come onto some angle of insight which would declare: *Here, this is to be done.* I wished a thousand useless longings, and amid them made whatever small tactics I could reason out. The main guidance I set in myself was that Dad should not be written off, not be allowed to write himself off, as an invalid. It may even be that in following this notion during his first few years of emphysema, not enough allowances were made for his illness. But he was surrounded in the family by three of the world's dogged souls, and he himself had persevered through past health woes.

Deeper than that lay the belief, also endlessly mulled in me, that it would be preferable for him to pace out an active but shorter life rather than an inert lingering. We could not talk about this in so many words—a failing in our family perhaps, yet none of us ever had seen much reason to say aloud what made itself plainly known—but my father had proclaimed as much with his earlier life.

Occasionally my estimates of how much Dad could be encouraged to do would overrun his capacities. During one of their visits to Seattle, Dad and Grandma were taken by us across Puget Sound on a fine afternoon to a play given in an outdoor theater. I had known that the theater seats were spaced down a hillside; what I did not know was that there was a descent of a few hundred yards before the topmost of the seating.

Grandma was perturbed, and fretful during the play. I had said, *We'll get him out of here somehow, don't worry about it.* Although Dad had continually said he was sure he could make the slope by taking it slow, he must have been edgy about it as well. Starting up, he at once went breathless.

Carol and I looked at one another: he was going to have to be carried out. I went to the stage, borrowed a straight-backed chair from the set. Seating him in it, Carol and I lifted the chair between us and started up the trail.

It made an awkward and severe load, which we denied over and over, and in our gritting paired exertion we took him out of there like a potentate. At the top, he could walk perfectly well on level ground. In double relief, I panted:

Told you we'd get you out somehow. And the episode did prove that, if shakily.

One thing more soon was proved: that when it was needed, we could draw together the strongest of family thews, live as a single household. The main decision, as so many others by then, was mine, and I came to it reluctantly, believing so entirely in the independence of lives. But there was the greater belief that my father must be helped in whatever way possible to live, and so in the autumn of 1968 I arranged that Dad and Grandma would come to Seattle to stay with Carol and me until the following spring.

Neither of them wanted the move. It would uproot them from everything familiar. Yet they saw that it was as I said: Dad could not undergo another mauling winter of chest infection. Seattle's mild coastal climate was the needed measure against that. Reluctantly, but on my word, they came.

When the pair of them had unpacked, I suddenly asked: *What did you do with Spot? Leave him with somebody?* Grandma answered slowly. *No. There was nobody right to take care of him and we knew we couldn't bring him with, so I . . . we had him done away with.* The day before they left, she had asked Dad, Spot's lifetime foe and idol, to take the aging dog to the veterinarian. *I'd rather have gone through a beating,* my father said now in my living room, but he had done the task, petted the bold old head as the needle's sleep crept through the dog, had him buried carefully on a ridge above the valley.

I turned and walked to the bathroom, locked the door, turned a faucet full on, and wept. For a jaunty white-and-brown dog, for my beset family which could not be spared even this loss—for being able to meet grief only in my own company this way.

I think now that Dad and Grandma settled into our expanded household with less tension than I did. Not that there wasn't much for them to wonder at in the unpredictable new locale. Day and night, ambulances would howl along a street below us on their way to the hospital which treated burn cases. Carol and I had stopped hearing the banshee sound of them after our first few weeks in the house. Grandma heard every one, *hmpf*ing each time to think of yet another disaster in this severe city-world.

Nor did she ever accustom herself to the telephone's blat from the kitchen; each time it jangled, she started in surprise, which in turn twitched Dad's nerves. From him: *What are ye jumping about?* From her: *Gee gosh, I can't help it, and what're you jumping about yourself?*

The telephone skirmish was daily, sometimes almost hourly, but betweentimes the pair of them passed the day more smoothly than could have been foreseen. Much of the morning they sat at the living-room table, Grandma playing her offhand solitaire, Dad pointing wordlessly whenever she overlooked a card to play, the both of them glancing every few moments out of the window to the city and its unending tributaries of traffic. A crew came to work on the railroad tracks nearby, and Dad studied their labors by the hour. He noticed that the heftiest of the workers arrived and went with great irregularity, and began an ironic game of foremanning him from the living-room. I would arrive home from the university for lunch and be told: *My man was ten minutes late again this morning. I'm gonna have to jack him up about this bein' late all the time and all the time.* The next noon, *He's gettin' better, my man is. Only about five minutes late this morning. I'll get a full day of work out of him yet one of these times.*

Dad had a grimmer game for himself each late afternoon. The doctor had ordered him to walk as far as he could every day. At first, he would come back from fifty yards down the street, desperate, out of breath: *Godamighty, I can't walk any more than a baby.* But the next day, he would try again. Grandma seldom went with him on these efforts, did not offer to go, was not invited. They both accepted that he would have to do this battle for breath by himself.

At last, an afternoon when I was on my way home from the university library and met him several blocks from the house and at the base of the slope which skirted away below our neighborhood. As I came up to him, Dad was panting but able to say: *I told myself I'd work up to walking this far, and I've done 'er.*

I tried to find my words for acclaim: *Hell, then you're just a lot stronger than you were. The doc will be tickled with you.* But he shook his head, as if he could not afford to admit triumph. *I know I can't do much. This is a helluva way to have to live, creeping along weak as a kitten.* I had no words at all for that, and we started for home, silently paired in his trudge.

To describe that half-year of the four of us under a single roof does not go far toward an understanding of it. I am not sure there is an understanding to be had, only reactions, reflexes. The time flowed well enough, yet none of us wanted to repeat the experience, nor did we. Carol picked her way through the situation the best of us all, turning the snappishness between Dad and Grandma with amusement, granting Grandma the share of chores she sought, even confounding one of Grandma's stone-cut sayings: *No kitchen is big enough for two women at once.* More than any of the rest of us, perhaps, Carol simply remained herself. Grandma, I think, felt entirely unrooted. She missed family and friends, missed the gossip and life-pattern of the valley, missed a house of her own, missed everything there was to miss of sixty years spent in Montana.

Dad seemed tugged between his past and the life I was trying to make for myself. He met our citified friends more easily, followed my university work more interestedly. Yet he did not manage to feel settled and adjusted either, uneasy with the torrents of people he saw rivering along streets and sidewalks, the lockstep of houses thousand upon thousand, any of the dimensions of the city.

For my part, I felt again the crowdedness I had tried to pull myself away from—from a too-small prairie sheep-wagon, from the half-house in Ringling, from so many unprivate places, so much of those Montana years. Relationships between me and both Dad and Grandma were richer and fuller than I had expected—they always were—yet I still fiercely wanted what I so long had wanted, a chosen space all my own in life.

With spring came the declaration from Dad and Grandma that they were ready to return to Montana. I agreed. The winter had worked out to plan: Dad had escaped all chest infection, he was very much stronger than when he had come, he seemed better able to cope with the emphysema. I drove the trip to Montana with them, to keep Dad's nerves steady for the time ahead of him.

In a matter of a few months, Dad's propped-up health plunged apart. The chest infection hit, there was hospitalization again. But worse, day-by-day signs of failure started to show now. He began to fall deep asleep any time of the day, for alarming periods, then be unable to close his eyes at night.

Grandma saw this in astonishment, then fury: *No wonder you can't sleep at night, sleeping all day long too. Gee gods. Get up and around and you'd get over that sleepy-headedness.* His usual answer was to sit forward for some minutes with his head in his hands, despairing, then to fall back again as if exhausted. I checked with his doctor at the clinic, and was provided the unbrambled version of

Grandma's viewpoint: Dad was in carbon dioxide narcosis, caused by his lungs' failure to rid themselves of their after-breath wastes. The carbon dioxide residue worked like a slowing drug in his bloodstream. The remedy was for him to get up, walk, ride an exercise bicycle, anything to get the deadening buildup pumped from him—exertion demanded exactly when he felt least able to make any.

This period of narcosis, with Dad asleep hour upon hour and his skin color with a dangerous hint of bluing in it, like some dark seepage beneath ice, was the most terrifying yet. It seemed very much like death practicing on him. We were in a time of quickening erosion—of the deadly gullying in my father's lungs, of my grandmother's failing chance to bolster his life, of my inability to find medical help which would make much difference now. My father day upon day lay back in his big chair in the living room in White Sulphur and gilled in air, as if out of breath from the long stopless run through life. But that it was not stopless, each of us knew too well. We could read that in the bulk of the oxygen tanks which came oftener and oftener into the house now.

I can chart my father's last years by the medical apparatus that attached itself to his existence. The first, the machine that blew a fog of medication into his lungs, sat at his bedside with some innocence. A bland metal-gray in tone and not much larger than a typewriter, the device awaited him several times a day, took in his puffs of exertion and traded out its mysterious mist, sent him away breathing less hard. But next to come were the dark-green oxygen tanks, huge as battleship shells, and their conveyor-like pace to his bedside was the tempo of doom for him.

He began their use sparingly, a minute or so of relief at a time into his lungs a few times a day. But across the months, the oxygen imbibing became oftener, longer. Grandma was at her most baffled and furious with this terrifying new addiction: *Charlie, the more of that you use, the more you just want to use!* He gave her a weary fury back: *I can't help using it, I've got to breathe.* And in the next minute she would have gone to the kitchen to bring him a cup of coffee and he would have thanked her softly, and the two-sided helplessness would have passed for the moment. The one winner was the oxygen, which the next day would tether him a few moments longer.

At last came the time when he slumped in the chair with the oxygen tether forever in his nose, slept with it. All had been reversed: from the outset when he was bolstered by a few minutes of oxygen each day, now there were only a handful of moments when he could bear to be without it. Everything now had thinned to the whiffs holding him in life, like a breeze scudding a dried leaf barely above the ground.

No longer could he even make a recuperative trip to Seattle; the doctor said there was medical risk in travel and Dad felt the greater risk in himself, could not bring himself to such a move. On one of my Montana trips, back again in the house in White Sulphur after the bleak task of having delivered Dad into another hospital stay, Grandma said out of the blue: *Dad asked me never to let you put him in a rest home.*

I said nothing for a long minute, which of course said that I had thought of it. What reply I eventually made to her I no longer know, but it was not definite enough for either of us.

That was the problem—to be definite in the unclearest of moments. Here was fact: my father was hopelessly afflicted, every breath a fresh agony. Here was proposition: warehouse him as the less-than-alive presence he was becoming. But then here was judgment: whose benefit would it be for? Not his own. Not Grandma's. Mine.

In the end, I turned decision back on itself. Not to choose the one crevice-crossing was to choose the other. I stayed by a conviction that had been forming silently in me—that the best that could be done in this desolate situation was to help this linked pair, Dad and Grandma, endure through it together in their own home. Across twenty years, I had watched the two of them wear grooves into each other until at last the fit of their lives became a mutual comfort, a necessity bridging between them. Their time together had passed through armistice into alliance and on to acceptance, then to affection, and at last had become one of the kinds of love.

I saw that now, even as I had missed seeing the early signs of the procession. Now my father leaned his very life on my grandmother, on her care of him. When his life toppled away, as it must soon, a presence would go out of my grandmother's existence like something lacking in the air of her own breathing.

This told me all the more that as long as he yet lived, as long as Grandma had the health and verve to care for him at home, she should. She was in some ways the oddest possible figure of mercy, put together as she was of a fast temper and oblique notions of illness and its consequences. Yet she still was sturdy, still had to keep herself busy every moment that she was not asleep. And there was that fiercest of all her capacities, her ability to prop other lives with her own. I lacked her knack for such entire sacrifice, her habit of putting all else before her own needs. The most I could do for my father was to warehouse him in my own home, assuming he could be gotten there, or within other walls. Grandma, if I allowed her, could do very much more.

What that tokened to me was that as long as Dad could remain in known surroundings—in the valley, in the house he had chosen and bought, with this woman he had come to such deep alliance with—for whatever little was left of his life, he should.

There were other unheard-of equations to this time. For one, Dad had become both thinner and larger—face and hands going gaunt, but the exertions of his lungs building his chest out to a broad shell, an encasement as if heft from everywhere else in his body had been summoned there. The great chest of course was a cruel fake; the muscles which had stretched out and out to squeeze air into the failing lungs still were unable to pull in the torrent of oxygen needed, and the more barrel-like Dad became, the more grudgingly breath dragged in and out of him.

For another, my father stayed in the moments of my days steadily now, even as his body dwindled from me. All of his way of life that I had sought escape from—the grindstone routine of ranching, the existence at the mercy of mauling weather, the endless starting-over from one calamity or another—was passing with him, and while I still wanted my distance from such a gauntlet, I found that I did not want my knowing of it to go from me. The perseverance to have lasted nearly seventy years amid such cold prospects was what heritage Dad had for me; I had begun to see that it counted for much.

Through all this ran the zipperlike whisper of history as well. Dad's time span, and even the late portion of it when I was growing up at his side, quickly was being peeled away by change. To my constant surprise, in our years in the north and the time I was away at college While Sulphur had swapped itself from being a livestock town to a logging town. Each time I drove in now across the long deck of the valley, the blue plume of smoke from the sawmill's scrap burners at the edge of town startled me, made me wonder for an instant whose house had caught fire. Out from town, along the forks of the Smith River and beneath the flanks of the Castles and Big Belts, the ranches were being reached by the continental metamorphosis from agriculture to agribusiness. No longer were there the summer's haying crews Dad had foremanned so many times, only a few men on galloping machines. Nor were there any longer the dozens of sheepherders, nor the roving shearing crews, because there no longer were sheep; we are a people swathed in synthetics now.

Even the sagebrush, the very coloration of that so-high prairie country, was beginning to be erased under potent new plows and tractors and farming theories, the topsoil which had defeated the homesteaders now laid back like a pelt being skinned off.

And beyond even that, the large valley ranches, which to my mind had croupiered an area that could have sustained many medium-sized ranches into a single fistful of huge holdings, were beginning to notice a bigness beyond their own: corporate America. *Ye know who owns the Dogie now?* Dad demanded indignantly when I arrived on one of my visits: *A-goddamn-Kansas-City-paper-box-company.*

Such matters began to align, in these first few years of the struggle with Dad's affliction, into the last and most unexpected of equations: I was discovering myself to be more my father's son, and my grandmother's grandson, than I had ever known. Exactly at the point of my life when I had meant to turn myself to teaching, to the routined assurances of scholarliness, I found myself veering inward instead. The university life was setting off in me the disquiets which had sent my father stomping time and again from the big ranches of the valley. I recognized in myself that, like him, I never was going to be comfortable about soldiering for the large enterprises of the world, and that unlike him, I had the cache of education to provide some choice in the matter. I was finding, too, that more of Grandma's fierceness of family was in me than was expected. The nation was in wars I automatically despised and feared—in Asian rice paddies, in its own streets—but what compelled all meaningful emotions in me was the obliteration raging against my own father.

As my decisions do, the one now came slowly, doggedly. I kept on through the seminars and exams, claimed the degree at the last dusty furrow of it all. But then I abandoned the offer of a job at one of the country's largest universities. Instead, I began to work full-time at writing, by the shaggiest and most marginal of its modes, free-lancing for magazines. I offered to Carol: *I know you married me for better or worse, but this is somewhere off the scale.* She answered as ever: *Do it.*

Academic friends plainly were puzzled and a bit disturbed, as if I had declared I was going off to be a wheelwright or a buffalo hunter. But when I undertook to explain myself during one of the Montana trips, Grandma simply offered her blanket assumption that whatever I did made some sense all its own, and Dad, I noticed, seemed to understand this drastic veer better than any other I had ever done. *At least,* he said, *ye'll be your own boss.*

My father's heritage of perseverance, I have said. At last, the emphysema began to gnaw even that from him. During another of my Montana stays, more than four years now since the diagnosis of what was at work in Dad's lungs, a neighbor stepped in to visit. As we sat in the living room and Grandma racketed in the kitchen to make coffee, the neighbor remarked to Dad how good it was to see him up and around, what relief it must be to be back from the hospital bed. At once Dad made a futile tossing motion with his hand and told her: *My heart's just hanging by a thread.*

I looked at him incredulously. Perhaps everything else inside his chest was becoming a horror, but time after time the doctor's examinations had found that engine of a heart had not yet shown falter, had withstood amazingly the fierce load on it.

Yet in one sense, at least, the heart truly was going out of him. The desperation of having to fight for every breath, of having to live tied by the nose to an oxygen tank, of regulating himself more and more by all the medication that demanded to be taken, simply had worn away his energy. So long and labored a dying had drawn nearly all worth from his body, and now it set in on his endurance of mind. Again, Dad began to yearn toward the surgery he had heard of when he first learned he had emphysema. Again I investigated, again gathered opinions, again told him what I had found: the surgery was considered doubtful, his clinic doctor advised passionately against it.

So forlorn about his existence—life was too generous a word for it now—that he had begun to base everything on the operation, Dad was wrenchingly depressed at the latest advice against it. *Whatever ye think, son. But I don't know how I can go on like I am.*

For weeks those words battered in me as I tried to weigh through the misery toying with him now, think what could be spoken into that tortured hopeless life. At last, in early January of 1971, I wrote one more of my careful letters. Saying: I had come to believe that here was one decision which I could not make for him. I would fly to Montana, we would attempt whatever slight relief there might be for him—perhaps another recuperative spell in the hospital. When he felt able to decide, I would listen and help him to weigh facts. But the words of this decision finally would have to come from him.

Out of that, a phone call, the day after my letter came to him: it was Grandma, saying that he had had the operation that morning.

The greatest fear I can imagine licked through me. As I held the phone my hand shook, the single time that had happened in my life. At last I gulped in breath and said I would come to Montana at once.

When I arrived the next day, Dad was breathing with less labor than I had seen him in for some time, but he told me there had been a glorious half-day after the operation when he had no sensation of breathing hard at all. *Ivan, it was like I was a well man again.* Then he had begun to feel the labor creep back. I sat with him the next few days, urged him into a small routine of life again. And heard the first cough from him like a scraping sound in the night.

By the end of a week, he plainly was coming down with the lung infection again. I despised the task as never before: it took me the large part of a day to talk him into another hospital stint.

When my plane time came and I stood to say goodbye to him, Dad was sitting on the edge of the hospital bed, his dismay at being there once more mixed with the relief of drawing on steady oxygen and the familiar care. He looked stronger than he had at home. I turned in the doorway to say my usual parting: *I'll talk to you on the phone soon. Take care.* He said as ever: *G'bye to ye, son.*

The hospital stay did bolster him again, did renew his strength and ease his lungs enough until, as usual, in about two weeks' time he was able to go home to White Sulphur and Grandma's care once more. He still struggled for breath, but seemed somehow slightly more enduring than he had been. And his prompt return home carried hope, for the chronic collapses back into hospitalization had told me how he would die—a last torturing confinement in the angled bed, tubes looped to his body, but breath eroding, eroding, despite all apparatus; within the white sheets a sharp panting for life like my mother's agony re-echoed, then a gasp to stillness. It would be the last terrible smother of his crippled lungs, and I could see it in every exactness but the moment on the calendar.

But he was home once more now, away from that not-yet-decreed moment, and even was escaping winter's usual pneumonia attacks. That and other delvings for reassurance were on his mind. In mid-February he sent to Carol and me his first letter in years. *Hi, you two. I am going to see if I can write you a short letter. I am doing pretty good, I think. My breathing seems to stay about the same. My legs still are so darn weak but I am slowly getting a little more strength in them. I am using the exercise bike all I can. . . .*

The page labored on in his taut, overcareful writing, but the news was in that slide of report: *doing pretty good . . . about the same . . . all I can.*

And soon after, the confirming lines of puzzle and suspicion from Grandma. *He doesn't seem to improve any. He's getting the same as before. Sleep days and up and down all nite. Usually eats three sandwitches during the nite with milk. But he doesn't eat a good meal. . . .* For the thousandth time I thought through the specter of his final hospital stay, and readied myself for the news that I would have to come once more and deliver him to the prospect.

I had forgotten that the great constant in my father was surprise. In early April, on the third morning after Dad's seventieth birthday, Grandma stepped to his doorway to begin him on another day of existing. At the bed, he was on his back with his head and upper body tilted to the right, his mouth open, as if having turned to speak an answer over his shoulder. In his custom now, the bedcovers had been flipped aside because of their burden on his laboring chest. His pajamas were scarcely mussed, and the square-cut face was freed of its straining look. And in the instant when his heart at last had convulsed in him and ended his life so silently and immediately that no hint of it could be heard in a room fifteen feet away, his right arm had flung wide, catching the tether of oxygen tube and tearing it from his nostrils.

By early afternoon I was in Montana, by dusk had made the burial arrangements, that night slept in the bed where my father had died less than twenty hours before. Grandma was teary-eyed, but steadier than I would have been from looking in on death in the dawn light. We both were startled, after the dragging years of near-helplessness, at the staccato pace of everything to be done now. Having arranged a furlough from her classes, Carol flew in from Seattle, propped us both with her efficiency.

Late in the second day, the minister who would read the funeral service came to the house. Across the years, I can think of little more remote from my father's range of mind than religion. Once in my boyhood, a pair of Jehovah's Witnesses had come to our door. Dad gave them his levelest look, proclaimed *We're staunch Presbyterians here,* and had the door closed on the visitors before they could blink. I gaped at him, and received his joke-calculating grin: *Never knew we was so pious, did ye?* I certainly didn't, and can think of no other time religion became a topic under our roof. The funeral minister now found that I was a bland target for his tries at commiseration. He soon asked what Bible reading I wished at the funeral service.

The one where God speaks to Job from the whirlwind.

Job 38, that would be? He sat higher in his chair. *It's not a . . . usual funeral choice.* I said nothing. *Well . . . The first few verses, I imagine? The readings usually are brief. . . .*

No, all of it. All the chapter. We're in no hurry after these years.

He nodded, offered a hand, was gone.

I did not believe in funerals and the customs of public grief, but I believed less in doing anything not understandable to Grandma. I braced, and on the morning before the funeral drove her across town to the chapel to see Dad in his casket. He looked milder than in life, calm and unscarred except for the star-print in the center of his square chin. She looked down at him, gave a sob, and said her one last sentence to him: *Oh Charlie, why did you have to die?*

Then the afternoon, and across the chapel, faces from two lifetimes—my father's, my own—hung row on row. I looked out among them as the preacher's words marched. *Where was thou when I laid the foundations of the earth?* . . . The lone black face of Taylor Gordon, nodding softly to the Bible rhythms. Clifford's head among the pallbearers, undressed without his rancher's hat atop it. *Hast thou commanded the morning.* . . . Sun-dark faces Dad had ridden with and foremanned on the Dogie and the Camas and a dozen other ranches; paler faces from the saloons and stores. *Hast thou entered into the treasures of the snow?* . . . Faces from the Basin, from winters a half century ago, from homesteads gone empty and echoing. *Canst thou send lightnings* . . . Faces absent, alive only in specific tales of death: Nellie queerly quiet in the metal casket of his car, battered by the rolling plunge from a hill road. At a canasta table, a heart attack astonishes McGrath; he flings his cards as if sledgehammered in the chest, topples backward as the jacks and queens flutter down upon him. Kate and Walter Badgett, each lying down in ancientness not to arise again, but of course Walter passing first, Kate watchfully next. *Wilt thou hunt the prey for the lion? or fill the appetite of the young lions.* . . . And last, always and always piercing through it all, the memory of my mother's deathday on the mountain, my father's life in a way having begun to end there where hers did. . . .

And at last, the procession to the cemetery, the brief graveside ceremony quickly done in bitter, wind-whipped April weather, and the last glimpse of Dad's casket within the walls of earth.

Nothing new can be said of the loss of a parent; it all has been wept out a million million times. During the funeral preparations and the days afterward, I could find in myself only the plainest, broadest of emotions—anger that Dad had suffered so steadily and so long, relief that he was released from the squeezing bars of his own ribcage, and that I was released from the guesswork decisions over his existence. Those, and the gratitude that of all interesting men I knew, this one had been my father.

Now there was Grandma's grief to be worked through. On some footings, she was as unshakable as ever. When the chore came to choose a tombstone for Dad's grave, she startled me by saying at once that she wanted to be buried exactly beside him, and to have her name on the same stone. *All right, sure,* I offered. Then she went silent for a minute and amended: *No, not together on the stone. Right alongside him, a stone like his one. We ought to each have our own gravestone but the same.*

But days after the funeral when the time neared that I would have to leave for Seattle again and we had talked through what she would do—how she would fend alone in the house, the bonus that her youngest son lived near enough to look in on her often, the luck of having neighbors who fussed over her—she suddenly put in: *Maybe I could of done better. Maybe I could of been better to Charlie, he was so sick.* . . . The words rivered out of me: *Good God, you waited on him hand and foot these years, you were the one person of any of us who could have done it. There's no blame on you and I never want to hear you saying there is. . . .* I broke off, choked by tears. My so-rare fury impressed her, and one woe of this after-death was dispelled.

Others took more time. When she arrived the next month for a stay with us in Seattle, I came back from putting her suitcase away to find her standing in the living room weeping. *Everywhere I look, I see Charlie here.* I had no fury for that, only the stab of knowing how late the emotion of familyhood had come to us. And for once in all these beset years, I did know the cure for something. Deliberately, sometime during each day with her, I brought Dad alive again in one conversation or another, made his passing a matter of fact among us rather than a storm center of grief.

As she always had, Grandma firmed herself up. As soon as she returned to Montana, there were the words in her first letter that I read like a line of a song: *I'm feeling pretty good now again and getting a little more straightened around every day.*

Now that my grandmother was alone, in the last of her odd widowhoods, again I would have to divine across seven hundred miles how a life was holding up, how much attention was wanted, what decisions and soothings and temperings were needed. Carol knew best the one clinching idea to reassure Grandma that her own life was far from over, a suggestion from the wife of one of my cousins during the swirl of the White Sulphur household after Dad's death. I worried the notion for a while, then began the phoning and letters needed and by midsummer could tender it to Grandma: *How would you like to go to Australia to see Paul? We'll send you.*

She had been in an airplane only a few times, had never flown alone, never seen an ocean, let alone been up over the expanse of one, never changed planes at vast terminals, never done eleven dozen impossible things she listed to me at once. As I had known, it took weeks to talk her toward the notion—that yes it could be afforded, yes I could handle mysteries of passport and visa, no she was not too old, although the fact of her seventy-eight years haunted me no little bit—until at last came the question which I knew meant she would do it: *Do you think really I can go there all by myself?* I laughed into the phone the one last word needed: *Really.*

Across half the earth in September of 1971, she was met in Australia by the son not seen for 25 years, and by the daughter-in-law and three grandchildren entirely new to her. Quickly her letters came in across the Pacific as if she was remaking the host land: . . . *The flowers are so pretty here. Nobody seems to pick them for boquets but I do their so lovely. . . . I been teaching the kids card games Rummy and Solitare and they want to play all the time now. . . . I went downtown with Joyce this morning. She said it was her pie day. I couldnt see and couldnt see why she would go buy pies when we both bake good and finally I asked her. She said No not that kind of pie she meant it was her pay day. They sure talk a broge here don't they. . . .* I grinned with the thought of her looking at kangaroos, living with this newfound family in their house so queerly stilted above a Queensland flood plain, going off with them to see salt mined from ocean water and to stand for her picture at a monument proclaiming something called the Tropic of Capricorn: *I don't just know what its all about but you will.* She sent me a clipping of what the newspaper there had written about her visit, and I read it thinking they knew only the scantest fraction of this caller.

When she returned in a month, Carol and I met her at the airport, hugged her in triumph and admiration, and hurried her to our house to sleep off 8,000 miles of flight. The next morning she did not wake up until past eleven o'clock, and was entirely scandalized: *Gee gods, why didn't you get me up hours ago?* I lifted my eyebrows and tried to tell her about jet lag, but for once she was having none of my explanations. *I never slept this late in my whole entire life,* she huffed, and was on her feet.

The single thing I knew I had done properly in Dad's last years was to keep him uninvalided as long as it could be managed. Given Grandma's restless insistence to be, as she would put it, *up and around and doing,* I thought that it was even more vital for her to stay active. I had forgotten what an ally a small town such as White Sulphur could be in this. Neighbors and friends and relatives kept an eye on her, mowed her lawn, delivered gossip to her kitchen table, delivered Grandma herself to what became a prized new pastime for her, a newly-formed Senior Citizens Club. When I visited the small house in Montana now, I looked at the tacked-up sheet of paper on which she scrawled the phone numbers of her support system, saw it lengthen steadily, and nodded in satisfaction.

The habit and patterns grew just in time, for in the spring of 1972, a few days less than a year after Dad's death, Grandma suffered a heart attack—the first blow on her health in her eight decades of life. I flew to Montana to do the cooking and housework when she came out of the hospital.

She was going to be, I knew, the world's most restless convalescent, and as soon as I had her seated in the house, I started on her: *We are going to make a deal. I'm going to do all the work in this house for the next week or so*—her lips already flying open in protest—*and you can help me with these.* I showed her a shoebox filled with file cards, the index material for a textbook Carol and I had just written. *All right,* she said, in immediate purpose, *show me just what there is to it.*

Across the next several days, she sat quietly and sorted and alphabetized as I hovered carefully out of the way. At last she pronounced, *I think that's all of it, Ivan.* I studied how much more vigorous and restored she had become, smiled and said: *I think it is.*

She recuperated briskly enough to go on living much as she had, but to her disgust needed to rely on heart-regulating pills. Whenever she felt the first signs of angina, usually needlelike sensations at the tops of her arms, she would pop a nitroglycerine pill into her mouth as if it were an aspirin, determinedly sit still for a few minutes, and be up and at some chore again. Outwardly, she aged hardly at all. I compare photos of her taken five years apart, and they seem to have been snapped within the same minute, the identical pursed smile beneath the resolute upper face and gray-white field of hair.

I found that now Grandma filled not only her own role for me, the one of stand-in mother begun twenty years earlier when she and I moved into the house in Ringling, but what had been Dad's as well: my compass-point to the past, to my own youth. Whenever she visited Seattle or I came to Montana, she began to talk readily of the gone years, to tell even of her marriage to Tom Ringer, and of life on the Wisconsin farm.

Her mind was not wandering back—it was as solid and set on the chore of the moment as ever—but she seemed freed at last of the tempers which had covered over such stories. True, there still came bursts out of her which could have resounded at any point of her past sixty years in the valley. Leave a light switched on in her house past early morning, and you would hear *hmpf! burnin' a hole in the daylight!* and the abrupt click. A long-haired white cat had recognized her front porch as a provision port, and he came and went, battered from alley fights and matted with cockleburrs, to the rhythm of her feedings and scoldings. But most of the time now, Grandma was in mellower mood than I could ever remember, as if old age was coming gently into her in compensation for the way it had ripped apart Dad.

I took the chance to have her retell what I had heard from her as a boy, confirm the details, imprint her private wordings. Before I quite knew it, the cadences of this book had begun out of listening to her. Listening and seeing, for the one scribe of my family's past had been the Brownie box camera. I dug out Grandma's photo albums which had gathered dust under one bed or another for sundry decades. I remember one early evening spent in the White Sulphur house, a set of hours as she went through for me an album which had belonged to my mother. Picture upon picture of my father and mother—in their herding days on Grass Mountain, on horseback at rodeos, dressed up in flat-cap-and-bonnet finery beside the square hulks of 1920's automobiles—brought sniffles or hard-swallowed sentences from Grandma, and by the time I had jotted my notes on the final page, the emotion she had been putting into the room had worn me out.

That should be enough for tonight, I said in a weary glaze. She turned to me in surprise: *But we got these others to get through. Hadn't we just as well to keep on?* And we did.

And then the moment, for there always is such a pivot moment, when it truly became clear how far along in life she was. At the end of September, 1974—she was eighty-one by now—she flew to Seattle to spend a few weeks with us. When Carol and I saw her coming slowly up the ramp from the plane, we waved, she gave us her pursed smile. Then she stopped and leaned against the wall of the ramp, and I bolted toward her. By the time I reached her, she was fumbling the bottle of heart pills from her purse. A pill and getting her to a chair eased the angina; before long, we were on our way, but with her now a more fragile piece of life than she had been minutes before.

Time and again in that visit, she had to sit and ease the heart symptoms. But she would not be kept idle, nor did I think she ought to be. She had lived under the same roof with Dad's helplessness; a repeat of that would be the cruelest affliction that could happen to her. And so I invented chores, tasks she could do while sitting. She clipped her way through mounds of newspapers to sort references for my writing files, and her only complaint was that it wasn't work enough. If two minutes of page flipping didn't yield a headline circled for clipping, her mild grumble would come: *Ivan, I'm not finding none to cut out.*

This visit of hers now had a sharp hook at the end of it. I had written articles about the World's Fair in Spokane, and Grandma longed to see it. The plan had been that at the end of her stay, Carol and I would drive her to Spokane, shepherd her around the Fair for a day, and she would fly home to Montana from there. Plainly her heart spasms were too chronic now for that, but just as plainly this might be her last outing in the world. And I believed more than ever, seeing the determination with which she would gulp a heart pill, sit briefly, and then be back at some chore, that her stride of life should be slowed as little as possible.

Near the end of her stay, I gave her another of my decrees: *There's just too much walking at the Fairgrounds. The only way I see that you can go there is in a wheelchair.* She gave me her most mildly regretful *Ohhh?*, as if I had just told her it might rain sometime in the next week. Then: *If you say so.*

I expect never to have another inspiration click to the perfection this one did. Grandma in her rented wheelchair, as Carol or I propelled her, instantly was eligible to go ahead of every line into every exhibit. She saw her World's Fair as effortlessly and grandly as if she were Queen Victoria somehow being trundled through time. *Gee gosh,* she said as Carol and I helped her into the car at the end of the day, obviously pleased with herself and the pair of us, *that was sure the way to do that.*

The next morning, in the last minutes before she was to board her plane at the Spokane airport, the awareness flew into me, as it always did now at these partings, that here might be the last set of moments I would see Grandma alive. Then total commotion: near us had been an orderly family, the mother saying goodbye to the husband and their four children as they set off for somewhere, and suddenly the woman was grappling with the man and shrieking: *I've got a restraining order! Don't let him on this plane with my children!* As he tried to pull away, she haltered him by his necktie and continued to shout. The children erupted into a bawling swirl, the smallest one was belly-whopped to the floor amid the wrestling.

The airline workers were slow and reluctant to edge in on the battle. I tried to talk Grandma calm as the brawl went on; the picture of her sagging against the plane ramp when she had arrived in Seattle blazed in me. But she said, *No, I'm all right, Ivan,* and sat watching and giving her usual *hmpf* until the airline people could herd the roaring family to a side room. Then it was time for me to help her down the ramp, and to her plane seat, and to smile a nervous goodbye to her one more time.

The phone call, the metallic blat of worst news, came three weeks later. Again the flight to Montana, the drive from Helena through the Big Belts to White Sulphur Springs, for this last of the burials in the valley's cemetery. Peter Doig, Annie Campbell Doig, Tom Ringer, Berneta Ringer Doig, Charlie Doig: in a somber space not much larger than a garden patch they all lay, nearly three hundred years of lives, not a life among them easy or unafflicted. A sum of so much of the valley could be found in them, and a sum which would keep emerging in me for however long I lived. Now Bessie Ringer, in her way the most sorrowing to see vanish, because she had been the most durable of them all.

Wonder built in me as I traced out her last day. The morning, Grandma had spent working on a quilt, another of her rainbow-paneled splendors, for a helpful neighbor who looked in on her often. Sometime she had telephoned to a friend at a ranch out of Ringling, asking to be brought a fresh supply of eggs when the woman came to town. At noon she was phoned by her son, and as usual in those checking calls, they talked for several minutes. In the afternoon a funeral was held for a member of one of the last families of the Sixteen country: Grandma did not go to the rites, but at the coffee hour held afterward at the Senior Citizens Club she helped with the serving and chatted with friends for an hour or more. Someone had driven her home, where she had her supper alone. In the evening, there was to be the weekly card party back at the Senior Citizens Club, and she phoned to ask for a ride with her best friend in the group—a woman who had run one of the White Sulphur saloons that had so often thorned Grandma's earlier life. They had nearly arrived at the card party when, in the midst of something joked by one or the other of them, Grandma cut off in the middle of a chuckle and slumped, chin onto chest. The friend whirled the car to the hospital a block away. A doctor instantly was trying to thump a heartbeat-rhythm into Grandma, but could work no flicker of response from her. She had gone from life precisely as she had lived it, with abruptness and at full pace.

Once more the funeral, the Bible rhythms, the lines of faces brigading back out of the chapel into the past. The relatives had raised their eyebrows when I told them the one funeral request Grandma had ever made to me: *I want a closed casket. Makes me spooky to think of everybody gawping down at me like that.* I flinched in turn when the minister's reading from Ecclesiastes began flatly: *The sun rises and the sun goes down, then it presses on. . . .* I had forgotten to specify the King James language to him. Then the wryness came to me. How could I expect my grandmother's exit to be any less touched by contention than her life had been?

At the graveside at last, in the cold coming-winter weather, the rites had to be hurried through, the casket rapidly roped down from sight, condolences quickly spoken in smoking breaths and as quickly taken by me. Carol's arm in mine made the single spot of warmth in the last of the cold minutes. As the groups of us began to turn toward our cars, the valley's mountain-chilled wind skirled hard among us. I recognized it from the afternoon of my father's burial.

This set of sagas, memory. Over and over self-told, as if the mind must have a way to pass its time, docket all the promptings for itself, within its narrow bone cave.

A final flame-lit prism of remembering: the February afternoon at a northern Pacific coastline, Carol and I with a pair of friends hiking beside the exploding surf. Gray, restless after-storm weather, my favorite mood of the fir-shagged wild shore. In a dozen journeys here, Carol and I repeat to each other, never have we seen the waves break so high and far. After a short mile, at Ellen Creek, the four of us pause. The creek's meek tea-colored flow has boiled wide, swirly, as the ocean surf drums into the mouth of the channel and looses giant whorls of tide up the start of the stream. John, ever the boldest of us, explores a route inland, across a log to the coiling creekbank opposite and there brushwhacking his way atop other logs and debris until he at last drops safely back to the ocean beach. I am uneasy, thinking through the chances of one of us snapping a leg in the rain-slick debris or slipping the ten-foot drop into the creek. The Ellen is a known channel that Carol and I have crossed and recrossed casually all the times before. With the storm surf nosing at it as it is, the stream may have risen now to thigh-high, but still a wader's depth. I suggest that I go across upstream of the surf line, find the shallowest route for Carol and Jean to come after; they agree. Boots slung around my neck, I slog rapidly into the water. At the deepest part the water surprises me for an instant by lapping up just over my belt, then as I begin the last dozen pulling strides to the shore, a vast slosh of tide swells across the top of my chest and undertow lifts away my feet.

Like a bug down a drain I am sucked feet first into the ocean, gravel beating up at me like shrapnel as the surf plows its roaring way, shore and sky and all else lost in the water avalanche. After forever, I am reversed, surged back to the tideline, slammed down, then rolled to sea again. Now I paddle to stay upright, and simply am turned and turned, toylike, within the next acres of water until I am struck against the shore again. Taken out into the froth yet again, this time I try to ride the surf with my body, eagling my arms wide; again I am pitched over and over, hurled to gravel, instantly lifted away and out. How many times this repeats, there is no counting—perhaps as few, and as many, as five. Even as my body is being beaten limp, my mind finds incredible clarity, as if the thinking portion of me had been lifted separately and set aside from the ocean's attack. While my arms and legs automatically try trick after trick to pull me atop the water and onto the precipice of shore, the feeling of death settles into me, bringing both surprise at the ease and calm of the process and a certain embarrassed chiding of myself that this is a silly and early method to exit from life. John later told that, as I came whirling out of the surf one more time, he saw on my face a look of deep resignation. My remembering of that eye-locked instant is of noting him, mouth open in a shout I cannot hear, beginning to run from forty yards away, and then in my next writhe within the dense falling wall of surf, discovering his arm across my back and under me, dragging my weary three-pointed stumble from the undertow. At the shallow moving seam of shore and surf, John exults in my ear: We've got it made now! *But I sense, as if a monstrous paw poised just beyond the edge of my vision, the next set of waves toppling toward us: we both are struck flat, but somehow hold the shore. Only then, in the wash back to sea of that aftermost wave, do my boots finally float free from around my neck, and John reaches casually as they pass and plucks them from the last of the water. Now Carol and Jean at our sides, flung to us through the flooding creek by their desperation and the luck of an interval between tidal whirlpools, their hands and John's steadying me until at last, up off the cold bite of the shore gravel, I stand again.*

That forenoon, a few dozen months into the past, has stayed much in my mind, and not only for the marvel of finding myself undrowned and for the gratitude of having had three lives offered up instantly for mine. By the time of that incident this book already had begun to take over my fingers, and my scuff against death inevitably called up in me the endings put to other figures in my family, with less reason than my mistaken wade into the Ellen. Spaced where I am, past having been young but not quite yet middle-aged, the odds of life-and-death still loom quite far from my usual thoughts. Yet this much has been brought home to me fully: that added now into the lineage of all else I share with Charlie Doig and Bessie Ringer is the sensation of having been swirled out of deepest hazard. The links are made instantly by memory. I am spun and spun within the frothing wave: creek water rises over Grandma's stirrups as she edges the roan to the flood-trapped cattle. Surf gravel beats up at me like shrapnel: the hooves of the black gelding pound across Dad in the corral dirt.

I feel, in my musing on it, as if the two of them too somehow stood up out of the slosh of death with me, the one giving his cocked grin of wryness at having survived one time more, the other muttering at the receding ocean and marching us all off into dry clothes.

Then my father and my grandmother go, together, back elsewhere in memory, and I am left to think through the fortune of all we experienced together. And of how, now, my single outline meets the time-swept air that knew theirs.